a liberating vision

politics
for
growing
humans

John Vasconcellos
Member of the California Legislature

Impact Publishers
POST OFFICE BOX 1094
SAN LUIS OBISPO, CALIFORNIA 93406

Library of Congress Cataloging in Publication Data:

Vasconcellos, John.
    A liberating vision.

    1.   United States--Social policy.   2.   Social institutions.   3.   Social values.   4.   Humanistic psychology.
I.   Title.
HN65.V37   309.1'73   79-16778
ISBN 0-915166-17-8
ISBN 0-915166-16-X pbk.

Impact 🕮 *Publishers*
POST OFFICE BOX 1094
SAN LUIS OBISPO, CALIFORNIA 93406

contents

V. ACTION: FOR GROWING HUMANS

VI. POLITICS: FOR GROWING HUMANS

"Where there is no vision, the people perish."

Old Testament, Proverbs, 29:18

To
  Sid Jourard and Robert Kennedy,
    who inspire me still,
      personally and politically.

For
  my friends,
    all growing humans.

preface

Friend—

In 1966 I was commissioned by the 300,000 residents of California's 24th (now 23rd) Assembly District to go to the Capitol as their Assemblyman, to help govern California and 23,000,000 human beings who choose to make our home here.

Since then I've been subsidized by the citizens of California to work full-time—wandering about, wondering about us humans: who we are as a people and where we're going. My hope and goal has been to make sense of my opportunity, this responsibility entrusted me by my constituents.

I'm grateful for the public support that's enabled me to devote all my time and energy these thirteen years to public affairs. The work is meaningful, wonderful, fascinating, fulfilling. Being a legislator enables me to look *where*ever I want, experience *what*ever I want, meet *whom*ever I want. It's a rare opportunity, a privileged life.

This book is my report and gift back to my constituents, and to all Californians, of what I've seen and learned, especially how I've learned to see.

It's also my offering to you beyond California—as we are all related as one human family. We ought not keep ourselves from one another by reason of geographical boundaries.

In my experience it seems that California is often where, for better or worse, events tend to happen *first*. It's the "test-tube state" (*Newsweek*). It's often our national frontier, the showcase for what's to come elsewhere. It's a place of particular possibility—where we humans (seem to) feel more free to be ourselves, even to experiment with our ways of being. The seeds of change, bursting forth first here, often become societal trends—with the rest of our country, even our world, following in fairly short order. In my experience, what's happening here (first or not) is already happening elsewhere—all around our world. My book might well be a statement of what's happening or coming for you—wherever you might be.

This book is my effort to analyze and describe, in a helpful and hopeful way, all I know of who and how and where we humans are today. I hope to explain what's happening now, what's gone wrong and how we can make it right.

I propose we develop a humanistic/holistic government and politics—in and for human beings everywhere. Having survived, even flourished, and proven myself effective these thirteen years—both at getting elected and at accomplishments in the Capitol, I hope I'm witness that such a humanistic vision is today viable and durable in politics.

I intend to facilitate our developing a personal relationship—as a basis for our coming together in a trusting way, to attend humanly and effectively to the dilemmas of our personal, public, political and social lives.

This book began as a compilation of articles, brochures, speeches and interviews. I began writing a brief introspective preface and a concluding epilogue. Both pieces grew—until they more than filled the book I'd planned to write.

One Sunday night several years ago I awoke suddenly, inspired to create a book. I got as far as the chapter headings, flashed on the title "A Liberating Vision", then lost interest. The title stayed with me. I like it for several reasons.

It draws attention to the significance of "vision": a way of looking at everything, a way of seeing. Through our vision of ourselves and our world, each of us makes sense of our lives and times, chooses how we shall live and act.

The vision I'm proposing (of innately innocent, inherently trustworthy human nature) warrants "liberation." I choose the participle "liberating" to indicate the active character of my vision, the responsibility it places within and upon each of us personally. Together "liberating" and "vision" are intended to cause you and me each to have to confront our own personal basic belief systems, our own assumptions about ourselves, our human nature and potential, and our individual responsibility for liberating ourselves. Each of us will be brought to the root of everything, and hopefully engage each other precisely at our roots. From there we'll be far more likely to
envision our liberation,
liberate ourselves,
liberate our vision,   and
enable each other's liberation.

Together they're intended to provide a basis for hope—within ourselves, between and among ourselves, for our society, for our future.

"Politics for growing humans" furthers my "liberating

vision." It calls attention to the inherent interrelationship between "politics" and "humans", and to the facts that:
government and politics are about growing humans,
growing humans belong in government and politics, and
a new politics is now ready and available for implementation, by and for growing humans.

Writing this book has been a surprisingly frightening experience for me. I've given hundreds of speeches. I like the way I do those. They now come readily. As much as I trust myself speaking, I'm unsure of myself writing this book. But this book, my *book*, has been a different experience. I found myself being defensive, writing all kinds of rationales for my writing, to counter your possible objections, to assure you'll like my book and still like me.

But I'm less unsure now than when I started. This book is proving a growthful experience for me. I'm realizing I don't *need* those defenses. Yet I want to share with you some of that trauma, and how I rationalized my writing—to myself.

I'm writing in the first person—contrary to tradition which conditioned me to never say "I." I do so because I find it more direct, precise and responsible. It's my personal story. This book is totally subjective—about and from the one subject I know more about than anyone else—me.

I talk to you in the immediate rather than the general second person. Right here and now it's only you reading my book, sharing my vision. By the nature of my position, you and I are related. I hope you'll read it in *your* first person, all the while wondering what it means for you personally.

I'm advised that I ought carefully distinguish my roles as legislator and as person, that citizens want a representative, not a personal friend.

I don't want to do that to myself, even for you. I won't any more separate my public/political person from my personal being. No role's worth playing. That fractures, fragments me, is suicidal. I already experience the recurring question: whether the position I've chosen to put myself into professionally too much keeps me from myself and other persons. I yearn for communication with other humans of a kind not available in a separated public life. I'm wanting more, not less, personal contact. The time and energy necessary for fulfilling personal needs and political responsibilities are each so enormous, it's only efficient to do them both at once, conjointly. No more separation!

Separation of person and position contradicts my vision: converging, fusing our personal and political lives. To engage in such separation is to perpetuate the very problem I seek to overcome. That's not enough for me, I want to be part of the solution!

Separating myself would be no more enlivening for you. It underestimates you, as traditional politics and politicians have usually done. I trust you more than that—to respond positively. Humans respond most often precisely as expected. I prefer to talk up, rather than down, to you. I'd rather be party to a positive self-fulfilling prophecy. I suspect and hope that you're more ready than commonly expected. Perhaps the ideas you find in this book may fill a vacuum you're already recognizing, wanting to be filled.

My book is incomplete, unfinished. It doesn't contain all I know and want to share with you. To conclude my manuscript for publication, I had to arbitrarily cut off new input— experiencing, dialoguing, thinking, intuiting. My book is a comprehensive synthesis of most everything I deem important now.

You may deem it incomplete for my not further exploring other aspects of human endeavor: spiritual, economic, environmental, psychic, mystic, whatever. I omit these because I have no significant personal experience with them from which to speak. My model is holistic, there's room for areas of your concern. I hope you'll add them in yourself.

I believe the crucial elements are present in my critique. I'm suggesting the foundations, hoping to make a good beginning. The elements need experimentation and expansion, interpretation and communication—in many directions, by many persons. It's appropriate to my vision to hand it over to you for that: add in other dimensions as you want, research and develop all of it.

Better I take the risk of acting, even making the errors risked in acting, than take the more enormous risk of inaction—waiting until my vision is "complete" by some definition.

Living my vision requires I reveal myself to you as I *am*, that I make my current self available, visible, vulnerable, inviting to you. I won't hold myself back, protecting me or you. To do or say or be any less would betray myself and demean your self. I refuse to perpetuate the distrust endemic to our old culture. That's likely the root of our problems—personal, societal, political—in the first place. Why lessen our chances of developing a mutually growthful relationship, enabling each other to grow? Besides, it may as well be "the real me" you like or dislike—not a "reasoned" facsimile thereof!

Of course it's up to you. You're responsible for your feelings, whether you'll tolerate, accept my being myself—or reject me for being myself, openly and honestly with you.

I'm incomplete, like anyone brought up by our old culture. Although I know many persons well, some intimately, I've yet to meet a "complete" person. I'm still in process of becoming a person. Thus it's natural and alright that my book is incomplete. Together, we'll keep on discovering and developing—our vision, critique and action—as we go on, growing ourselves together.

My book is unpolished. I was trained to write and speak only polished words, phrases, clauses, sentences, paragraphs, chapters. I've edited it several times. That could go on forever. I don't want it to. I haven't the time, energy, desire and discipline to do all the polishing myself. I'm still unpolished myself, and prefer to devote myself to that task. It's time for me to publish, not polish. It's up to you to polish for yourself.

Nor are words sufficient for my purposes. We don't yet have words precise enough to express adequately what I want to tell you: the ineffable matters of the heart. Words are fragments: they hardly fit, much less portray holistic vision. Even pictures (a vision) though better, aren't sufficient. It's only enough that we feel and act. Words are the best I have to offer you here and now, at a distance. They can point the way. I invite you, from your own experience, to fill in between my words, color our pictures, realize our vision. Only you can do that for yourself.

I hope I manage to express and convey what I *know* deep inside me, from my experience—in a way liberating, even compelling for you personally. I offer various lists in my book. They are extensive, but not exhaustive. I hope you'll find them illustrative of what you can make true for yourself. They're presented in what seems to me logically progressing order, to facilitate your further exploration, experimentation and verification of their value for you personally.

In critiquing our institutions, I describe them and the groups of persons who make them up—as I've been impressed by them.

Not every person in any group fits my group impression. You needn't wear the shoe unless it fits you. If you feel it pinch, will you wonder why?

As I've searched and grown, personally and politically, I've met, listened to, read the writings of many persons, famous and not. I used to cite others extensively. I came to realize I did so in proportion to my feeling insecure, unsure of myself, unwilling to take responsibility for uttering that particular statement all on my own. Now I cite primarily when someone has spoken more poetically than I, or as a lead for your further exploration.

In constructing my own belief system, I've borrowed and assimilated much from many. I've made my own synthesis. I take full responsibility for it. Grateful as I am to many, I won't attribute much of anything to anyone. I trust that any person who's been my teacher will be enough pleased that I have learned—that any person whose ideas are valuable for humans will be satisfied that I'm spreading them further. If you recognize yourself, your words, in here, I hope you'll be pleased.

Whoever and however and wherever I am, I'm well aware I couldn't have and haven't done this all by myself. I wouldn't be who I am today without the remarkable personal presence and love of Art, Dan, Fred, Jim, John H., John L., John V., Joni, Judith, Ken, Leo, Mary, Pat, Patti, Richard, Sid, Stan, Stanley and Teresa. Each was particularly instrumental in my personal growth. Nor would I be who and where I am today, personally and/or politically, without the generous efforts of other persons too numerous to mention. I trust they know and appreciate their own contribution to my life.

Nor would my book be what it is without the loving critique of my friends Alex, Barbara, Bob, Bobbi, Dan, Dorothy, Greg, Jim, John C., John L., Joni, Margaret, Maxine, Michael L., Michael T., Pat, Richard and Tara, the quiet writing places provided me by Dorothy, and the faithful, sensitive manuscript typing by Bobbi as I've been pulling this together.

I hope you're here—to stay with me—
throughout my book—and after.
I invite and welcome your response.
I invite and welcome you.

JOHN VASCONCELLOS
Spring, 1979

introduction: preview of coming attractions

"Tell me what your vision of the future is, and I will tell you what you are."

—Frederick Polak

I want to summarize the major points of this book:

First, we human beings live in a unique time of change and crisis, peril and potential.

Second, our traditional politics—right or left, liberal or conservative, Republican or Democrat—is obsolescent, lacking credibility and effectiveness, neither fitting our people today nor responsive to the problems of our lives and times. Our politics isn't working.

Third, we humans must learn how to live together more intelligently, gently, caringly, all as members of one human family—or we will likely perish from our earth.

1

Fourth, we humans have lost our way and our faith, and are engaged in an endless, fruitless, exasperating quarrel—over the wrong questions. Only if we search out and surface the right questions, engage ourselves and our dialogue there—do we have any real hope of overcoming our exasperation, our differences and our problems.

Fifth, the central emerging issue
personal and political
human, moral, philosophical
theoretical and practical
of our lives and times
is "How do we grow healthy human beings?"
How do we provide an environment
in which a human being
can most readily, fully
grow and develop him/her self
to be/come

self-aware *and* self-esteeming,
self-realizing *and* self-determining,
free *and* responsible,
whole rather than fractured,
hopeful rather than cynical,
open rather than closed,
revealing rather than concealing,
gentle rather than violent,
motivated rather than apathetic,
democratic rather than authoritarian,
cooperative rather than competitive,
competent and excellent,
ecologically responsible,
loving rather than hating,
moral rather than immoral,
political rather than apolitical?

Sixth, our resolution of that issue depends upon
our most basic assumptions about ourselves:
the vision each of us has and holds
about our own human nature and potential,
who we are and who we can be/come.
Upon that assumption, with that vision

each of us chooses and creates our selves,
our own lives and being, and
conceptualizes, designs, creates, and operates our institutions.

Seventh, the central emerging event
of our lives and times,
personal and sociopolitical,
in thought, in feeling, in fact
is the effort by millions of human beings
of every sex, age, race, color, creed,
nationality, wealth, inclination
to redefine and transform
that very most basic assumption, foundational vision
about our human nature and potential:
from negative to positive,
guilty to innocent,
untruthworthy to trustworthy,
cynical to faithful
and

upon that shifting assumption
to redefine and transform
our own nature and potential and being,
our own human growth and development,
our own relationships,
interpersonal and institutional.

Eighth, the central personal/sociopolitical *event*
of our lives and times
therefore specifically relates to
the central personal/sociopolitical *issue*
of our lives and times.

If the issue between and before us
were how to grow trees in Anarctica,
our differences wouldn't matter much.

But our issue is
how to grow a healthy human being.

If you believe that's accomplished
by beating her/him into submission

and I believe that's accomplished
by loving him/her into liberation—
our difference becomes
momentous, explosive, perhaps irreconcilable.

We're like a family
in which mother and father
have contrary beliefs
about child-raising.

Ninth, precisely in that engagement
of event and issue,
we'll find explanation for
what's happening in our lives and society now,
what's going and gone wrong
in our lives and society now and in our past,
how we can make it right
in our lives and society now and for our future.

Tenth, our new vision
of our human nature and potential
provides us the basis for
a *new* human bill of rights,
an essential foundation for making things right in our lives.

Eleventh, our new vision
provides us a new basis for undertaking responsibility
for ourselves, our lives, our society—
to grow and develop ourselves
into fully-functioning human beings;
for choosing to act, to involve ourselves,   and
to participate personally and fully
in our human struggle for
a more decent, peaceful society and future.

Twelfth, our new vision
provides us the basis
for mobilizing human political action—
an essential foundation for making things right in our society.

Thirteenth, "personal" and "political" are inseparable:
the sum of our personal visions determines our politics;
our public-policy decision-making,
affects who I be/come.
The politics I do is who I am!

Fourteenth, we need, it's time for, we can create
a new human politics—
constructed
by liberals
who are into liberating human nature—
beginning with ourselves—
                    and
                              by conservatives
                    who are into conserving human nature—
                              beginning with ourselves—
a common place of beginning,
                    for beginning
                              to get ourselves together.

Fifteenth, each of us is personally responsible
for choosing between our two visions of
our human nature and potential.
we each must confront our own most deeply held beliefs:
are we human beings, by nature, good or evil?

Sixteenth, how each of us chooses
depends upon our experience of ourselves.
That provides us the vision
each of us carries into all our relationships,
interpersonal and institutional.
Each of us must confront ourselves!

Finally, it's now time each of us humans choose and act!

I hope to clearly demonstrate each of these points. Regardless of my success, I trust you recognize that you're responsible for your own understanding of what's happening, and for choosing how you're going to live your life.

I.
BACKGROUND:
PERSONAL SKETCHES

chapter 1

setting my sights — high

> *"Some...(persons)...see things as they are and ask 'Why?', I dream things as they never were and ask 'Why not?'"*
>
> —George Bernard Shaw

> *"I offer my dreams as dreams, leaving it to the reader to discover whether they have something useful for waking people."*
>
> —Jean-Jacques Rousseau

I want to share with you my goals in writing this book. I invite you to examine their significance in and for your life:
My goals are...
...to get the word out;
...to deepen our public dialogue;
...to propose a viable and compelling vision;
...to suggest an enlivening agenda;
...to improve the credibility of our government and politics;
...to enlist you in politics *and* personal growth;
...to mobilize ourselves;
...to humanize politics;
...to alleviate suffering;
...to do something for you; and
...to do something for me.

9

I want to get the word out, as widely and quickly as possible, that:
there's a vision that explains, in a concrete and hopeful way, what's happening in our lives and society;
there are many persons sharing our vision;
there's something we can do about realizing our vision;
it's time we got ourselves together.

There's nothing so powerful as an idea whose time has come — except persons whose time has come,
especially when the "time of persons" has come.
It's that time now.

To facilitate getting the word out:
a. I'm publishing this initially in a paperback format;
b. I've pledged my first year net proceeds to SELF-DETERMINATION: A Personal/Political Network, a four-year-old, 1600-member alliance of growing humans, for personal and political action toward our most serious public need:humanizing politics. (Get more information and membership application by writing Post Office Box 126, Santa Clara, California, 95052, or calling 408-984-8134);
c. Feel free to reproduce and/or use any part of this (non-commercially), if you follow the procedure noted on the copyright page (ii).
d. Will you share it, and more of yourself, with a family member, friend, neighbor, colleague, adversary?

I want to expand and deepen our public dialogue—so it matches the expansion and depth of persons in our times.
I'm tired of the shallowness and demagoguery of most politics—resulting from complicity between politicians and citizenry, each responsible, each underestimating the other's willingness to fully confront the crises of our times. Too many of us are trapped in trivia—wasting our time, energy and ourselves on shallow questions, activities and relationships. Too often we argue the wrong issues, get lost in our surface differences, attack only the surface symptoms of our problems. Only if we ask ourselves the right questions are we likely to discover the true answers and thereby resolve our problems.
Our society is sick and dying, if not sickening and deadly, at

its very root. We must attend to it right there. Nothing less will
suffice. There's little point in undertaking modest reform
proposals. They're little more than institutional tinkering at a
time when our institutions are in fact crumbling at their
foundations.

Every decision you or I make, of personal *or* public policy,
derives from our most basic assumptions about ourselves. Each
of us must
recognize, own up to, examine,
disclose, discuss
our own most basic assumptions. We best deepen our relationships and our dialogue by deepening ourselves. We must
engage each other at that deep level.

I want to propose a viable and compelling vision, one
which is:
faithful and hopeful,
reconciling and unifying,
credible and compelling,
liberating.

We live amidst widespread breakdown and turbulence, confusion and fear, cynicism and despair. Institutions that used to
provide us stability and security are fast crumbling, leaving us
insecure and afraid. Sometimes institutions in fact made us
insecure, then provided us false security. Paradoxically, their
crumbling, while making us aware of the falseness of their
security, likely leaves us unsecured.

We too readily cling to what is known, our status quo, even
though it doesn't serve us well any more. We're so besieged and
baffled. Absent a plausible explanation for what's happening,
one that enables us to maintain our faith and *see* our way
through, we're likely to retreat, even into reaction. We're
susceptible to simplistic preachments and demagoguery, even
fascism.

The best if not only antidote is a positive and plausible explanation for what's happening in our lives. It must enable us to
recognize that what's happening can be valuable for us personally. Then instead of feeling threatened and struggling against
what's happening, we can understand, feel reassured, and participate creatively to give more human shape and speed to what's
happening. Then we can be hopeful rather than despairing.

The best such explanation I've discovered is Willis Harman's *An Incomplete Guide to the Future*. Those in Carl Rogers' *Inner Power*, Ted Roszak's *Person/Planet* and Mark Satin's *New Age Politics* are on target, helpful, inspiring. I believe my own, from my unique personal and political experience, complements those.

We live amidst contrary basic belief systems.
I want to propose a vision
for getting ourselves together,
individually and societally,
personally and politically,
to enable us to grow,
to go beyond our past ineffectual recriminations,
to reconcile—
to truly come together in our present presence.

I hope to shift our dialogue from negative and win-lose and divisive to positive and win-win and cohesive.
I hope to bridge the two worlds—personal and political—in which I walk almost daily, enabling each to better recognize the other. I hope to provide an overall connecting vision so we can regain our sense of human community. We're all in this together, there's no place else to go, we can't afford to waste ourselves, fighting each other. We desperately need a basis for reconciliation, consensus, coalition and action.
I want to articulate the hopes and ambitions I believe natural to *every* human being—regardless of sex, age, race, color, creed, nationality, wealth, inclination, size, shape, whatever. I want to legitimate a positive vision too much thought to be only private, dreamy, philosophical, naive, and mistaken.
So much of our lives is self-perpetuating, self-fulfilling prophecy. Our expectations affect our experiences. My vision calls forth certain choices which, in turn, influence the future course of events. I hope my vision can externally reconcile persons of our traditional and new cultures, and facilitate the internal reconciliation of persons in transition between the two.
I hope to provide a critique so simple and clear that your response will be "Of course! Aha! Sure!"

I want to suggest an enlivening agenda that speaks directly to the dehumanization so prevalent today—a humanistic, holistic agenda. By ''humanistic'' I mean regarding human nature and human beings as innately innocent; by "holistic" I mean regarding the whole human being as positive.

I want to present an agenda of personal, human, moral, social and political concerns. I want to draw attention to a question not usually thought of as political: "How do we grow a healthy human being?" I want to persuade you that we can and must attend to that question now.

Coming to explore, understand and develop ourselves is the most revitalizing, invigorating activity we humans can engage in. There's already much (re)searching by scientists (by the hundreds) and by laypersons (by the thousands) going on about our human growth and development and behavior. We live in "the age of human discovery." We ourselves have become our frontier, the object of our research, and our own laboratory. We're also the subjects of our research, and the best experts. Who knows more about me than I do? We're the new pioneers. It's time we begin acting like pioneers: visionary, bold, willing to explore and experiment—with ourselves!

I want to enable government and public employees, politics and politicians, to become credible again, to persons both within and outside public service.

It's become chic to be scornful, skeptical-to-cynical, about our government and politics and all persons in them. Polls show blatant distrust of politicians, ranking us somewhere near the bottom on the scale of "trustworthiness." Political institutions which once enjoyed respect are held in low esteem today. Voters are apathetic. Only 37% of the eligible persons voted in our 1978 national elections. Fewer and fewer persons are registering in either major political party.

I find all that sad. That's dangerous to our very form of government.

Whether we characterize ours as a "republic" or a "democracy," its survival depends upon a wise and involved electorate, enlightened public officials, faithful public servants, and reciprocal trust and credibility among us all. Right now we're lacking all these. Our government's in trouble! We're all in trouble!

I want to participate in recreating that trust and credibility. I've experienced˙ so many good persons in and out of government, with so much good will, caring, talent and energy. It's time we recognized each other and act together. I want to make politics explicitly about people, and the hopeful implications of becoming human. Then we humans will be motivated to involve ourselves in politics.

I want to enlist you in politics and in personal growth, the natural rights—and responsibilities—of us all.

Too many humans are observers rather than participants in life. I'm into taking responsibility, developing a sense of responsibility, and living responsibly.

I want to facilitate freeing ourselves from some myths which may be blocking our acceptance of political responsibility:

a. "All the trouble will go away, pass me by, at least not engulf me." There's plenty of human history of people waiting, hiding, hoping—and perishing on account of their own inaction. Let's not be naive.

b. "Someone else will do it for me, save me the trouble, save me from the trouble, rescue me." This time the trouble's so pervasive, not even the charisma of a Kennedy can rescue us. We all must participate. If I'm not part of the solution, I'm part of the problem. If I'm not the solution, I am the problem.

c. "Someone first has to give me permission to speak and act. I need ratification and/or reward." Hopefully, the vision I propose will enable us to recognize we don't need permission to be ourselves, to care, to express and involve ourselves. Too many persons in our society feel they first need permission from some authority to act. Often I find myself fulfilling my responsibility by giving other persons permission not to have to ask for permission.

d. "I don't belong in politics. I'll feel like an intruder." I can't let anyone make me feel I'm a freak, outsider, intruder. No one has exclusive right to legitimacy in politics. I—and you— belong in politics and government as legitimately, as rightfully as anyone. I—and you—ought feel legitimate, reclaim the trapping of legitimacy.

e. "Politics will dirty me." How little faith in myself, to believe that politics will affect me more than I will affect politics.

f. "It wouldn't change anyway: it's never going to get better, no matter how hard I try, what I do." That's the safe, protective coloring of a cynic which, in its paralyzing effect, perpetuates how things are. It's another self-fulfilling, self-perpetuating prophecy. As I see our world, our situation is tenuous, hanging in the balance. A difference can be made.

g. "I can't make a difference anyway. Who am I?" Inculcating that attitude in me is the most profound way persons currently holding power keep things the way they are. They maintain their position and power by discouraging me away from acting, turning me off to exercising my own power. As I see it, our situation is so balanced, that each of us can make, can be, the difference. Our situation will get better only if and when you and I believe it can, that we can matter—then act to make it happen.

I hope to persuade you to recognize, *for yourself*, that you have a right and a responsibility to participate, a role to play, in politics. I'll offer suggestions on how you may go about becoming political.

And I want to facilitate freeing ourselves from some myths—possibly blocking our acceptance of responsibility for ourselves, our own human growth and development. Our capacity to engage ourselves effectively in politics depends upon the level of our own human development. And there's no reason each of us shouldn't become the most fully-functioning human being possible.

I want to mobilize ourselves.

I want to provide a focus (vision) and a framework (vehicle) for mobilizing ourselves toward realization of our human vision. Let's build an alliance—to get the word out, to enable us together to realize our vision, personally and politically. Our world's best kept secret is that there are so many of us "closet humanists." We're so many hiding humans. It's time we all come out—with ourselves intact.

I want to humanize politics—to cross-fertilize our human potential, consciousness and liberation movements with our public-policy decision-making.

There are so many of us in government and politics looking for a solution to our social problems. Healthy human development may provide it. There are many of us into our own personal growth, looking now for an outlet for expression and involvement. Politics ought provide that. We humans must recognize the political dimension of our personal vision. We politicians must recognize the human dimension—beginning with our own. Then we'll begin solving our problems. Our selves and our society are inherently connected. We need to change and heal both simultaneously.

Hopefully, my vision provides an engaging, hopeful, credible basis for motivating political theory and action.

I want to participate in alleviating suffering in our world.
I want to help humanize our society and institutions—so newly arriving human beings will be ever more nurtured and free, self-possessed and self-esteeming. Then they needn't experience the pain of self-repression and of self-recovery that I have.

I want to enable persons already damaged to heal themselves. I want to provide assurance to persons in transition: it's okay to make changes in our lives. You aren't alone, others are also in transit. We can help each other. Let's give ourselves permission to grow heartily!

I want to do something for you personally. I want to make an announcement. I want to share with you some good news: my vision.

I want to facilitate your improvement of your life. I hope my book enables you to further liberate your vision, compelling you to further liberate yourself. My vision is a way you can take toward discovering yourself.

I want to tell you who and how I am—that we might go beyond an exchange of our intellects, and reach into each other's heart.

For persons already sharing my vision,
I want to inspire you, say it more clearly, make it more moving for you—
that we may come together in relation, cooperation,
searching and struggling to
create authentic selves,
live meaningful lives,
experience tender relationships,
build a more decent human society.

I want to present a possible vision for you.
I want you to know there are kindred persons
in the halls of government and politics.
I hope my work, especially on myself,
provides you encouragement.

For persons who don't share my vision
I want to confront you with it,
cause you to reexamine your own vision.

And I want to provide us occasion
for recognizing and revealing the root of our differences,
that we may engage humanly, profitably, at that level.

I know I haven't the right to condition you or your existence. I believe I have the right, perhaps the duty, to confront you in a way that challenges you to be/come more than you now are, even all of whom you can be/come. I ought never force my answer on you. I ought always raise the right question between us. I can't change you or your consciousness. Only you can do that—for yourself!

Finally, *I want to do something for myself.* I have (unmet) personal needs.

a. I want to learn and grow more, expand myself and my vision. I seek, invite your critique, our relationship.

b. I'm intrigued by the challenge. I want to see whether I can accurately and persuasively analyze the principal moral deficiencies and dilemmas of our society. I want to see whether I can cause you to reflect anew upon our human and political crises, and your own capacity and responsibility for involving yourself in their resolution.

c. I'm weary. I want some respite. I'm tired of the ever-escalating, increasingly taxing person demands and sacrifices incumbent upon (at least my way of) being in public office today. I've been proposing my vision through fifty speeches each year these past twelve years. I'm tired of racing around, arriving in different cities, entering new buildings, encountering seas of unfamiliar faces, wondering how to be present in a significant way in thirty minutes or less. I'd like to make my vision available to you at less cost to me personally.

d. My writing brings together my whole past life and experience up until now. It clarifies what I know, *and* my life and being. It also clears my mind, leaving room within me for new thoughts, insights and realities to emerge.

I'm wanting to put what I know together, get it out of my head, onto paper and, hopefully, into yours. I want to make way for something new and better for me personally, some way that allows me more time and space for being myself, attending to my personal needs. I want to clear my decks for action, feel unencumbered to make a fresh start—perhaps with a new way of being in the Assembly, perhaps with another way of being in politics, perhaps with a way of being less explicitly in politics.

I recognize that what I know is changing even as I write. But when we hereinafter meet, I hope we won't have our same old arguments, nor even have to repeat the ground I cover herein. We can go past what's here, engaging each other so as to enable us to grow into further insight, hope and human action.

As I write this, I find myself almost into hysterics at the incongruities of this passage and in myself. It's like saying: "I'm weary, give me respite, full speed ahead!" As I write, I'm gaining insight about myself and my incongruities.

e. I want to enlist you in our political struggle. There's so very much to be done. I want more support and participants. We must band together, form a reservoir of our talent and energy, work together to bring about our vision.

f. I want to enlist you in my personal struggle. My mission from the outset has been as much personal as political. I've met most of the persons currently enriching my life amidst my being public. I travel, speak, and write, looking for persons to provide me companionship, reassurance, occasioning my further personal expansion. I'm looking to be more and more involved with persons who share my vision, are open and willing to share themselves with me, to be/come allies, friends, even more. I hope my writing makes me known to you. I'm hoping you'll make yourself known to me—so we may share, together grow more human.

One caution: be prepared to find me other than you might expect from reading my book. Since I'm daily into expanding myself, by the time you read this, I'll already be more than I am while writing this. I've experienced myself changing and growing during the nine-month course of my writing this book, even on account of its writing. I've found it especially powerful, growthful, empowering—to work on my book with a friend, reading to each other. My book deepened, we each deepened, our relationship deepened, work became play.

Yet I'm anxious because I may be less than you'd expect (perhaps because I'm less than I expect). I'm still a creature of our traditional culture, not yet able to live all I know, believe and propose. I'm better at this intellectually than at living it, better talking than being it. My head is more willing, my flesh yet weak. Considering my earlier bias toward intellectual development, it's no surprise I'm not up to date with myself, existentially.

Even as I've become a knowledgeable and prominent public spokesperson for human growth and development, I have my problems, personally. That gap causes some persons to judge me hypocritical, to say I ought not speak. I find speaking helps me clarify and close that gap. I'm still in process, in progress, struggling to become a whole person.

Overall, I hope my book will facilitate my realizing all my goals. I've set my sights high. I'm going for it all.

chapter 2

a personal invitation

"Today we are witnessing the frightening things that political leaders with one-channeled minds can do. What alarms us is their simplistic view of social and political reality. They know only one solution: and this solution is totalitarian and spurious. Their lack of tolerance and fear of dissent reflect their own lack of freedom. One-channeled minds can never comprehend that truth may have many channels."

—Gordon Allport

As I was completing my second term in the Assembly, I briefly contemplated running for Lieutenant Governor in the 1970 elections. I told only one friend, Marc Christensen, my teen-age co-chairman in my first campaign, about my thoughts, then discarded the idea. Later Los Angeles attorney and political activist Bill Norris told me he and friends were looking for a candidate for Lieutenant Governor, asked if I was interested. I said I thought not, but would consider it.

I drove home that night, found Marc—without notice—awaiting me. The coincidence got me wondering. The next day college friend Tom Farley, member of the Colorado Legislature, called to say he was running for Lieutenant Governor. More wondering. The following week, still wondering, I flew to Los Angeles for a funeral, stayed overnight with political activist friend Gary Townsend. We discussed the Lieutenant Governorship at length. Finally I went to sleep.

An hour later I awakened fully, thoughts racing through my head. I got up, wrote them down into a statement which concluded "That's why I'm running for Lieutenant Governor." Twenty-four hours later, I had no more desire to run for that office, so I simply changed the conclusion to "That's why I'm running for reelection to the Assembly."

It is still my favorite of my writings. I offer it (updated) to you now, as we begin our effort toward a truly new, human politics.

I invite you to participate in politics—a politics of personal responsibility and human community.

I've spent my 12 years as an Assemblyman/Legislator— wandering about our state and nation, wondering about the state of our humanness—we are 220 million human beings now—trying to discover the reasons for the problems that confront and bewilder and nearly overwhelm us all.

I believe our greatest problem is that we have lost our faith— we have lost faith in ourselves, we have lost faith in each other—and I want to be a part of rediscovering our faith, in ourselves and in each other.

I'm tired of watching the gaps that divide us—between persons young and old, between persons poor and rich, between persons of different colors—continue to grow. It's time we close gaps instead of widening them.

I'm weary of seeing the walls that separate us continue to build. It's time we build bridges, instead of walls.

I'm tired of observing persons sitting back in apathy, or moving out in violence, persons resorting to force or fear or name-calling or sloganeering, persons hiding behind simple answers or blaming it all on someone else.

It's time each of us assumed our personal responsibility to ask new and deeper questions—to instead wonder why the other person is acting as s/he is, to go personally to the other and listen and learn what's behind that conduct, and to wonder how to become involved with that person in a way that responds humanly to his/her pain.

I'm weary of sensing the escalation of negative feelings between the various groups of our society. It's time we reconcile, time we seek a new sense of community.

I'm tired of feeling the circle of cynicism in which we are enmeshed—our politicians not trusting our people (to handle the truth), our people not trusting our politicians. It's time we break that circle, and create a circle of faith.

I'm most weary of the game people play, and of the games some politicians—of all parties, at all levels—play.

It's time for a truly new politics—

I am committed to a politics of openness and honesty, a politics of personal encounter and a politics of shared search—inviting each American to recognize his/her personal responsibility to participate, fully and freely, openly and honestly, in finding our way back together.

I feel no need, and believe it destructive, to simply indict our past, or even our present. I sense each person has done the best he or she then knew how. And we have come a long way—even to where—perhaps for the first time in human history—we are painfully aware of how much we have not done, and of how much more we can do, and must do—with and for ourselves, and every person in our society.

And I feel little need to put anyone down—including other persons running for office: I want to be a part of picking ourselves up.

I want to tell it—not like it was, but like it is.

I want to say—not what's politic—but what's real.

I want to speak—not what people want to hear—but what I know, and how I think and how I feel—openly and honestly.

I want to be myself—and, whether anyone agrees, if everyone will be themselves—openly and honestly—with me, and with each other—I have deep faith we can find our way together.

Somehow we have lost ourselves in our surface differences—young and old, black and brown and white and yellow and red, male and female, straight and gay, tall and short, rich and poor. And we have frozen up behind our walls of fear, anger, hostility, hate, despair.

It's time we recall that deep down inside—far more important than our surface differences—we are each and all human beings. We share the same hopes and dreams for ourselves and, I trust, for each other, for lives of freedom and harmony, decency and dignity, equality and peace.

Unless we begin there, we truly have little hope of resolving our problems of racial prejudice, violence, drug abuse, unemployment and welfare and high taxes, automation and technology, crime and delinquency, pollution and population and environment, poverty and hunger, health and education, power and manipulation, family disintegration, traumatic change, institutional reform, the experiential gap between persons, even war and peace.

Each of us—each person in America—must recognize and realize his/her unique potential, his/her unique responsibility, in our common search.

Each of us must wonder more about what more each of us can be—and become—and do—to get ourselves together.

Each of us must wonder how we can discover more of ourselves (some now say we each operate at five to six percent of our human potential), how to discover more faith, more trust, more sensitivity, more compassion, more caring, more love—toward, with and for, each and every person in our entire human family. Much more: each of us must assume and recognize our personal responsibility—discover our commitment—to become involved, to participate, to solve our human problems.

As we enter our future—the direction is ours to choose. Many say—with ample evidence—that we verge on disaster, or apocalypse, or revolution. I say "perhaps"—but I say more—that we stand on the threshold of realizing our American dream—for every American—if we but have the necessary faith. Though our problems are immense, our potential is far greater.

I want to be a greater part in realizing our potential, and in rediscovering our faith—that we may truly come together again.

I invite each and every person to become an active, experiencing participant with me, in our common endeavor.

Will you join me?

chapter 3

a
transparent
self

> *"This above all: to thine own self be true, and it must follow, as the night the day, thou canst not then be false to any...(person)..."*
> —William Shakespeare

My old friend,
mentor and *a* parent of "the real me",
Sid Jourard
(whom I still mourn and miss)
taught me

there are two things especially valuable
we humans
can do with and for each other:

I can
tell you
who I am

                    and

I can
listen to you
tell me
who you are.

I've since discovered
a third:

I can
be present with you
in a way that
invites your opening,
discovering and disclosing
more of
who you are.

This chapter is my effort toward such a personal relationship between you and me. I want to take the time and space to introduce myself to you. It's important, to me and for you, that you sense who I am and where I'm coming from, as we embark upon our joint search for a liberating vision, for our liberation, for ourselves.

My friend,
mentor and *a* parent of "the political me,"
Robert Kennedy
was the first politician
I heard speak about "love."

This book is my effort
to describe and propose
a "politics of love."

I've earlier given you my goals in writing this book. But there's a more basic reason for my writing. It represents my realization that everything I do is the product and expression of my current being. I (and each of us) always do what I want to do. I'm doing this simply because I find myself *wanting* to. The reasons I commonly think up to justify my actions are usually only rationalizations, even excuses, for doing what I want to do (having been conditioned throughout my upbringing to believe I ought not, above all, do what *I* want to do.

"*Why now?*"
I've been presenting these ideas in frequent speeches and infrequent articles for years. Others have been urging me to write a book. Yet it's only happening now. Why now? Again, my

most basic insight is because I *feel* like doing it now. But there's more I can discern.

I sense a timeliness, even an urgency, now. I sense we humans may be at, if not already past, a point of no return—in our struggle for making our lives and society more human.

We live in unprecedented times: enormously changing, conflicting, chaotic and confusing times. We've come forward so far, so fast, that many of us are weak and off-balance, bewildered, even frightened ("future shock").

Something tremendous is happening, or at least trying to happen, within our individual lives and in our world at large. We share a peculiar and unprecedented time and space on our earth. We've come to a threshold, a crossroads—confused if not conflicted (within and between ourselves) as to which direction to take. We live in a precious, pregnant moment, in which we likely will choose to either claim or forfeit the greatest opportunity in history to expand our human existence and ourselves. We must seize this moment—and glorify and maximize it!

Further impelling "now's" are the pervasive apathy in our politics today, and our increasing polarization. The traditional center seems fast disappearing in American politics, with no more middle ground on many issues. That's dangerous—unless we deal with it creatively, to clarify our differences, to help us understand and resolve those problems which divide us.

The overwhelming passage of Proposition 13 by over 4,000,000 Californians in 1978, and the wave of similar issues in other states—further focuses our urgency. I fear such may dishearten and demoralize those persons who believe in and call out the best in us humans, appetize those persons who believe in and call out the worst in us.

As a heavily involved participant and observer, I want to offer what I have to contribute to the understanding of our present crisis. Even a slightly increased insight might make the difference between faith and despair, paralysis or action, for each of us, for all of us, even for our human race.

There's further reason "Why now?" I sense a readiness in myself. I took my 1978 vacation to get away for twelve days by myself alone. That gave me time to review what I'd earlier written and decide whether I wanted to put it all together now. I'm surprised by the similarity between what I was saying years ago and what I'm saying now. It's still current. I've been living my vision pretty faithfully these past twelve years. I've field tested it. It's validated, ready for consumption. I find myself much more assured, and sure, of myself and my beliefs.

Combined, my growing sense of urgency and my growing sense of myself lead me to act now. It's a time for speaking out. It's time for me to speak out!

"Why me?"

I could superficially respond: I've been requested to write by friends, other concerned persons, prospective publishers. Such urgings help me overcome my self-consciousness about writing, but by themselves are insufficient to move me to write.

My deeper response to "Why me?" is because while we humans have much in common, each of us is unique. All of us, as human beings, are alike by (our) nature. Yet each of us is who we are (and different) on account of our own unique formative interplay of genetics and experience. I am who I am, the sum total of my life so far. So I have a unique story to tell.

Sid Jourard uses this insight beautifully—in exploring how we humans ought properly deal with persons different from us. He suggests that each of us is largely the result of our experience—if I'd had your experience or you mine to date, we'd be the same. I ought recognize our differences as a matter of experience and development. To put you down for being different is silly; worse, it's counterproductive, for I then only add to your negative experience. Instead I ought accept you as an integral person. I could then be present with you in a way that adds positively to your experience, to your becoming more than you now are.

I'm reminded of my behavior toward conservatives in the Legislature. When first elected, I carefully avoided close contact with them. I deemed them "bad persons" who might contaminate me. As I grew personally, I came to recognize my avoidance as a symptom of my personal insecurity. As I grew secure enough within myself to risk exposing myself to them, I found them to be humans, just like me. We developed some trust, much affection even occasional agreement. I am more for having done so.

Although I'm still self-conscious about saying it, I believe that my experience of the past thirteen years makes me and my story unique in an especially timely way. I've spent these years in elected public office, *and* in personal struggle with what I believe is the major problem, struggle and aspiration of our times: discovering what it means to be/come fully human. We're redefining and expanding our sense of being human, and searching out how to live a new way, according to our new and expanded image of our human nature and potential.

I've been living a daily dual odyssey: personal *and* political, searching out who I am as a person *and* how to be/come the best elected official I can. I live daily, at times painfully, the trauma and anguish of the search for self that typified our age. We explorers of our own human nature and potential have a special contribution to make toward our larger society. In resolving our own problems, we'll most likely become insightful and able to present viable solutions for the regeneration of our society as a whole.

Too often the pain of personal crisis and growth leads persons to depart the 24-hour-per-day fishbowl rigors of being in public office. I've managed to maintain both efforts because I've received ample support from fine friends, good staff and skilled therapists. So far I haven't met another person in elected office at any level who has so long and consistently addressed his/her own personal growth. I'd be delighted to.

My quest began January 30, 1966—a turning point in my life, marked by radical change in my personal and social condition. On that critical day I held my first Assembly campaign meeting *and* embarked on my personal odyssey as well. I left my old self behind for good. I began living the existence of a nomad—cut loose from my old ways, on the search for new ways of being, professional and personal.

I'd begun my political career running for class president in the 8th grade. I lost by one vote—mine, a sign of my then lacking self esteem, a lesson well learned, never repeated. During high school I twice ran for student body office. I was so nervous that when I rose to address the student body, I could only stutter " V-v-v-v-o-o-o-t-t-t-t-t-e-e-e-f-f-f-f-o-o-o-r-r-r-r-m-m-m-e-e-e. " They didn't. I had my first victories at the University of Santa Clara: I was successively elected class vice-president, class president, student body secretary, student body president and law school student body president.

As I was completing my undergraduate senior year, I was

called in by the senior adviser, a brash New Yorker Jesuit, Steve
Earley. He said he wanted to discuss my life plans—and I began
backing out the door. He assured me he wasn't going to suggest
a religious vocation—and I stayed. He suggested I go into
politics as a career—on account of my performance as student
body president. He expected the Democratic Party to be the
"wave of the future" and then Attorney General Pat Brown to
soon become Governor. He proposed preparing a resume about
me and taking it to Pat Brown. I listened curiously. Having no
career plans beyond completing my R.O.T.C.-required two
years in the Army, I didn't object.

Steve is persistent and persuasive. Due to his urging (helped
by his Roman collar), Brown invited me to come meet him. I did.
He then invited me to attend the State Democratic Convention. I
did, and served as doorman in the Assembly Chambers. I
started "at the bottom."

Thereafter Brown annually invited me for a visit, and each
time spoke of looking for some opportunity to provide me
political experience and exposure. Nothing happened until the
1960 Democratic Convention in Los Angeles. Pat Brown went to
Mass at the nearest Catholic Church, and encountered my old
promoter Steve Earley saying Mass. Steve put the pressure on,
asking Brown when he was going to find me that opportunity.

The following week Pat invited me to join his personal staff, as
travel secretary. After two weeks of hesitation I accepted, and
took a leave of absence from my law firm. I held the position
from September 1960 through August 1961. During that time I
accompanied Pat Brown just about everywhere, spending more
time with him than did any other person, except his wife
Bernice.

In fall of 1961 I returned to my San Jose law practice, and
involved myself in numerous political, civic and religious efforts.

In 1966 I was elected to the Assembly of the California
Legislature, where I'm now serving my 7th term. During those
thirteen years I've served on Committees on Local Government,
Constitutional Amendments, Criminal Justice, Educational
Goals, Health, Housing and Human Resources. More signifi-
cantly, I've served all thirteen years on the Assembly Education
Committee, and for the past nine years have chaired California's
only legislative effort specializing in postsecondary education.

Just as significantly, I've served eight of the past nine years on the Assembly Ways and Means Committee. Six of the past seven years I've chaired its five-person Education Sub-committee, which reviews budgets for all of California public education from preschool through postgraduate. In 1977 and 1978 I was appointed by the Assembly Speaker to serve on the two-house, six-person conference committee which reconciles and finalizes the entire California budget. In 1979 I was named to the Joint Legislative Budget Committee.

I'm addicted to politics. My political odyssey has provided me enormous experience in the real world of practical politics and politicians.

Concurrently with my political journey, I've been experiencing a personal identity crisis. I began searching when the carefully cemented structure of my existence began to crumble. As I've been virtually "coming apart," I've undertaken continuous and varied efforts to grow myself into a more whole, healthy human being. I've been searching for a more authentic and nourishing life, and am still engaged in a continuing quest for my full self-identity.

I began by reading Sid Jourard's *The Transparent Self* in 1966. Several years earlier it was given me by surgeon friend Phil Ernstrom. I glanced through it and found it made little sense to me. In 1966 when I began searching desperately, I rediscovered Sid's book. Suddenly it made total sense. It became my "bible".

In 1966-67 I spent an hour once a week for a year with Leo Rock, priest/psychologist trained in the Carl Rogers school of reflective listening. He listened in a way that assured me it was okay to be who and how I am, even as I plumbed bottom trying to reconstruct my life and being. I struggled with the process of releasing myself from one belief system (traditional Roman Catholicism) and discovering and internalizing a more viable system (commonly referred to as "humanistic psychology", not to be confused with "Humanism.")

Since I'd been especially raised to value intellectual activity, I read extensively, even exhaustively—everything I could find in humanistic psychology. I gradually assured myself, gave myself permission that it would be okay to go further in exploring and experiencing myself, beyond my head, even "out of my mind."

I built myself up to go adventuring, though slowly, even reluctantly. In February of 1966 I made my first trip to Esalen, a growth center in Big Sur, California. I went with friends Dave and Joni Leahy. We drove there very slowly, afraid of the unknown (of ourselves as much as of that place). We were afraid even to reveal our fears to each other, 'til years later.

Since I'd grown up to be impressed with "big-name people," I spent one weekend a month that year touring the touted gurus of the human potential movement: Dick Farson, Sid Jourard, Abe Maslow, Jim and Liz Bugental, Jim Fadiman, Rollo May, John Heider, Carl Rogers and Leo Rock—in order of appearance. Those weekends moved me increasingly beyond the intellectual/cerebral into the experiential/emotional/encounter mode.

In 1971, at the urging of friend Gary Townsend, I took a significant, and I believe essential next step—to rediscover and revitalize my body and energy, that I'd been so long out of touch with. For the next three years, I spent an hour every week or two, with Berkeley bioenergeticist Stanley Keleman, trying to liberate and integrate *all* of my human being. Many mornings I'd spend on the Assembly floor or in Committee, then drive the freeway for an afternoon in Stanley's workshop. Some culture shock!

At one point he refused to work further until he forwarned me. He knew politics was nearly my whole life. He saw so much rage so deep within me, he worried that if he opened me to it, I might lose control and wash out of politics. I told him: "I have no choice, let's go on." There followed a period when I was so explosive, two Assembly colleagues were assigned to attend me during my tantrums, until I calmed down. I've since outgrown the worst of my rage, although there are still times I become outraged by what's transpiring in our Legislature. (Perhaps you know *that* feeling!) I added a half dozen sessions with physical therapist Margaret Elke.

Since 1973 I've spent an hour or more each day, often concurrently with other activities, in a self-discovered process of stretching and twisting my body from deep within. It serves to loosen and expand my body, my being and my consciousness.

So I'm addicted to (my) personal growth as well as to politics. My personal odyssey has provided me enormous experience in human growth. I have a seemingly inescapable dream and drive to totally liberate myself. My old need for achievement has become now my need for knowing and growing myself. I'm fascinated by the process of growing myself into a wholly healthy human being.

I consider my continuing personal growth necessary to my fulfillment, possibly even to my survival, personally and politically. Skeptics claim that personal growth and political involvement are inconsistent, even contrary. I challenge that: it's just not true.

In my search-for-self odyssey, I came to recognize that our culture and institutions had enormous influence on me and my development. I increasingly recognized the convergence of the personal and the political in our times. I developed a critique and theory of government and politics that revolves around the question: "how do we grow a healthy human being?"

Since my personal and political struggles now share the same focus—how to grow a healthy human being—what I learn in one is invariably valuable to me in the other. I'm trying to converge/fuse my personal and political lives, recognize and reconcile their inherent relationship and oneness, and make that explicit in my life. My parallel experiences led me to further recognize the necessity that people understand the convergence of the personal and the political. I began generating efforts toward its wider recognition, acceptance and implementation.

In 1969 friends and I spent an afternoon exploring the personal/political convergence with growth center founder, (the late) Bob Driver and his friends in Del Mar, California. Later that year in San Francisco, Bob and I explored it further with Esalen founder Michael Murphy and Director of Development Stuart Miller and my friends Pat Callan and Dennis Connors. In 1972, in six San Francisco dinner discussions, six of us (Murphy, Callan, writer George Leonard, Esalen lawyer John Clancy, psychologist Joe Adams and I) explored it further. In 1974 friends Stan Commons, Steve Reed and I founded SELF-DETERMINATION: A Personal/Political Network—an operational effort to promote understanding and implementation of the personal/political convergence.

Throughout my legislative career, I've continued my convergence efforts—seeking ever more to develop and legitimize a more humanistic, holistic politics. I seek to converge and cross-fertilize the tenets and goals of humanistic psychology with our public-policy decision-making.

In both senses, personal and political, I'm an "insider." My uncommon dual experience gives me a particular capacity for proposing a vision which would reconcile persons with politics and government, and reconcile politicians and public employees with personal growth.

I also speak from another, more common dual experience: I have deeply lived and experienced both our traditional and new cultures. I was raised in our traditional culture's institutions— home, church, school, law practice, civic activities, government. I lived it faithfully until age thirty-three. I was and am successful by almost every standard of our traditional culture—high grades and awards throughout school, highly respected law firm, active lay church leader, seven times elected to the Legislature, given key assignments here. I have a good position and title. I'm established. I'm part of the establishment.

These past thirteen years I've lived increasingly into our new culture—exploring, experimenting with and experiencing alternative ways of being, personally and politically, inter-personally and institutionally.

Additionally, how I live moves me back and forth between them daily, often hourly. And my work requires I become trusted by persons in both cultures, and effective in reconciling the two. I have friends in each culture. And even as I seek to live ever more by our new culture, I find a goodly part of our traditional culture persisting, still operational within me. Curiously, my old traditional, duty-bound, high-achieving, save-the-world vocation sense commits me to my work and its many opportunities for doing good. My new sense of myself, more positive and overflowing, is intrigued if not captivated by the opportunity for further enabling the liberation of persons, including myself, in our society.

There are additional responses to "Why me?"

One is my own sense of personal responsibility: I care.

Another is my sense of political responsibility: I take my public office seriously. It's a position of influence and leadership. A leader has responsibilities. The primary one is to enable other persons to recognize and realize their innate capacities for becoming *their own* leaders.

A significant related responsibility of a leader is to help hope happen again within our people. That requires that I become able to explain what's happening outside and around us in a believable, reassuring and hopeful way. I must become able to occasion, catalyze and facilitate events happening inside people, so we grow ourselves more, discover our own hopefulness.

My capacity for and the character of my leadership is dependent upon my vision and experience of myself as a person. To be such a leader requires enormous self-possession, high self esteem, and a deeply faithful vision of human nature, grounded in deep and reassuring experience of myself. Each of us who assumes responsibility for growing other persons (through family, education, religion, health, politics, however) has a personal responsibility for growing her/him *self* more and more whole!

To properly carry out my leadership responsibilities, I must be regularly attending to my own continuing growth and expansion as a person. Only then will I discover faith enough in (my own) human nature to recognize that you are innately trustworthy, that such capacity is in you to be evoked. Only thus will I grow whole enough to not need "followers", not to be with you in ways that perpetuate your dependence upon me, the "leader." I only need power over you to the extent I'm not yet in touch with my own power/energy within myself. As I get more in touch with myself, I'll less need and desire power "over" you. I'll more want to empower you.

It's important too, that you discover that you only *give* me power over you to the extent you're not yet in touch with your own power/energy within yourself. As you get more in touch with yourself, you'll less need and desire to give me power over you. You'll more want to empower yourself!

As I attend to and experience myself growing personally, I sense my increasing capacity to see, to articulate, to influence other persons. I observe myself growing politically—almost in proportion. Sometimes now it seems I can see what's on our horizon, just around our corner, what's coming for us humans, where we're headed. If I can see and report back my observations clearly enough, hopefully you'll be better able to see and to recognize and to say it just as well, and to utilize it in your life. People tell me I have the facility to put into words what they are so far only thinking and feeling, personally and/or politically. I am willing to do so.

I want to share with you two letters I've received in that regard. The first is from then-college-sophomore Marc Christensen, written upon Martin Luther King's assassination:

5 April 1968
Friday 2:00 a.m.

Dearest John,

Don't know why my thoughts have turned to you now. We were just talking about Dr. King—and for one passing moment I felt afraid, alone and confused. Not so much because of some disbelief, John, what kind of country do we have when a man can't walk freely without being shot? Worse yet a man who knew only peace? How do we stay optimistic at these times? How can we tell people to love, to trust, not to fear?

I guess my mind and heart come to you not because I thought you'd have any answers but because you'd be searching too—searching down deep for a little bit more courage, a little bit of hope, and a smile.

This may sound weird when you read it—but it's been a weird day. And these are very weird times. Somehow I can only think of the President when he said— "When the going gets tough, the tough get going." John, let's really work for a better world, really try hard.

Thanks for listening.

Your friend always,
MARC

The second is from then-18-year-old friend John Ungerleider, as he concluded a month's internship with me in the Capitol in July, 1976:

John—

It seems absurd and a somewhat tragic commentary on society to have to thank somebody for verifying one's right to dream. It is crucial to me though, and gives me great strength. So I thank you.

PEACE,
JOHN

Our times call out for appropriate vision and action—and for some things to be said, which aren't being said or heard well enough. My own being cries out likewise. I want to try and say those things. I believe I have something significant, valuable, hopeful to say to you. Being in a position of political leadership in a time of crisis—I ought no longer hold back, for any reason. Life, especially political life, is tenuous. I am perishable without notice. I may as well "go for it."

I'm choosing to create from my life this public document—grounded in my belief that my existence is significant, personally and politically. I offer this document with mild anxiety that you may not like my writing. I worry that the way I record my vision may turn you off. I also worry about your not liking my book. It's so much me, you'd then not like me. I ask that you respond to my substance, rather than my form.

I am willing to take those risks. Our present situation demands such effort of each of us humans, especially if we hold public office. Too many politicians are too neutral and bland, modeling and perpetuating our very problem. I'd rather take the risk.

On the other hand, I do this with another, greater anxiety: you may like my writing and me more than I'm ready for. I'm unsure whether I want the increased attention my writing may bring. If my book is successful, I may be more in demand, by more persons, for more public involvement and appearances. A part of me shudders at that possibility.

Already I've experienced some of that attention. In a restaurant one evening, a dozen persons acknowledged me. One sent over after-dinner birthday drinks. The waiter said he'd voted for me. The manager told me he was flattered I was dining in his restaurant. Students write theses about me and my politics. As I exited a friend's office Christmas party, an unfamiliar woman recognized me, threw her arms around me, giving me a Christmas kiss. Whether I cut my hair, shine my shoes, wear a necktie are already topics of media attention and public conversation.

I find such attention flattering and exhilarating. I find it simultaneously frustrating and exhausting. It's like being an entertainer or other celebrity, always in public, on display, having all the time to "be on," always at an elevated metabolic pitch.

At times I love it all. At times I find myself hating it, wanting to give up and get out—except there's no place else to go, and I don't want to let that get me down, force me out. Sometimes I feel like living my life as an "ordinary person," even becoming a hermit. Sometimes I want to return to the silence of the state of nature (rather than the din of the state of civilization), where beings seem to more readily live in peace.

Already too many persons too much elevate me onto a pedestal, then "dutifully" keep *their* distance. It's not comfortable, I get mighty lonely up there. I'm a person, wanting to be with and among other persons.

I worry about getting caught up in being a popular leader. The crowds and acclaim of press and public are heady and tempting. Hopefully I won't get caught up in it, needing it, playing to it. There's no surer way to lose track of myself and my commitment to myself. I hope that acknowledging this worry—openly, to you—helps me resolve it properly. Hopefully my personal growth efforts get me more in touch with my natural self esteem, so I less need power, admirers or followers.

Also, I'm depending on you to take your own responsibility. You only need a hero/ine to the extent you haven't yet realized your own innate capacity for becoming your own hero/ine. My vision is truly one of *self*-determination.

Many persons in our culture are accustomed to look to persons in positions of authority for direction and permission. I hope to occupy my position in such a way that if you look or listen to me, for direction or permission, I'll use that forum to support you looking into yourself, for permission, for trusting *your own* innate authority for becoming your own leader. It's wonderful to share power—by empowering others.

I occasionally feel uncertain about the use I'm making of my position of power. I hope that I'm correct in my vision, not misleading anyone. I won't however, let that uncertainty become an excuse for my inaction. Again, your responsibility comes into play.

I recognize an irony: the more I acknowledge my uncertainties and hesitations, the more attractive I may become, both as a person and as a leader. Overall, I'm basically shy. I'm still somewhat unsure of myself, insecure. But rather than avoid myself and my responsibility, I want to recognize, confront and outgrow my shyness, my self-consciousness. I'm going to just let myself out, be who I am, do what I want, and trust you with myself.

Sometimes this all seems too grand and bold and risky: I feel it too much for me, I want no more of it.

Other times it comes clear to me our time is ripe, that you and I are ready, that no other effort is worth making, personal or political.

At all times I recognize my vision as the natural expression of my own continuing growth as a person. I know then that if you and I come together fully, we can and will enable our vision to happen, to come to life!

II.
SCENE:
SOCIETY
IN
CRISIS

chapter 4

kaleidoscope: change, crisis, chaos

"There is a disintegration of the hope, which is the inner genius of the American spirit, that...(persons)... can solve their inner problems and that evils can be overcome."

—Walter Lippman

"At all levels of American life people share similar fears, insecurities and gnawing doubts to such an intense degree that the country may in fact be suffering from a national nervous breakdown."

—National Committee for
an Effective Congress

I increasingly find myself
sensing that we human beings
share lives in the most unique time
of our entire human odyssey
from however we came to be here
to wherever we're destined to be going.

Our times are unprecedented simply by reason of the enormous changing that has become the fact and fabric of our daily lives. Alvin Toffler's *Future Shock* dramatically demonstrates that. Our personal experience is more than ample evidence of changing, changing, changing.

Three changes are especially significant and profound in our lives and society. They interrelate, adding to each other's effects, and converge beneath, upon and within us human beings.

First is *the coming of our "affluent society."* Ever since the dawn of human history, most humans have spent most of their lives doubled over, struggling to produce enough food, shelter and clothing simply to assure physical survival. In times of such scarcity, persons necessarily had to curtail themselves, conform, fit together artificially. We may suppose that only a few kings, philosophers, bishops and artists had or took the time to ask themselves "Who am I?" "What's the meaning and purpose of life?" "Who are you?" "How do we relate to and with each other?"

That's no longer our situation. With our tremendous technological genius and the productivity of our economic system, we've developed ourselves to the point where we can produce more than enough of the basic physical goods for everyone on our earth. Having the capacity to assure our physical survival (problems of distribution acknowledged), we enter a different society. In an affluent time, we humans can be less curtailed, conforming and repressed—more curious, diverse, unique, individualistic, expressive.

More and more of us are using this occasion, taking the time to ask ourselves those questions about our lives and being, our own purpose, each other. That's a truly great step for humankind. We ought be grateful and work to extend that opportunity to every person.

The second and simultaneous change is *the coming of universal/mass education.* For the first time in human history we have the impact of virtually everyone being educated through grade school, most through high school, even a generation in our country whose majority has been to college. Though far from what it could and should be, education does expose more minds to the analytical, critical questioning process. Our increased *capacity* for questioning interfaces with our increased *occasion* for questioning. The convergence becomes empowering!

Third and also simultaneous is *the coming of our mass media,* especially television. Our average 18-year-old has spent more than 18,000 hours watching television. I lived my first eighteen years with no television—a radio allowed occasionally. The boundaries of my childhood world could be measured in blocks. Today's persons have our entire world to look to. Through television we observe the lives of people everywhere on our globe: their joys, sorrows, suffering, and protest. They're all in our front room every evening, part of our daily family exposure: Viet Nam, Watts, Peking, Guyana, Camp David, South Africa, wherever. No longer are we isolated from what and who's going on in the rest of our world. Our entire world is now opened to us. We ought open ourselves to our entire world.

Television allows us to see history pretty much as it's being made, before it's censored (at least in our country). It provides us all our world to wonder about, matching our increased occasion and capacity for wondering. The convergence becomes overpowering! The convergence of technology and affluence inspire a greater standard-of-living expectation. The convergence of universal education and mass media demystify life, authority and ourselves. The convergence of all three leads to a changing experience and expectation of both our external and internal worlds. A new human awareness, consciousness emerges and takes its place within and amongst us. We're becoming a new people, new persons.

In addition, the availability of television in virtually every home in our country lets persons at our society's economic bottom—our "have-not's"—see for the first time what others have, what they've been missing. Moreover, they're urged to believe they won't be *okay* unless they have it. They're urged to want it and, more, to *expect* it. There results an increasing—and appropriate—thrust toward material equality.

But it isn't only *economic* have-nots who are envisioning themselves and life and human existence in a new and different way. Television also shows "what we've been missing" to persons excluded from the mainstream of our society's wealth, influence and opportunity just because they're *different* from our majority cultural stereotype: Anglo, young, tall, handsome, straight, hard-working, able-bodied, male. We witness and experience an unprecedented thrust toward human equality: our liberation movements.

As well, persons in our mainstream are getting a glimpse that there's more to ourselves and life and human existence than we've heretofore known. We witness and experience an unprecedented thrust toward human expansion: our human growth movements.

The result: all groups want more! The "have-nots" want as much as other humans have, the "haves" want as much as we humans *can* have. We're into an era of *rising* expectations.

Neither our "have-not's" nor our "haves" (material or psychological) are going to be put aside or ignored for long. We are all brothers and sisters, members of our human family. We all deserve to grow. We all ought revel in our growth.

Many, many humans are experiencing and envisioning ourselves and life in new and different ways. We're sharing in an attempted redefinition of human life and compassion, politics and possibility. We're searching, reaching toward a new vision and a new ethic. We're wanting to move away from elitism and competition toward a more human and democratic society.

As a nation we're in ferment: our people are restless, on the search, on the move. We find ourselves living in a world in flux, a new world, with new culture and new persons. Everything about us is changing: our world, our society and institutions, ourselves. We're fast approaching a "critical mass" of change, a change in magnitude, a change in character; more than change—a transformation—both in our outside world and within ourselves.

It behooves us to discover how to make sense of all our changing, so we may better live and work amidst it. These powerful forces and conditions, that bring us into a new world with its new culture and new persons, and affect our very beings and lives, are now permanently amidst us. There's no going back: there's already too much changing, we cannot cease our changing. As our world's physical resources are consumed and dwindle, we may find our material affluence diminishing. But our worldwide drive toward universal education will never cease. We aren't going to close our schools and universities. We aren't going to disassemble our machines and technology. We aren't going to throw away our television sets.

We aren't going to move backward toward oppression and denial. Women aren't going back, nor are blacks, browns, gays, disabled, or older persons going back into their places of isolation. There's no going back for persons who have tasted freedom, opportunity or personal growth. Persons who have improved the quality of their lives aren't going to settle for less. Persons who have more deeply experienced themselves are here to stay.

Nothing's certain any more, nothing seems inevitable. Not even taxes since Proposition 13! Not even death according to some new beliefs!

Our changing relates to another profound hallmark of our times: crisis. Nearly everything's in crisis: our society, our institutions, our selves. Our institutions aren't working well. Our problems are getting out of control. Our attempted solutions often prove more counterproductive than effective. Our major social problems seem intractable. Contrary to our best intentions, despite our best efforts, everything's disintegrating. Our decision-makers don't seem to understand what's happening, or why, or how to make it right. Personal lives and relationships are in unprecedented disrepair.

It doesn't take an economist, sociologist or statistician to observe and conclude that things aren't working. At this point anybody can see that, everybody lives amidst that.

We can catalogue the failing character of nearly all our major institutions and ourselves:

Our families: fewer marriages, almost as many divorces, battered spouses, abused children, child runaways and suicides;

Our health: epidemics of physical (e.g. cancer) and emotional dis-ease, skyrocketing costs of health care;

Our education: learning failures, truancy, dropouts, vandalism, assaults on teachers;

Our safety: rampaging crime, violence, recidivism;

Our economics: unprecedented inflation, balance of payments deficit, dollar decline;

Our employment: unemployment, underemployment, strikes;

Our environment: pollution of our air, water, earth;

Our mineral resources: diminishing, exhausting;

Our personal lives: alienation, loneliness, apathy, boredom, pain, cynicism, drug abuse, suicide;

Our sexuality: dysfunction, rape, incest, pornography;

Our personal relations: empty and unfulfilling, absent love, fearful of contact and intimacy;

Our group relations: racism, sexism, ageism;

Our political relationships: apathy, loss of credibility and morale, polarization on key issues, citizen revolts;

Our international relations: wars, enormous armaments.

Our people constantly face dehumanizing situations that demonstrate that the very dignity of humans is in doubt and jeopardy. Our important social institutions (family, church, school, university, government) are besieged financially, rapidly losing our allegiance, finding their legitimacy challenged. Our economic, political, cultural and moral systems are all in disrepair. Those persons and institutions which have been the source of our values, authority and direction have been under bombardment and have suffered a remarkable loss of credibility.

An immigrant woman I met while walking precincts in 1974 put it simply: "Something's gone wrong with America, it's not living up to its promise any more." Our American dream has become a nightmare. We seem to have lost our sense of community, our way, and our confidence. The public's confidence in our major institutions dropped in 1978 to the lowest level since 1972, according to a survey by the University of Chicago's National Opinion Research Center. People expressing "a great deal of confidence" constituted, for various institutions and years:

	1973	1974	1975	1976	1977	1978	Average 73-78	Rank 73-78
Medicine	53.8	60.3	50.4	53.8	51.4	45.9	52.6	1
Scientific Community	36.7	44.9	37.6	42.6	40.8	36.1	39.8	2
Banks and Financial Institutions	— —	— —	31.9	39.4	41.8	32.8	36.5	4
Organized Religion	34.6	44.2	24.3	30.5	39.9	30.5	34.0	6
Military	31.6	39.6	35.2	39.0	36.2	29.4	35.1	5
Education	36.8	49.0	30.9	37.2	40.5	28.4	37.1	3
U.S. Supreme Court	31.3	33.2	30.7	35.2	35.5	28.0	32.3	7
Major Companies	29.2	31.3	19.2	21.9	27.1	21.6	25.0	8
Press	23.0	25.8	23.8	28.3	25.0	20.0	24.3	9
TV	18.5	23.4	17.8	18.6	17.4	13.7	18.2	11
Congress	23.4	17.0	13.3	13.7	19.0	12.9	16.6	12
Executive Branch of the Federal Government	29.2	13.6	13.3	13.4	27.8	12.5	18.3	10
Organized Labor	15.4	18.2	10.1	11.5	14.7	11.0	13.5	13

Our trust in our institutions, our leaders and our old ways of living is waning. We who embraced the American ideology of independence and upward mobility have done all "the right things," yet our rewards are not forthcoming. We've tried so hard and sincerely to make it all work. We're seething with resentment, frustration and fright about our present predicament and "the system." A phrase from the popular film "Network" illustrates our exasperation: "I'm mad as hell, and I'm not going to take this any more!"

We find it hard to accept that we're no longer the masters of our destiny. We can't act with our accustomed freedom, assurance and boldness. We find it hard to accept that we can't simply and immediately solve the continuing crises in our lives. According to a 1976 Harris survey, 59% of our people feel alienated, disaffected and/or disenchanted with our country; 63% believe that the people running our country don't really care what happens.

In his *An Inquiry Into the Human Prospect*, Robert Heilbroner explores our human prospects and reluctantly concludes there are none. Is our trend reversible or are we already too late, past the point of no return? The evidence suggests we're going through a long period in which there'll likely be no quick and easy solutions to our problems. We can't wish or frighten or talk or fight away our problems. But we *can* solve them, and believing so makes it easier and quicker. Suddenly it's become late for us humans, we have no time to lose. We ought have a sense of urgency.

The word "crisis" derives from the Greek, meaning "turning point." In a physical illness, the "crisis", the "turning point" can be for bad or good, worse or better, death or life. Our society is now at a point of turning. We needn't be alarmed. We can consciously take responsibility for directing its turning toward *life*.

In fact, a "crisis" often provides a unique opportunity for our awakening. Our despair can grow sufficient to cause us to suspend—even for a moment—our usual way of seeing things. We then can experience a curious moment of unusual openness and receptivity, when we'll let an alternative notion enter our consciousness.

As with our changing, our crises require our attention. Each of us humans must now focus our attention, energy, time, and resources—our entire lives—on the main issues of our times,...or there may well be no more humans. And we can *do* that!

Our question is: What can and shall we do about our crises? It's not enough to complain about how bad things are, or fantasize about how we'd like them to be. Avoidance doesn't serve us, acknowledgment does. Let's not waste our time and energy in efforts that don't serve our purpose. Let's not divert ourselves in blaming, scapegoating, looking for someone else to hang it on. That way we fool ourselves into believing it's out of our hands. That doesn't do any good. Worse, it divides us. We need instead to come together to solve our problems.

Let's not let ourselves be entranced by simplistic answers or demagogues. In our situation, we're especially vulnerable to falsely-assuring, security-oriented proposals. They're fulfilling only for the demagogue, who has nothing better to offer us, so plays on our fears to make him/herself popular and powerful.

Let's not be preoccupied with our past, studying ancient matters to the *neglect* of those confronting us today. There's no going back. The circumstances that produced us and our times are irreversible. Let's not be preoccupied with our future. Instead of using our resources to hold conferences on "human potential in the 21st century," let's realize our human potential *now*.

Let's not waste time in speculation about future trends, or how long a current undesired trend will last. Let's instead recognize that we create the trend, by how we create ourselves, and how long a trend lasts depends upon how immediately we're willing to involve ourselves in reversing it. The best way to improve our future—even to assure we'll have a future—is to engage ourselves in our present. *Now* is our only real chance to live, and our only place to live.

Let's be motivated by hope rather than by fear. Being frightened into doing "what's good for ourselves" curtails our ability to see or act wisely in our own behalf. Let's choose to be hopeful rather than hopeless, to rechannel our fears and frustrations into positive faith and action.

Let's not wait for a catastrophe (if we've not already experienced one) to bring us to life, and move us to involve ourselves in corrective action. We don't need an external enemy to unify us humans. As a world, we need to recognize our unity. We are unified in our common human nature, unified in our desire to make our lives better.

Let's not wait for some charismatic leader to bring us to life, move us to corrective action. Our world's healing won't result from some benign president or enlightened legislature, at whatever level. Each of us must recognize our future lies in our own hands. We ought each assume our responsibility for participating in the effort to overcome our predicament. You and I are either part of our solution, or we are part of our problem.

Let's not expect adopting a different ideology to be the answer to our world's problems. Changing ideology isn't as effective as changing ourselves. There's no one better qualified than ourselves to improve our own lives. We simply need to recognize that truth, and act upon it.

Let's not set ourselves apart from our human struggle. What happens to other humans happens to us. We've got to overcome our apathy, let ourselves care. While in Israel, I shared the touching experience of Jerusalem's Holocaust Museum with Shimshon Zelniker, a University of California professor directing the University's "Junior Year Abroad" program at Hebrew University. He lost family in the Holocaust. As we exited, my compassion was made more poignant by his comment: "And to think the thing that most disconcerts people in Southern California is bad surf."

Humanity is not outside, but within us, each and all. Precisely because we see the truth, we're responsible for telling it, acting on it. It's vital we create a sense of *possibility*, that life can be improved. And we must create a sense of *faith*, that each of us can make a difference. Then we'll begin seeing opportunities everywhere.

Let's not underestimate our capacity to face and understand our reality. Let's assume each other person has as much faith and good will, and cares as deeply about improving our lives and society as we do. We can do something more creative, effective, deserving of ourselves! We've grown enough now to be able to look calmly at what's true today.

We've been pretending, like the Emperor's New Clothes. Let's publicly admit, to ourselves and each other: we live in a time of enormous crisis. Our choice is either to surrender to how it is and despair, or to take the chance to risk and improve it.

We must deal similarly with the chaos of our times. In Greek *chaos* means "a situation in which a latent order, not yet recognizable, is emerging." We can't escape our chaos by refusing to look at it either. Let's overcome our timidity and descend into the midst of our chaos. We must take responsibility to look at and into our reality, and recognize and realize the order latent there.

In January of 1979 I spent six days in Egypt. The average income is $200/year, the illiteracy rate is 40%, 30% of the population has a drinking-water disease they'll die of. Of Cairo's 11,000,000 perscns, 60,000 families live in the cemeteries, the best housing they can afford. The dead are housed better than the living. There are twelve persons in the average residential room.

I then spent eight days in Israel. The interest rate is 30%, the inflation rate is 50%, and they live literally under the gun all the time. Yet neither country is experiencing the type and magnitude of our social problems. We're the most materially prosperous nation in our world, and in a time of prosperity. We Americans constitute six percent of our world's population, consume 30 percent of our entire world population's annual usage of our mineral resources. We have the most able, educated, talented, good-willed and wealthy citizenry and nation ever to exist on our planet. Yet we can't seem to get it all together. Something is missing—perhaps a matter of faith.

Our inability to solve our problems suggests we're doing something mighty wrong in our efforts—that we're not looking in the right direction for solutions.

To dissipate our fear and confusion, we need to become able to make sense of all that's happening. We need an explanation to solve our problems, even to survive—and to maintain our faith and hope amidst it all. Then we can recognize that what's happening can be valuable for us personally. Then we can participate with/in it fruitfully, to provide a sense of direction. Then we can enable our transformation to happen more readily, and gently. Then we can resolve our crises and our chaos!

Let's be hopeful—rather than embarrassed—on account of our past efforts. We've demonstrated our capacity for accomplishing enormous good. Let's be proud of all the good we've accomplished in our 200 years as a nation. Let's admit our mistakes, and use them as opportunities for our learning.

It's time we substitute a program for our problems. We may begin by envisioning how we'd like our lives and society to be. What kind of world do we want to live in? What kind of people do we need to make it that way? What's keeping us from having them? What kind of processes would enable us to get there? How do we get ourselves from here to there?

In seeking answers, let's engage ourselves and each other deeply, authentically, candidly. We've grown enough. We have to look deeply if we want to discover truly responsive solutions. In attempting to solve our problems, we ought begin at the beginning, the root causes, not lose ourselves in arguing shallow surface questions. Too often that covers and avoids our basic issues. If we will search out, surface, and engage our basic questions, ask ourselves "Why?" we may see what's happening below our surfaces, the reasons for what's moving there.

An in-depth analysis of our social condition will be possible when we become willing to go beyond our surface differences as *persons*, searching out our common *humanness*. That requires us to acknowledge, confront, perhaps even challenge and surrender our most basic assumptions—about our own human nature and potential, our own human lives and relationships. We must become willing to examine, question, challenge everything, including ourselves and our most deeply held beliefs, assumptions and values. We have to reexamine and challenge ourselves and how we live. We ought even be prepared to change our minds, and ourselves.

There are, to my mind, several major questions that we must attend to if we're going to make things right again, in our lives and society, now and for our future:

• *How do we grow our moral capacity* to keep pace with our other developed capacities, and our developing world?

• *How come we're so fascinated with things,* property, money, wealth, and economic development—*and so unconcerned with persons* and human development?

• *How can we (re)discover our capacity for community*—beyond that traditionally forced by adversity? I was struck during my visits to Egypt and Israel that in both countries, especially advantaged persons seemed to be living a sense of caring about other persons, especially the disadvantaged.

• *How do we grow healthy human beings?* Better stated, what environments can and should we provide to facilitate and enable human beings to grow ourselves to become
self-aware and self-esteeming,
self-realizing and self-determining,
free *and* responsible,
competent and excellent,
ecologically responsible,
whole rather than fractured,
hopeful rather than cynical,
open rather than closed,
revealing rather than concealing,

gentle rather than violent,
motivated rather than apathetic,
democratic rather than authoritarian,
cooperative rather than competitive,
loving rather than hating,
moral rather than amoral,
political rather than apolitical?

* *Where do we look for leadership today?*

Our predicament is aggravated by the acceleration in the process of discarding beliefs that is common in our society now. We've evolved radically differing beliefs about how to go about fixing everything—all held by sincere people. And designing a program necessarily involves determining and proposing "how" we should deal with our problems.

Where should we look for solutions? An obvious place is our basic political system. Is it sound? After much wondering, I find myself believing it is. It works. In recent political history, two of our previous three presidents, one of each major party, were forced out of office. The third was defeated by a near-unknown outsider. The Viet Nam war was ended. Racism and sexism are no longer our public policy. Change *does* happen within our political system.

Even more reassuring, our entire system of government is founded upon the finest assumptions about us human beings: "We hold these truths to be self-evident, that all men are created equal, that they are endowed by their creator with certain unalienable rights, that among these are life, liberty and the pursuit of happiness." Section I of California's Constitution begins: "All people are by nature free and independent, and have certain inalienable rights, among which are those of enjoying and defending life and liberty; acquiring, possessing, and protecting property; and pursuing and obtaining safety, happiness, and privacy."

For all its faults and failures, I don't believe the *structure* of our political system is our primary, central problem.

It is unfortunately true that most of what our public officials discuss is shallow and unimportant, not conducive to solving our major problems. Too much of what our Legislators, Governors, even our President does—is unimportant, "politics as usual."

We need *extraordinary* politics!

Where shall we look next? Many persons suggest our economic system: that if we could more equally distribute wealth, all would be okay. I grant our economic system warrants examination, change, correction, improvement. But far more than economics is gone awry. There is a central, deeper cause of our myriad problems, including those which are economic.

Where then shall we look? I submit that the correct, best place to look is right at *ourselves and each other*. We need to look at how we envision and experience ourselves, our human nature and potential. We've been so entranced by exploring outer space. We need as well to search out our inner space— ourselves—all that's happening within, between, amongst and to us human beings today.

Our situation and problems derive from our general personal, cultural and social context, and we'll discover our solutions emerging from within the same context. Our stream of human events offers clues.

All of what's happening in our lives, whether it appears to us good or bad, is the *choice* and expression of some of our fellow humans. It's no accident our institutions are failing. People don't reject institutions arbitrarily, for no reason, without reason. In making our choices, we humans are saying something important. What is it? What are we wanting and asking for? Protesting and complaining about? What do we really want? Is there anything helpful and hopeful in all of this?

I can recognize some valuable clues. The counterproductivity of so many of our efforts to date suggests we may have something basically wrong. We may be operating in reverse, working off the wrong assumptions. The fact our efforts to solve one problem often create or aggravate others suggests they may all be interrelated.

It begins to look like we have *one central underlying root* problem. It's something basically wrong. It's an upside-down reason that accounts for everything so coming apart and for our incapacity to put it all back together again.

Something enormous is trying to happen! I can see a pattern emerging. I hope to share it clearly with you in the chapters to come.

chapter 5

microscopes,
telescopes,
macroscope

*"If there is any period which one would desire to be
born in, is it not the era of revolution when the old and
the new stand side by side and admit of being
compared; when all the energies of...(persons)...are
searched by fear and hope; when the historic glories of
the old can be compensated by the rich possibilities of
a new era. This time like all is a very good one if one
but knows what to do with it."*

—Ralph Waldo Emerson

To fullfill my responsibility to myself as a person *and*
to fullfill my responsibility as a legislator to you,
I've spent these thirteen years trying to figure out
what's happening.

From my searching and experiencing, I've come to recognize
patterns and trends—leading to a theme now emerging. It
explains what's happening: we have one world macroproblem,
and we're in revolution to resolve it. You and I should personally
involve ourselves in correcting it.

I've found several ways of looking at our reality, and recognizing what we humans are up to. Some ways look closely like a *microscope*, others look from a distance (over time) like a *telescope*; one way is a *"macroscope"* for viewing our big, overall picture. These perspectives help me understand: what's happening now, in our lives and society; what's going and gone wrong, in our lives and society, now and in our past; and what's right and how we can make it right, in our lives and society, now and for our future.

I invite you to consider these perspectives with me.

Perspective #1: Our Two Cultures (Philip Slater's *The Pursuit of Loneliness: American Culture at the Breaking Point*)

Our contemporary conflict can be understood as the clash of two contrary cultural models. I'll refer to them as our "old" and our "new" cultures. We humans are in transition between them, experiencing a transformation of our old culture into our new culture. Our society is torn between conflicting, contrary cultures—each experientially grounded, with its own value system, its own ethical and moral imperatives.

Each human being has life experiences profoundly different from, perhaps opposite those of other persons. This uniqueness of experience often leads to radically different, even contrary selves. It leads as well to contrary assumptions about life and human nature, expectations about being human, and value systems.

Our old culture developed in a world of scarcity—first from our basic human struggle for survival, later from the insecurity of our great economic depression. Our new culture has been generated since World War II—in a time of remarkable affluence. The experiences and perceptions of many persons who have grown up (some for a second time) in this new kind of world are radically different from persons growing up in our old culture. As a result they differ in values, attitudes, human expectations and sense of possibility.

Initially our new culture was a phenomenon among our young. Because they were brought up in a world as different from their parents as were the children of our initial immigrants, they grew up differently. As they did so, they created a culture fitting themselves. Curiously, many already older persons recognized the possibilities of our new culture for themselves, and began exploring it. As a result, many persons of all ages are living new lives today.

For persons whose gut experience is scarcity, the common basic assumption is distrust: they expect little from life, take nothing for granted. Their logical resultant moral imperatives are security, accumulation and competition. For persons whose gut experience is plenty, the common basic assumption is trust: they expect much of life, take everything for granted. Their logical resultant moral imperatives are freedom, sharing and cooperation.

Our old culture therefore emphasizes work, accumulation, elitism, intellectuality, conformity—values necessary for personal and collective survival in more difficult times. Our new culture softens—perhaps even rejects—the work ethic, rejects conformity, is more sensuous and democratic in its orientation, more trusting of diversity, feelings and the human body—with less fear and shame and guilt. These values are possible in more easy times. They're even necessary for human personal and collective flourishing in such times.

Such different cultures result in contrary minds, insights, beliefs, moral imperatives, attitudes (about almost everything):
trust and distrust,
freedom and security,
accumulating and sharing,
property, material possessions and money,
competition and cooperation,
work and leisure,
authority and responsibility,
consciousness and pleasure,
drugs and music,
war and peace,
God and religion,
nature and our environment,
self-fulfillment and self-denial,
repression and liberation,
human emotions and the human body,
sensuality and our senses,
sexuality and love.

The most fundamental divergence of our two cultures is in

their views about the character of human nature, and the existence of human potential.

The implicit bias underlying our old culture and its institutions is that our human nature is inherently evil, sinful, guilty, untrustworthy, irresponsible, violent. In this bias, the most we can hope for is to contain ourselves. Some persons instead propose that our human nature is neutral, we arrive like a "blank slate," to be written on. In either event, a human must look outward and upward—to institutions (parents and family, religion and churches, schools and education, government, bosses)—for authority, values, fulfillment, salvation, instruction on what to do, even on how to be.

Our new culture instead assumes the human's fundamental goodness, innate innocence, spontaneous trustworthiness, gentleness and responsibility. Such a human would instead look inward and downward for authority, values, fulfillment, salvation, instruction on what to do, how to be.

No wonder we're experiencing cultural and institutional and personal crisis. Our institutions were conceived and constructed out of our old experience, our old culture, our traditional ethic. And they served well! They produced affluence, technology, automation, universal education, mass media, rapid and intercontinental transportation, outer space exploration. We've experienced tremendous intellectual growth, fostered more by liberals, and tremendous material growth, fostered more by conservatives. Together they provide us a new and different world, externally and internally. We can each take pride in our contributions, and in each other's.

Our institutions served our traditional values so well they evolved and are giving birth to a new world and new experience. These are fostering in turn an evolving new culture and consciousness, an evolving character of humanity, and eventually new persons. There results something very different in the way we human beings experience life and ourselves, and in

how we think and feel,
how we believe and trust,
how we hope and love.

Our new culture persons stand on the shoulders of our old culture—with expanded visionary capacities. We can see further.

Sadly, old culture persons are often threatened by and bitter toward persons of our new culture—with their expanded opportunities, vision and aspirations. Too often they view our new persons as wasteful, lazy, disrespectful, ungenerous, ungrateful. Instead, they too deserve to delight in and enjoy our new culture—the fruit of *their* culture and labors, generosity and sacrifices.

Sadly, our new culture persons don't often appreciate enough those foundations upon which we stand to see. Instead, with newly expanded vision, we often see only our old culture's repressive processes—as the greatest threat to personhood, wholeness and integrity. Instead we could appreciate the foundations of our growth.

Unfortunately persons of both groups are almost always righteous regarding their own culture, negative regarding the other's. We ought all recognize it's not a matter of choice or preference or "right and wrong" that underlies our split cultures. It's simply a matter of experiencing differently the evolving character of our world and of ourselves.

(Slater's proposed solution is incongruous. He puts down the rise of individualism, proposes self-denial as a necessary basis for our return to community. His solution derives from our old culture's negative model of human nature. It fails to recognize that our evolving new human is becoming more naturally loving and sharing, more naturally desirous and capable of community.)

Perspective #2: Our Three Cultures (Will Schutz)

In the beginning we lived amidst our traditional culture. In the 1960's we witnessed the emergence of our counter-culture, wherein many persons saw another vision, different from our traditional culture. They separated themselves from our old culture and tried to destroy it. A cultural revolution began.

Now we're merging the best of our two cultures, into an *encounter* culture, where instead of fighting cultures, we persons are encountering each other.

Perspective #3: Our Culture and Nature

We usually talk of revolution in the political sense: changing who gets to operate our political institutions, to exercise power in our society. Political revolutions usually don't make that much difference, changing only who holds the power, not so much how they use it. "They" are usually still persons of the same old culture.

More recently we've been shifting toward a cultural revolution. We're recognizing our old culture's constraining grip upon us. We're throwing off our external bondage. We want a culture that matches our changing selves.

Now we are grown to where that isn't enough. We're recognizing culture's constraining clench within us. If we're still enculturated persons, we'll not act much differently. We're into changing ourselves. It's dawning within us that culture as we've known it is, by definition, cynical about our human nature. It superimposes itself upon our nature. It implies our human nature isn't of itself sufficient. We're moving into a pro-nature, anti-culture revolution. We're breaking out of our internal bondage, liberating our own nature from the imposts and ravages of all enculturation. It's a natural progression.

Perspective #4: Our Shifting of Power
We find ourselves experiencing a profound shifting of power in our lives and society. We're well into a startling, but increasingly evident *demystification* process.

In prior times much of life and power was held in secrecy, mystery and mystique. Rulers held their power without having to justify it or themselves. People were taught to be awed by authority and to blindly, automatically trust it. I was raised (or lowered?) in a church where the authority figure (priest) conducted the main ritual facing away from me, speaking in an ancient foreign language.

Now all our world is transforming as we begin to see through the old myths of power and authority. More and more persons are refusing to swallow arbitrary authority and power. We used to always have to prove ourselves satisfactory to the authority figures. Now we're asking questions, putting the burden of proof on those *in* authority, to demonstrate their trustworthiness. The pressure's on—them.

We're outgrowing mystery. We're wanting all secrecy exposed, everything (including ourselves) out in the open: no more blindness. We're trusting our own authority, asserting our own power. That's a healthy sign, a healthy state of mind. It leads to healthier persons, healthier politics, and a healthier society.

A remarkable second step in our power shift is an ever-growing *horizontalization* process (Joe Fabry). Our society, institutions and ourselvès have been constructed on a vertical model. Power was held vertically—whether it was the parent, priest, principal, President, Pope—or their counterparts. The operating assumption was that someone up above knew "better than I" what was good for me. Our institutions operated and depended upon that someone holding the authority and power, having the truth and answers. S/he made decisions for the rest of us, handed them down, often in the form of rules and prescriptions for us to follow. If we didn't, we were punished, even banished from the kingdom.

At first, power was held individually—by a dictator or monarch. Later it was held collectively—by the oligarchy, the "new power elite," or representative bodies. The rest of us were taught to avoid ourselves, look outward and upward to that authority for instructions on what to do, even how to be. We learned, in turn, to look downward, on other humans, giving instructions. Either way, we always have a crooked neck. No wonder we're all so much in pain!

To accommodate our instruction, we constructed ourselves vertically: placing value upon our heads above our emotions above our bodies.

Stemming from the same changing of our experience, humankind is evolving horizontally. Vertical authority is under attack internationally within our traditional institutions—family, church, school, university, government, business, unions, workplaces. We're much less willing to accept what some other authority says is true or right.

Instead we're looking inward and downward, into ourselves, our own feelings and bodies, to discover what is true and right. We're trusting our own being for the answers on how to live, what to do, how to be.

This eruption is upending ourselves and every institution in our society. It takes many forms and names: "democratization," "decentralization," "local control," "maximum participation of the group affected," "self-determination," "parent advisory councils," "community self-assessment of needs," "net-working."

A third force in our power shift is an undeniable

individualization process. Based upon our old negative
assumptions about human beings, the intention and function of
our traditional institutions were to fix and fit, edit and tailor us
into the common institutionally-approved shapes. They saved us
from ourselves! Institutions conditioned us to avoid ourselves
and serve the institutions. We chose to conform. We put on
uniforms, marched in lockstep in an assembly-line world. We
relied on external standards rather than our internal needs and
wants. The implication again was that the institution knows
more than the individual.

With our evolving, expanding sense of ourselves, the focus is
radically shifting away from institutionalization to individualization. We humans are developing a deepened sense of ourselves,
our minds, bodies, feelings, needs and wants. We individuals
are bringing a heightened sense of our individual rights to our
institutions. We'll be faithful to institutions only insofar as
institutions are faithful to individuals, to us individually. We are
saying "I will be who I am, I won't be conditioned, oppressed,
repressed any more."

The purpose of institutions today is to celebrate the
uniqueness and serve the needs of each individual human being.
We're shifting from institutionalizing and programming
individuals to individualizing institutions and programs.

A primary purpose of our traditional education was to
socialize the children of parents of differing cultures. We
believed that being uniform, we might better band and bind
ourselves together to form a strong nation.

Now, in contrast, California's Education Code (Section 33080)
declares: "Each child is a unique person, with unique needs,
and the purpose of the educational system of this state is to
enable each child to develop all of his or her own potential." The
Code goes on to propose individually prescribed programs for
developmentally disabled children, for mentally gifted minors,
for limited and non-English speaking children, and for every
child, through the state's School Improvement Program.
Comparable shifts toward individualized programs are evolving
in health, job training and other fields.

A fourth major factor in our shifting of power is our
personalization ethic. In order to survive in a world of physical
scarcity, we humans chose to limit ourselves. We suppressed
our bodies and emotions to concentrate our energy in our

intellects. We believed that better equipped us to conquer our threatening external environment (Tom Hanna's *Bodies in Revolt*).

Until recently there was little general attention given to what it means to be/come a person. Our shift toward individualization inspires further exploration of what an individual is and can become: an exploration of our human potential.

In our new culture, we humans can relax ourselves some, let ourselves be/come whole, fully-functioning persons. We're recognizing, honoring, opening and developing all of our selves—our minds and emotions and bodies; our insides and instincts and impulses and intuition; our subjectivity and sensuality and sexuality—as well as our intellectual capacity.

Along with our new experience of our radically changed external world comes a radically different experience of our internal world, ourselves. In outgrowing our old culture, we see something new emerging in the way we envision and experience ourselves. It is a radical change in how we human beings see our human nature and potential, who we are and who we can be/come. From that foundation we are differently envisioning human growth and development, human relationships and human institutions.

Our institutions must become *person*-centered, tailoring themselves and their programs to development of the whole person of the individuals they serve. Such a goal is reachable only insofar as the persons operating institutions have become aware of their *own* potentialities as unique and whole persons.

The cumulation and culmination of these four processes is a profound shifting of power and authority from the awesome, mystical, vertical throne on high—to ourselves. They lead to the *empowerment* of the individual, liberated, integrated, whole human being. They lead to us persons owning and exercising our own power and authority in determining our own lives. Let's all celebrate and participate in our empowerment!

We need wisdom, trust and patience to see and steer our way through this profound shifting of power. We often make false starts, explore blind alleys. Yet move and explore we must.

Social movements usually unleash counter-movements, in behalf of greater "stability" as traditionally defined. Ours is no exception. We already hear cries for more order, structure, and control. But our forward movements won't reverse themselves, as we won't reverse ourselves. We may have some slowing while we assimilate, but we won't go back to how it was: secrecy, mystique, vertical power structures, institutionalization, depersonalization, dehumanization. Our forward thrust has an inertia that can't be stopped. We're like the genie once out of the bottle. Our efforts to fully live our new faith will ease, hasten and assure our ultimate self-realization.

Perspective #5: Our Shifting of Responsibility

Until recently we've expected leadership (for our living, revolution, salvation, whatever) to come from "on high." We've hungered for leaders like John Kennedy and his charismatic Camelot crew to come riding on white chargers to rescue us all, save us even from ourselves, especially from our taking responsibility. Upon the assassination of Robert Kennedy, priest friend Larry Largente said: "The lesson is—we have to be/come our own leaders."

Now we're recognizing that leadership must come from ourselves, from the bottom of our being. We're becoming our own leaders, choosing our own lives and being. We're the true "grass roots" movement, growing from the roots of our own being.

Perspective #6: Our Expanding Ourselves

Growing out of these same developments, we've been finding ourselves amidst five great concurrent efforts toward human expansion:

...*Our liberation movements*—black, women's, brown, gay, gray, children's, handicapped. My 6-foot tall friend Patt Schwab initiated "tall women's liberation" as her 5½-foot short friend Ralph Keyes started "short men's liberation." Each is a statement by persons who perceive themselves to be mostly outside the mainstreams of power, influence and opportunity in our society. Each is simply saying: "To be different is beautiful. It's okay to be who I am. I'm inherently valuable. I won't be judged worthy by whether I look or act like you."

...*Our human potential movement.* Thousands of persons have undertaken hundreds of varieties of personal exploration, experience and expansion: encounter, sensitivity, bioenergetics, rebirthing, inspirational breathing, reflective listening, co-

counseling, re-evaluation counseling, structural integration (Rolfing), functional integration (Feldenkrais), Alexander technique, psychosynthesis, AT (assertiveness training), T.A. (transactional analysis), Erhard Seminar Training, reality therapy, massage, reflexology, meditative therapy, chant, jogging, Lifespring, yoga and many, many more.

Each is a statement by persons mostly within the mainstream of power, influence and opportunity in our society. Each is simply saying: "There's more to me than I have known. I want to explore and experience and expand myself. I want to be/come a whole person, a fully-functioning human."

...*Our sexual revolution.* Millions of persons are exploring human sexuality: demystification, intimacy, touching, sensuality, playfulness, oral sex, multiple orgasm, masturbation, erogenous zones, beyond genitality, open marriage, serial marriage, swinging, group marriages, communal living, homosexuality (male and female), sexual therapy, sex-change operations, pornography, whatever. We're making statements about denied, repressed human bodies. Each is simply saying: "I want to inhabit and experience my entire body more fully and naturally, without fear or shame or guilt."

...*Our drug epidemic.* Millions of persons are experimenting with drugs: marijuana, cocaine, amphetamines, barbiturates, alcohol, hashish, LSD, PCP (angel dust), glue, heroin, methadone, poppers, mushrooms, Ketamine, Valium, uppers, downers, whatever. They're making statements about our denied, repressed natural energy and feelings. Each is simply saying: "I want to feel differently, more or less. I'll reach for a chemical to get up on, high on, down on, onto." Many want to feel more, to "expand their consciousness," to find a new "high." The latest poll indicates 42 million Americans have used marijuana. Many want to feel less, to deaden, dull or desensitize themselves to the pain in their lives. The ghetto black in Harlem who sees a totally unacceptable existence may choose heroin. A middle class housewife who doesn't want to face certain realities of her existence may choose Valium. An up-and-coming business executive, unable to stand the pace and pressure, may choose alcohol. All are choosing to avoid their true feelings.

...*A spiritual awakening.* Thousands of persons are exploring their spiritual dimension: church reformers, renewers, ecumenicists, charismatics, psychics, parapsychologists, astrologers, palmists, Tarot readers, I-Ching-ers, meditators, Moonies, Hare Krishnas, reincarnationists, herbalists, fasters, whatever. They're making statements about our spiritual emptiness. Each is simply saying: "I want to explore and experience a further (spiritual) dimension of myself, my humanness."

Some persons find some of these statements, or their expression, crazy, self-indulgent or outrageous. Yet we owe our fellow humans respect for their persons, and their choices. We ought recognize the common thread and thrust running through them all: exploring humanness. We're all saying "I want to own, know, develop and experience myself—fully."

Some persons claim these movements have "run their course," that they were novelties and fads at most and are now passe, receding in popularity. Such claims are only wishful thinking, revealing more about the critics' unwillingness to explore themselves.

These movements are still here amongst us, going strong, growing into epidemic proportions, contagious in character. So are they still going strong within us, the persons who've been participating in them. We're only now less noticeable. That's because these practices have made their way into our cultural mainstream, our everyday cultural practices. They're no longer headline events.

Our liberation movements have made remarkable strides. We've pretty well abandoned our public policies of racism and sexism. Several states have decriminalized adult in-private consenting sexuality and the possession of marijuana. California and Seattle have strongly repudiated attempts to legitimize discrimination against gay persons.

In the United States George and Nena O'Neill's *Open Marriage* sold three million copies, Alex Comfort's *The Joy of Sex* sold over five million, his *More Joy of Sex* over one million. Books on human growth and behavior and relationships commonly make our best seller lists. My hometown newspaper, the *San Jose Mercury*, has initiated a daily section entitled "Living." TransWorld Airlines offers, as in-flight entertainment, "Father Harry of the God Squad" exhorting us with music to more touching, feeling and letting go.

It was only in 1962 that the Esalen Institute (a parent of the growth center movement) opened in Big Sur, California, and that the Association for Humanistic Psychology was formed. There are now two hundred growth centers in America. AHP now has over 6,000 members, and draws a thousand persons to its monthly regional conferences. Human growth programs have made their way into the extension programs of our major universities.

And human growth is going international. Yaacov Catalfe, educational counsellor in Israel's Kibbutz Neot Mordechai, quotes Sid Jourard and uses Uvaldo Palomares' "magic circle" with children. Teacher friend Carolina Russell has a 15-year-old Columbian student who bemoans his inability to find books in Spanish on existentialism. Professor friend John Bruckman discovered an 18-year-old Berliner college woman deeply into humanistic psychology. The dean of teacher education at Cairo's Ain Shams University is a humanistic psychologist. A Baguio City, Philippines shop sells T-shirts whose across-the-front inscription is "Feelings." Psychologist friend Alexis Johnson opened a growth center in Spain. Gestalt therapist friends Judith and George Brown regularly offer workshops in Scandinavia. Friend Joao Amaral, first President of the Azores, tells Californians he hopes to learn from our experience as he leads his people toward self-determination.

The human potential movement is mushrooming, becoming a habit sweeping our entire world. Human potential is bursting forth. We humans are coming out of our "closet." We are taking responsibility for becoming free, autonomous, fully-functioning human beings.

There's a new world calling, awaiting our discovery, awaiting us. That world is in ourselves. It *is* ourselves. Its call seems as precarious as that of the sirens. Yet it's as alluring. It calls us to our depths. We owe it to ourselves to respond. Let's not stop our ears, cover our eyes, nor block ourselves. We're into the age of human exploration. Let's sail onward—supporting each other's journey of exploration.

Perspective #7: Our Declarations of Independence

200 years ago
our major political issue
was our struggle for liberation
from political bondage—colonialism.
Amidst anguish, pain and violence
we won that struggle.
Today no one doubts its legitimacy
nor ours as a free nation.
We call that struggle
our "Revolutionary War."

100 years ago
our major political issue
was our struggle for liberation
from external physical bondage—slavery.
Amidst anguish, pain and violence
we won that struggle.
Today few doubt its legitimacy
nor ours as free persons.
We call that struggle
our "Civil War."

Today
we're struggling no less
amidst anguish, pain and violence.
Our major political issue
is our struggle for liberation
from internal psychological bondage—repression.
We the people
are recognizing
there's far more to each of us
than we were let believe.

We people are exploring
our innate innocence,
our inherent trustworthiness.
We are persons
realizing our capacity for
openness, authenticity, caring, intimacy.
We persons are changing
our assumptions about our human nature

upon which
we define and design ourselves,
create and operate our institutions.
We are human architects,
redesigning our selves.
We are humans,
recreating ourselves.

We're saying,
"I'm no longer willing
to be owned or conditioned
by you or anyone.
I will determine
who I am.
I want to be,
I will be/come
myself."

We are winning this struggle.
Some day no one will doubt its legitimacy
nor ours as whole persons.

Let's call our struggle
our "Human Revolution."

Let's ask ourselves,
"How can we
make our revolution gentle?"

And let's begin right now.

Perspective #8: Our Struggles

Our former revolution
was for our freedom as a nation.

Our current revolution
is to become a nation
of free and whole persons.

Our former civil war
was between us humans,
our north and south states.

Our current civil war
is within us humans,
between our positive and negative states.

World War I
led us into a violent struggle
to "make our world safe for democracy."

Now
we're leading ourselves
into a peaceful struggle
to make our democracy and our world
safe for *human* beings.

Perspective #9: Our Goals

Woodrow Wilson offered us a "New Freedom."
Our emerging new freedom is the freedom to be ourselves.

Franklin Roosevelt offered us a "New Deal"
—with "Four Freedoms".
Our emerging new deal is
freedom from fear of ourselves,
freedom to be/come ourselves.

John F. Kennedy offered us a "New Frontier."
Our emerging new frontier is ourselves.

Jimmy Carter offers us a "New Foundation."
Our emerging new foundation is
a positive assumption about our human nature.

Perspective #10: Our Noble Experiments

We humans have been
experimenting with our society,
to create a democracy
where all persons are
equally recognized, respected, cherished,
and empowered as participants
in the wholeness of our society.
We characterize this as
"our noble political experiment."

We persons are now

experimenting with our humanness,
trying to create
a "democratic character structure"
where intellect and body and emotions
are equally acknowledged, valued and celebrated
and empowered as participants
in the wholeness of ourselves.
Let's characterize this as
"our noble human experiment."

We'll become able
to live democratically
among ourselves
to the degree
we become able
to live democratically
within ourselves.

Let's not too quickly
surrender our dreams
for a democratic society.
Let's not abandon our "noble political experiment"
at the precise moment of
our "noble human experiment."

Perspective #11: Our Space Travels

In the 1960's,
led by John Kennedy,
we found ourselves
setting our sights high,
soaring into the reaches of outer space.
Many of us doubted.
But as a nation
we focused our attention and resources,
on a few highly trained experts,
the rest of us only paying the bill.

We succeeded beyond our wildest dreams—
breaking the bond of gravity,
entering outer space,
and getting ourselves back again.

Now we find ourselves
turning our sights inward,
plunging into the universe of inner space.
Many of us are doubting.

If as individuals
we focus our attention and resources—
we who are the experts,
with plenty of experience in being human—
we'll again succeed
beyond our wildest dreams,
breaking the bond of repression,
entering inner space,
and getting back to ourselves.

In 1492 Christopher Columbus ventured to the edge of our
then-known world. Instead of falling off its edge, he found it
round and safe.

Today we humans are venturing beyond the edge of our
known world. We're discovering our wholeness and complete-
ness, that we have no edges to fall off of. We're safe as well.

It's appropriate we have no leaders on this venture.
It's appropriate
we lead ourselves—
to ourselves!

Perspective #12: Our Expanding Consciousness

Previously we've little wondered
how to expand our human consciousness.
Unconsciousness was our way,
a result of our expected and accepted repression.

Now we're wondering,
opening and looking inside ourselves,
rejecting our repression,
 accepting and expanding our selves.
We're growing more aware of ourselves,
waking up, becoming conscious.
It's our awareness revolution.

Perspective #13: Our Expanding Sense of "Who Am I?"

Until recently
our Western culture
was premised on Descartes' notion
"I think therefore I am."
We demeaned and disregarded
the rest of ourselves,
especially our emotions and our bodies.

Our outbreak of the 1960's
was characterized (Franklin Murphy)
as our revolution from
"I think therefore I am"
                to
"I feel therefore I am."

We recognized our emotions,
legitimized our instincts, impulses and intuition.
We undertook encounter groups, sensitivity sessions, therapy.
We created a culture that
supports our experiencing and expressing them and ourselves.

Recently we've deepened our revolution from
"I think and feel therefore I am"
                to
"I am my body."
(Stanley Keleman; Tom Hanna's *Bodies in Revolt*).
We're undertaking body awareness, movement and integration
efforts.

Now we're recognizing:
I am whole and one,
intellect and emotions and body altogether.

We're trying to heal
our traditional culture's mind/body split,
return us to our wholeness,
return our wholeness to ourselves.

Perspective #14: Our Renaissances (L.S. Stavrianos' *The Promise of the Coming Dark Age*)

Some centuries ago
we experienced our Dark Ages.
From within them developed our Renaissance,
the birth of a new culture.

We're now into a new dark age,
recognizing and experiencing our own darkness.
We're experiencing a new renaissance,
the birth of new persons.
We're called "new age persons," "seed persons," "new
consciousness persons."
Ten years ago Carl Rogers called us "persons of tomorrow."
We've become persons of today.

We're into rebirthing experiences
from Jimmy Carter's "born-again Christian"
to Marin County's "tub rebirthing"
to the rebirthing of inspirational breathing.

Let's each of us become a renaissance person—
birthing ourselves anew—
the basis for fully developing ourselves as human beings.

It looks darkest just before dawn.
If we open our eyes to seeing,
we'll discern hopeful signs emerging—
the most hopeful of which is
ourselves.

*Perspective #15: Our New Copernican Revolution (Willis
Harman)*
      In 1968 school counselor friend Chuck Parent sent me Willis
Harman's paper "The New Copernican Revolution." It put a
framework on all that's happening in our world. It clarified my
thinking. It excited me then. It still does now.
      In the 16th century Copernicus and Galileo recognized an idea
which all humans now accept: our earth and sun revolve around
each other contrary to what we humans had believed. That
recognition rocked our world. It radically undermined orthodox
religion, science, education, all our culture and institutions. We
had to reevaluate everything in light of our new information. We
reconstructed everything to meet our new understanding.
      In the 18th century Charles Darwin recognized an idea which

most humans today accept: the evolution of our species, from our "animal" origins. That recognition shocked our world. It radically undermined all our culture and institutions. Again we had to reevaluate everything in light of our new knowledge. Again we reconstructed everything based on our new understanding.

In the 19th century Sigmund Freud recognized an idea which many persons today accept: the second layer of our humanness: the instinctual, impulsive, intuitive, compulsive, neurotic. Again our world was shocked, this time ourselves included. All our culture and institutions, *and* human relations, were radically undermined. We had to reevaluate everything in light of our new insight, to match our new understanding. We're reconstructing everything, including ourselves.

Now we're experiencing the next stage in our human evolution—our "New Copernican Revolution." This time we ourselves (rather than some other, famous person) are challenging the orthodox conviction about our most basic life assumption: our belief about our human nature and potential. Many of us (not yet enough) are challenging our traditional culture's assumption that, at root and by nature, we humans are evil. Many of us believe that we are instead, at root and by nature, innocent.

We're rocking ourselves, and all our world. We're radically undermining our culture and institutions. We're revolutionizing our human relations, with ourselves and with each other. We're reevaluating everything in light of our new sense of ourselves. We're reconstructing ourselves, and everything.

This revolution fits and completes our preceding revolutions, progressively expanding our understanding of ourselves and everything. We humans have come a long way: from changing our sense of our outer world, to changing our sense of where we came from, to changing our sense of who and why we are now, to changing our sense of who and how we can be/come more in our future.

Some writings have especially helped me understand what's happening, what we humans are up to these days:

Willis Harman—*An Incomplete Guide to the Future*
L.S. Stavrianos—*The Promise of the Coming Dark Age*
Robert Theobald—*An Alternative Future for America II*;
   Beyond Despair—Directions for America's Third Century

Philip Slater—*The Pursuit of Loneliness—American Culture at the Breaking Point*
Theodore Roszak—*The Making of a Counterculture*
Tom Hanna—*Bodies in Revolt; The End of Tyranny*
Norman O. Brown—*Life Against Death*
Robert Heilbroner—*An Inquiry Into the Human Prospect*
R.D. Laing—*The Politics of Experience*
Joseph Fabry—*The Pursuit of Meaning*
David Cooper—*The Death of the Family*; *The Grammar of Living*
Wilhelm Reich—*The Mass Psychology of Fascism*
Ernest Callenbach—*Ecotopia*
Mark Satin—*New Age Politics*
Peter Marin—*In A Man's Time*
Marcia Seligson—*Options*
Charles Reich—*The Sorcerer of Bolinas Bay*
Pamela Portugal—*A Place for Human Beings*
Will Schutz—*Here Comes Everybody*
Francisco Jose Moreno—*Beyond Faith and Reason*
Stanley Keleman—*The Human Ground—Sexuality, Self and Survival*
Robert Coles and Daniel Berrigan—*The Geography of Faith*
Francis Schaeffer—*The God Who Is There*
Joe Powers—*Spirit and Sacrament*
Erich Fromm—*Escape From Freedom*
Michael Rossman—*New Age Blues*
Richard Bach—*Jonathan Livingston Seagull*

I also recommend Carl Rogers' *On Personal Power* and Theodore Roszak's *Person/Planet*—which I've refrained from reading because I expect they're too like my book, I'd confuse my own writing.

Please use your local library and/or bookseller to find those items which interest you.

Now, from our perspectives, let's look at what's happening in our lives and society.

chapter 6

outgrowing our
tunnel vision:
the first sight
of liberation

*"If the doors of perception were cleansed, everything
would appear infinite."*
— William Blake

Our perspectives provide valuable clues to:
...*What's happening* in our lives and society today;
...*What's going and gone wrong,* in our lives and society, now
and in our past;
...*How we can make it right,* in our lives and society, now and
for our future.

How we look at things, how we see what's happening,
depends on who we are. What's happening is that we human
beings have been changing our external world. And we're
changing our internal world, ourselves, in keeping with our
changing external world.

We human beings are outgrowing ourselves
and our vision of ourselves.
We're growing ourselves into expanded human beings,
with an expanding sense of humanness,
expanding our sense of our human capacities,
of who we are and can be/come,
of what we need and want—
for ourselves and for all humans.

We're redefining and we're redesigning ourselves. We're standing up, looking around *and* within, wondering who we are, what life means—and how we can realize its meaning, how we can realize, fulfill and satisfy ourselves. With our changing sense of ourselves, we're changing our sense of our rights—
to love ourselves,
to have ourselves respected and accepted,
to have our needs and wants responded to.
We're outgrowing our old assumptions of limitation;
our aspirations are rising.
We want more of—and for ourselves!

Especially significant is our expanding capacity to see. We've been liberating our vision. We've improved our vision. We can see more clearly. We're more aware, insightful, perceptive. What looks like failure, is instead signs of our success. So much of it *looks* bad because we can *see* better!

We live in a paradoxical world and time—of new despair and new hope. How we see and characterize what's happening depends on who we are—our assumptions, values, perceptions and expectations. Persons of our old culture see upheaval, confusion, strife. They conclude that our society and institutions are breaking down.

Our new vision persons see it differently. Our ferment is a creative, healthy human ferment. We humans are ripening, maturing, growing up. We're coming of age. Our society isn't breaking down, it's breaking up—as we break ourselves open and break out of our old society's mold. When we undertook our Revolutionary War, English rule broke down. When we undertook our Civil War, slave ownership broke down. It's the same today. Society is coming apart in ways that release life-affirming energies. What looks like anarchy from our old vision is instead the troubled birth of a new, becoming-more-human social order. We're into a creative, not destructive, form of disintegration. We're integrating ourselves. We're experiencing labor pains.

What's becoming clear is that our old vision worked so well, that we're outgrowing it. Our predicament, plight and peril are not the result of our failing, but rather the result of our succeeding. We've freed ourselves from the daily anxieties and limitations of struggling for immediate survival. The good conditions and successes of our society have allowed us, even caused us to grow. Our economic successes, education, technology and television enable us to expand ourselves, so we see and want more—for ourselves.

We've improved our longevity, tolerance, housing, transportation, jobs, wealth, public health, material standard of living, medical care, help for our needy, beaches, parks, telecommunications. We've been so successful we've managed, even unwittingly, to set the stage for our own outgrowing ourselves, our own further evolution. We've made so much progress, we're making more sense of ourselves and of our lives, according to a pattern not yet commonly recognized. It's time we attend to recognizing a positive human pattern of evolution, amidst all that's happening. It's time we attend to our own further evolution, toward our full humanness.

We've outgrown our institutions that gave us birth, precisely to the extent they're still operating off assumptions we've since outgrown about ourselves. Our society and institutions are lagging far behind us. Within a period determined by years rather than by aeons, there's been a fundamental change in the conditions under which life's been going on since its beginning. The end of what we call normal, usual and sacred is close at hand, and cannot be evaded.

There are many signs, as just before the spring buds break through, that we're approaching a critical mass of awareness. Many persons are feeling expectation, as though our world is a super-saturated solution, anticipating that small change needed, to transform it into a crystal. We're ready for an unprecedented leap toward greater wholeness and consciousness. We're in the midst of a major evolutionary transformation of humankind. Our future may well bring the unfolding of an awesome and joyous new vision of our human nature.

As our times differ from all prior times, they differ as well

from future times, from all that may come after for us humans.
We are now approaching a unique and major crossroads and
threshhold in our entire human history. We'll likely never pass
this way again. We stand perched at this point—reaching for
some truly new and different sense of who we human beings
are. That discovery may be just as profound as the day we
emerged from the sea, or stood up straight for the first time.

There's a new world coming into being, based upon a coming
together of new persons. We're living at the end of one age, the
beginning of another. We're no longer anchored in the old,
whose foundations are fast slipping beneath and within us.
We're not as yet secured to the new. It's so new, we can't yet
even imagine what it, and we, will be/come.

We're recognizing that a grim tragedy lies behind the tinsel
splendor of modern civilization, its ceaseless rush of living, the
marvels of our science, its gospel of progress. It offers neither
stability nor certainty, nothing substantial to our struggling
humanity. Beneath its dazzling surface, material attractions and
madly feverish activity, modern civilization hinders rather than
helps our expanded humanness, our craving for a better life.
We're coming to recognize its moral inadequacy and
extravagant pretensions, to see through its treacherously
deceptive, hypnotic and self-destructive tendency. We're no
longer willing to be victims of a vast debilitating myth, kept alive
by our homes, churches, schools, governments, armies,
hospitals, prisons, workplaces, and all our institutions.

We humans aren't rejecting our institutions arbitrarily,
without reason. Our reason is simply that our institutions are
failing us. They're failing to recognize that we have grown.
They're failing to meet our needs. They're not facilitating our
fulfillment of ourselves. Too often instead our institutions are
getting in the way of our getting ourselves and our needs
fulfilled.

There's general dissatisfaction. We're experiencing the ever-
widening gap between what our institutions are providing, and
what we humans are needing, wanting and demanding. Our
minorities, women, gays, handicapped and older persons are
wanting full recognition of themselves and their rights to
participate fully in our society. Our changing mainstream
persons are wanting more recognition of their full selves, and
more attention paid thereto.

A recent ABC News-Harris Survey of 1,186 American adults presents strong evidence. *Eighty-nine percent* of those surveyed say they want "experiences that make you peaceful inside." *Ninety-one percent* would like opportunities to use their own creative abilities. Significantly, *eighty-one percent* opt for being "involved in efforts where people cooperate rather than compete." Given a choice between "breaking up big things and getting back to more humanized living" on the one hand, and "developing bigger and more efficient ways of doing things" on the other, *seventy-two percent* chose more humanization! A majority favored both "learning to get our pleasures out of non-material things" and "learning to appreciate human values more than material values."

Syndicated columnist Sydney J. Harris, reporting the results of the poll, commented on its implications for our future:

> "Americans seem to sense that our economy has entered a post-industrial era, where services are becoming more valued than physical goods. And the key to turning out better services lies in human resources. Unlike raw materials and physical resources, human resources can be totally renewable on a regular basis, if they are nurtured properly.
>
> The future that Americans envision is going to depend far more on the country's ability to find economic growth in the people-intensive service areas than in the physical goods areas. The daily experience of trying to cope with inflation and energy shortages appears to be bringing about this basic change in values and ushering in a new era in America."

We all complain about the depersonalization and dehumanization of our society and institutions. No wonder. They just haven't grown to match our growing humanness. Instead they contradict and compress us. But we've outgrown as well our willingness to be oppressed, contained and repressed. We're standing up for ourselves, closing our mouths to junk being stuffed inside us. We're opening our mouths, to speak for ourselves—not just when spoken to—to say "No more." In times of scarcity and ignorance, we humans can be kept down.

In times of affluence, universal education and mass media, we humans will rise—and should be encouraged—up.

We're leaving our old system behind. We humans do not live by bread alone. We're shifting from quantity to quality of life issues. We aren't satisfied with survival. We want to thrive, grow, fulfill ourselves and our human potential.

We more traditional persons can rejoice with pride: we built the platform on which our expanding persons can see beyond us further. We expanding persons can rejoice with appreciation— to our traditional persons who made it possible, often by great generosity and sacrifice.

We've solved many of our easier, external, mechanical problems. The problems of success are often harder to solve. We get complacent, assume our old ways will continue to work for us, since they worked so well before. It's harder than ever to change our ways. But with our new vision, we can see how things should and could be better for us humans.

We're resentful and frustrated that they're not.

Certainly we're already changing and growing. Our question is whether we're growing rapidly enough to keep pace with our changing world and our changing persons in it. If we don't change ourselves, we'll become obsolete, in and for our world, not unlike the dinosaurs who once inhabited it.

We deserve more than that. We can do more than that for ourselves. In preparation for our growing, let's look at our old vision. With our liberated, expanding vision, we can now get a sharper focus on it.

backlighting our old vision: are we inhuman by nature?

> *"Perhaps the sentiments contained in the following pages are not yet sufficiently fashionable to procure them general favor: a long habit of not thinking a thing* wrong, *gives it a superficial appearance of being* right, *and raises at first a formidable outcry in defense of that custom. But the tumult soon subsides. Time makes more converts than reason."*
>
> —Thomas Paine

To fully appreciate our new vision, its promise and significance, we must fully appreciate our old vision, its process and practice.

Let's look at our old vision in several progressive steps:First, its *content:* its assumptions about us humans and our nature; Second, its *intentions* toward us humans, based upon its assumptions; Third, its *operations*, methods based upon its intentions; and (following in Chapter 8) Fourth, the *effects* and *results* of its operations upon us humans.

First, our old vision *contains* the following assumptions about us humans:

- That in fact and by nature, we're not okay, we're afflicted by original sin. We are, innately and inherently, evil, sinful, corrupt, base, guilty, unworthy, untrustworthy, dangerous, aggressive, violent. In our society a human charged with crime is legally presumed innocent until proved guilty— beyond a reasonable doubt. How come I'm assumed guilty by nature, guilty until proven innocent, until I prove myself innocent—without any doubt?
- That the best we humans can hope for about ourselves is negative: to contain our evil;
- That we humans don't know what's good for ourselves, and need to be protected from ourselves;
- That our subjectivity—instincts, impulses, intuition, feelings, emotions—is inaccurate, untrustworthy, dangerous;
- That our human bodies are dirty; that seeing, touching, showing, sharing them is bad;
- That we can love at most one other human being—the "myth of the quantifiability of love."

In short, our old vision offers a stunted, cynical, demeaning, self-denying, self-defeating and pathogenic vision of our nature and potential.

Second, based on its assumptions about us, our old vision, *intends* with respect to each of us humans:

- To dehumanize us, dissociate us from our own nature;
- To cause us to distrust and deny our nature, to not be natural;
- To separate us from, keep us from knowing our own innocence and goodness;
- To repress us, to cause us to not be our natural selves;
- To fix us, to make us okay;
- To make us believe and feel we are unworthy and untrustworthy;
- To make us feel guilty about our natural selves, to contain ourselves;
- To mystify us, make us unaware of ourselves, keep us from knowing ourselves, to keep us ignorant about the world within us. The content and intention of our old vision were brought home to me in a discussion with Max Rafferty, then California's Superintendent of Public Instruction, about sensitivity

training. Max told me it was bad because it operates on the premise that a person ought get to know him/her self. "That's wrong," he said. "What life's about is ignoring and denying one's self and serving other people."

- To cause us to distrust our own experiencing, to disconnect our capacity for recognizing what's going on within and around us (R.D. Laing's *The Politics of Experience*);
- To shift the source of authority from the untrustworthy within us to "out there, up there";
- To cause us to distrust and repress our "dangerous" instincts, impulses, feelings;
- To cause us to disavow and disown our "shameful" bodies;
- To subjugate us, so we could be "saved";
- To intimidate us, so we'll not rise up;
- To perpetuate our old vision itself. One day my former calendar-person Sherry Stansberry visited her obstetrician. While waiting she was reading Frederick Leboyer's *Birth Without Violence*. On seeing the book, her doctor got angry and told her it was "a lot of crap." He explained: "Life in our society is violent. We ought take full advantage of our first opportunity to impress that fact upon an infant, to prepare him for it all." Here we see something significant: how personal vision determines public action and perpetuates, even recreates itself in a self-fulfilling prophecy. And it's all undertaken by totally sincere persons with the very best of intentions: to fix me, make me okay, able to cope with life, so I'll grow up to be/come a good and worthy person, a responsible citizen, make my way in our world, fit in, get a good job, have a nice family, get to heaven.

It's a sad fact: our systems founded on our old vision can't stand really *alive* persons, our natural passion for life. They need us anesthetized so we won't feel the pain they inflict upon and within us. Jonathan Kozol's *The Night Is Dark and I Am Far From Home* illustrates how American education has this intention and effect.

Our old culture is masochistic. Persons who live by it have a death wish. In a way, they're getting their wish: their culture's dying.

Third, based on its intentions toward us, our old vision has ways, methods, devices, techniques of *operating* upon us: The most evident are: .

- Our old vision creates institutions for managing people and human affairs. It operates them on the basis of its negative assumptions about our nature. We get the "command/ control" model of institutions. In the guise of reassuring us, they repress us.
- It creates customs, mores, manners, formalities—inducing and conditioning us to wear masks, to cover and hide our natural beings, especially our bodies and our feelings. We don't dare show our real selves.
- It creates myths and models for us to live by. We have masculine (macho, tough, "big boys don't cry") and feminine (soft, weepy, emotional) models for how we should or shouldn't be.

We have the myth of objectivity, regarding how we should look at life: that we can and should abstract ourselves from our selves; that we see, observe, understand and report more accurately the farther away from ourselves we get. That's unhelpful and impossible. I see best up close. A microscope reveals more detail than a telescope. What people call "objectivity" is only shared subjectivity.

Our old vision appeals only to reason. It idealizes "intellect" and "rationality," pays great homage to the abstract concept of "reason," makes "reason" into an object of faith, is nonrational in its commitment to reason alone. It frowns on, even forbids using our reason as a tool of *self*-observation, for exploring our own humanness and insides. To me it's obvious that our bodies and emotions operate logically. Our old vision doesn't teach me to think independently. It conditions me so I'll "independently" think just the way it does.

- It creates taboos: "Don't ever..., or else!" Our old vision's most subtle is "the taboo against knowing who I am" (Alan Watts). That serves to keep us in the dark about ourselves, to maintain our darkness, to keep us from knowing fully who we are, what we want, what's happening in our lives, who's friend and who's oppressor. Mystifying us about ourselves makes us susceptible to mystification by others.

Our old vision has very explicit taboos regarding our bodies, touching and sexuality. My body isn't to be seen, nudity is forbidden. Until recently women couldn't nurse their babies in public. How unnatural! My body isn't to be touched.

Don't touch things, anyone else, especially don't touch myself, especially not THERE. The more I make my body suffer, the more good it does me. I'm taught to hate my body, be ashamed of it.

I vividly recall: getting sick to my stomach after a 7th grade basketball game because I had to change clothes in a boy's locker room; being traumatized having to communally shower in an all boys prep school; quitting frosh football on the second day of practice on account of my terror. The first evening of my 1969 Esalen trip I was unable to bring myself to go to the mixed hot baths. The next night my terror was outweighed by my desire to converse further with a new friend. I'll never forget my enormous sigh of relief and release when I climbed out of the tub, leaned over the railing above the ocean, looked up to the stars and realized the heavens hadn't opened, descended their wrath on me.

The taboo on touching shows in how we (fail to) greet each other in our society, touching at most our hands, perhaps stiffly our bodies, occasionally our mouths. It's evident in the snickering when anyone mentions massage.

The most pervasive taboo is on our human sexuality. Our old vision lowers a curtain of silence over the entire subject, over us as well. The most important learning in life is how to be loving, to make love, to be a lover. We don't teach that at home. The only sex education I received at home came from my father, a public school administrator, the night before I was sent off to boarding school. He took me aside and said: "Now about sex, there's just one thing I want to tell you: don't do anything you wouldn't want done to your sister." I was then fourteen years old. She was four.

Then we battle against it being taught at school. At prep school they expanded my exposure to sexuality to an entire semester (called "Modern Youth and Chastity"), and shortened my instruction to "Don't!" Our old vision teaches us that sex is dirty, then insists we save it for the *one* we love. It epitomizes the three monkeys: "See no evil, hear no evil, speak no evil," as though sexuality were evil, just like our "human nature." Then it expects us to be all fine, fully functioning, all at once, the night the institution (church or government) legalizes "us."

Another taboo, less commonly understood, operates on our

emotions. Our old vision distrusts my natural, life-supporting emotions. So it wants to instil its own instead. Its technique is two-step: First, it teaches me to distrust and deny my experience of my natural feeling. When a child comes in crying with a stubbed toe, the parent insists: "Don't cry, your toe doesn't really hurt." So I'm without any (trust) of my natural feelings. Then our old culture conditions in the feelings *it* wants me to have in a given situation (Alexander Lowen's "conceptual feelings," the feelings I'm taught to *think I should* feel in a situation).

• Along with its major methods, our old vision has several clever and effective operating techniques—"enforcers." They include fear, shame, guilt, conditioning, intimidation, repression, editing, fixing, scorning, containing, bribery, destroying autonomy, monitoring, discouraging.

Perhaps the most subtle is bribery: gold stars, M&M's, promotions, grades, heaven or hell—all offered and granted or withheld. Our old vision does things for me with a string, to get me to behave its way—then keeps me moving like a puppet. There's always a price to pay, usually mighty high, often it's myself. The most devastating form of bribery is (the threat of) withholding love: "If you do that, I won't love you, I'll go away." "You wouldn't do that if you loved mommy/daddy."

Another form of bribery is (the threat of) punishment, even banishment: corporal (spanking, a hard handhold, a cold touch), facial (frown), exclusionary ("go to your room"). The formal punisher/briber is the law: "Don't—or you'll go to jail!" Our old vision even declared a "natural law," for whose violation I'd incur the supreme punishment, banishment from heaven, forever burning in hell.

An especially debilitating technique is discouragement. I'm often told: "That's just human nature." "That's just the way life is." I usually correct it: "That's not human *nature*, that's human *behavior* as we've come to know it, as we've conditioned persons to be—other than ourselves and natural." Let's wonder why it is that way, and how we can change it.

A less sinister technique is monitoring to insure I perform. Instead of trusting my being, letting me be, assuming I'll prove responsible—our old vision acts as though if I just "was," I'd never do anything responsible. At dinner with then California Governor Ronald Reagan, we discussed whether university professors ought take roll in class. He argued they should because "People are naturally untrustworthy. They need to be checked on to make sure they perform reliably." Again we see personal vision dictating public action.

Perhaps our old vision's most insidious technique is making us humans dependent. Old vision institutions intimidate and repress us, make us feel guilty, rob us of our natural autonomy by teaching us to distrust our experiencing—then own us forever after. My church persuaded me I was by nature a sinner, that it had the monopoly, the only key to absolution and salvation, dispensed on its terms. I got beholden, locked in tightly.

Our old vision has a vast array of methods, well designed and efficiently funtioning, to achieve its purposes. It's especially clever, even diabolical, in combining its methods and techniques, getting us to be and do as it wants. Generally it operates by getting me to "knot me," to make me not me (R.D. Laing's *Knots*).

Our old vision's operations are especially poignant as they apply to children, the most malleable and defenseless of us humans. Children are born into our world as beautiful, free animals. Our old vision doubts, denies, disputes, does everything it can to dispel that belief, destroy that fact. Old vision parents believe a child arrives evil, needing to be fixed and saved. Their idea of a responsible child is one who learns not to do what s/he naturally wants, but what *they* want done. They transmit their cynicism, including their fear of emotion, body and sexuality. They recreate their distrust of their own experiencing. They deprive their children of their good sense of themselves and their bodies, robbing them of their innate innocence, curiosity and passion.

They become "two-sense families"—where members can look at and listen to each other, but no touching, tasting or smelling (David Cooper). We appropriately call our old vision parenting "child-*rearing*": everything done is backwards, turns the child around, away from his/her own nature. It has the opposite effect from what they'd like. It's mathematical, logical: if a child arrives innocent, and we assume her/him guilty, whatever we choose to do to "fix" the child will instead screw him/her up.

A new human arrives in a natural state of dependence. Whether s/he grows up into a dependency consciousness, is determined largely by whether the parent is self-sufficient—responding naturally to the infant's needs—or insufficient, dependent, and needing to make the infant dependent on her/him as a means of reestablishing his/her own worth and sufficiency.

"Growing up" in our old vision occurred in a home where I was taught to be "seen and not heard," in schools where I was to "sit down, shut up and sit still," and in a church whose central ritual was, still is "Oh, Lord, I am not worthy" (though reduced since my childhood from three times to once per ritual). Wilhelm Reich's *The Mass Psychology of Fascism* proposes that our homes, churches, schools and governments—all well-intentioned—conspire to rob children of their natural sense of themselves, their autonomy, making them ever after willing subjects, slaves of the state.

Certainly we ought preserve the family—as a way of growing healthy children—so long as parents want to conserve children and their natural being.

In our culture
bringing up a child
usually has the effect of
bringing down the person
who is the child
within
(David Cooper).

Our old vision is pathological. It assumes we're sick when we're not. On that assumption it ministers and mandates to us in such a way it makes us sick. It conditions us to give up, surrender ourselves, to go along, to give in. That serves to anesthetize us, put us to sleep, perpetuate our asleepness. We live amidst a conspiracy of cynicism and self-fulfilling, self-perpetuating prophecies about our very nature.

Socialization is,
by definition and intention,

dehumanization,
depersonalization.

We find ourselves
chopping down life,
cutting down persons
to make them fit
our culture and our assumptions.

After which
we're no more human.

We humans
should no more
stand for that!

chapter 8

hindsight:
results of
our old vision

"Original sin is located in the unconscious."

—Norman O. Brown

"The crisis of our times may well be one of coming to grips with (hu)man's capacity for transcending all manner of bondage."

—Franklin Shaw

Let's now look at the profound effects our old vision has upon us humans.

The overall effect of our old vision's operations on, and treatment of me is, of course, to make me what I am: other than myself, other than natural, all screwed up. Many of us are walking wounded, victims of our upbringing. Its effects and our resulting behavior patterns are devastating, almost endless. I have identified at least seventy. Each of us has become:

1. *Dehumanized*, alienated from our human nature. No surprise! That's the intention of all major institutions founded on our old vision: home and family, church and religion, school and education, government and politics. I end up self-denied and self-denying.

2. *Depersonalized*, impersonal, needing titles and roles, less into being a person, more into being a "professional." My parents' primary sense of their identity and worth is in being (called) Mother and Dad, rather than Teresa and John, the persons. We end up dealing with other persons as numbers rather than as persons.

3. *Cynical*, about my own human nature, my own humanness. My idealism's repressed, perhaps the worst scarring by our old vision. I'm therefore cynical about you and all nature: I expect too little from life and myself and you. Without my natural hopefulness, I'm despairing, a "no-exit, dead end" existentialist, abstracted from myself and my own goodness, living in my head, missing life, concluding life's absurd (Colin Wilson's *Introduction To the New Existentialism*).

4. *Distrustful*, untrusting of myself, my feelings, subjectivity, instincts, impulses, intuitions. Afraid to open up. Priest friend Tenn Wright told me "If I shed all my masks, I'll be like an onion without any skin, nothing left of me." A milder belief simply compares life to peeling an onion: "each layer I peel off, I cry more." I'm left not knowing I'm innately trustworthy. Unable to trust others, I'm guarded, defensive, closed, uncooperative with my fellow humans, wasteful of energy and time. Culture is institutionalized distrust of our human nature.

5. *Suspicious*. Since there was a price tag on most things given to or done for me, I'm wary of anyone offering to do anything for me (especially for free).

6. *Unsure of myself*, lacking in self-assurance, self-confidence. Unsure of what I want and what's best for me, I expect someone else to know better. I'm insecure, lacking self-possession, needing formality, masks, roles, defenses. I look for authority outside myself, play life safe, take no risks. By hiding behind objectivity and arbitrary rules, I become an obedient child who looks and waits all my life for permission to live, to be myself. I feel powerless, since I've surrendered my natural power, energy to you/others.

7. *Dependent*, not independent or autonomous. Leaning on others to advise and instruct me, and to establish my personal and social values, I'm easily manipulated.

8. *Irresponsible*. So conditioned away from myself and my natural capacity for being responsibly self-determining, I've lost touch with my natural capacity to take responsibility. Too often

when a child takes responsibility, s/he's punished. Few persons have freed ourselves to be/come fully responsible. We see ourselves as victims, and perpetuate the wrongdoing, both within ourselves and by passing it on to someone else.

9. *Less than whole*, parted, separated, fractured, fragmented, not together. I've become only one-third of a person, on account of our acculturation. Men are "allowed" to be intellectual, women emotional, neither sexual.

10. *Complex*, no longer simple or a unity. We've "complexified" ourselves in ways neither natural nor necessary, hardly healthy. Recognizing how we've complexified ourselves, it's a wonder we humans relate with each other at all!

11. *Split*, body and mind, into a pluralistic character, vertically constructed: head over emotions over body. My mind's okay, the rest of me is not. Exalting intellectuality over instincts and reason over emotion, we've put them in opposition to each other, rather than allowing them their natural oneness and harmony. The structure I want outside myself is a projection of the structure I carry within myself, so I need and want and create vertically structured, hierarchical institutions.

12. *Hateful toward my body*. Uneasy, uncomfortable in my body. Accepting of taboos against my body, feeling it ugly, I become embarrassed about being seen naked, afraid to touch and be touched, and threatened by nudity (usually banning it). Naked we came out of our mother's womb, how come such flurry to assure we're covered (in some cultures from head to toe) ever after?

We're compulsively into too many, gaudy clothes, to make ourselves attractive, to cover our bodies, especially the parts most energized, most intimate. Low on nonverbal communication, body language, we become against free speech/expression for our bodies, and constitutionally protect as free only verbal speech. Money talks, and is constitutionally protected under Supreme Court decisions; body talk (nudity, dance, sexuality, touching) isn't.

We're into liberation movements, all being about our bodies: color, age, sex, shape, size, inclination toward touch. We're attracted to body relaxing and recovering therapies: bioenergetics, Rolfing, Feldenkrais, Alexander method, touching, massage, hot tubs.

13. *Confused* about what is obscene, and what is permissible

to show and see in person or in media: enjoying bodies, creating life, love-making, sexuality—or violence, destroying bodies and life. A case in point: objections to our 1978 Christmas stamp, depicting a famous Madonna and naked Christ child as "obscene" (babies do arrive that way, even Christ). Yet it's "typical" to be vicariously excited by four-letter words about my body, its parts and functions and touching.

14. *Repressed in my body*, blocking my energy from circulating freely and naturally throughout my entire body. I create muscular "character armor": stiff, dead zones which encircle me like rings, at different levels of my body (Wilhelm Reich, Alexander Lowen). The result: such distortions within and distorted expressions outside myself as ulcers, strokes, hurting, drug-dependence, acting out, lashing out, violence, taboos on touching, starved, deficient, needy, needing to be touched—physically or psychologically—for reassurance and replenishment.

15. *Shameful, ashamed of myself*, my private parts especially. Needing privacy, I become secretive, unwilling to be open, let myself be known. We've so repressed our private parts, the pressure builds, becomes compelling, private becomes pre-occupying, leading to a remarkable bias in favor of our private sector, suspicion and hatred of and alienation of our public sector.

16. *Not comfortable in just being*, unable to handle our silence, needing to talk much, unaware of nonverbal communication, making up for it verbally by verbose, incessant talk, interminable, shallow, saying nothing of substance, a tower of babble. Our sportcasters act as if we have no capacity for observing for ourselves, always filling in the silence, talking non-stop. Friend Jim Mathis talks little. I get anxious midst our silence, and ask "Is anything wrong?" He replies: "No, if it was, I'd tell you."

17. *My natural being repressed*, making me unnatural, engaging in unnatural acts.

18. *Uncomfortable*, heavily into material comforts, ill at ease with myself, embarrassed, fearful, uncomfortable in the company of each other, making little real contact with each other.

19. *Self-conscious*, because I'm inhibited, not being my natural self.

20. *Graceless*, having lost touch with my body's natural capacity for carrying me through life, and for responding appropriately, gracefully.

21. *Tight, rigid*, immobile, inflexible, backaching.

22. *Cold, remote*, distant from myself and from you.

23. *Asexual to anti-sexual*, not fully, naturally sexual or erotic, afraid, ashamed, guilty about my sexuality. How well I recall the terror with which I approached the mandatory Catholic confession ritual, on matters regarding my sexuality. I've been conditioned to be unable to fully, freely, comfortably talk, touch, look, show, share, move, be sexual. I'm afraid of touching you, for fear my touching will be interpreted as sexual, a "no-no". Thus we've become constrained about touching persons of *both* sexes.

Having repressed and contained our natural sexuality, not allowing it its natural way and expression, we create distortion, build up pressure, tension, leading to a heavy emotional charge on our sexual appetite. This buildup leads to our becoming compulsive, driven, preoccupied, and leads to our sexual energy coming out in weird, kinky ways, exploding. Our most satisfying curse words are associated with the disgust with which we associate our sexual organs and acts.

We've come to live our sexuality through our heads (dirty jokes, fantasizing) and through our eyes (looking at every person walking by, wondering, looking at pictures, even of children). An anomaly: that which is most taboo, demeaned, shameful, repressed, my sexuality, is the most enduring, empassioned proof of loyalty in a human relationship. Sharing my body with another person becomes the highest form of proving my loyalty, our love. We most cherish our minds, yet don't construe sharing *them* as betrayal.

Unsure of our own natural sexuality, we want the government to proscribe which sexual acts are right or wrong. If the government doesn't proscribe certain acts, somehow they're legitimate.

Having lost touch with our natural sexuality, we're needy for substitute gratification, irresponsible sexually, emotionally crippled, confused, neurotic about sexuality, susceptible to pornography.

We need sexual contact: someone else to touch us,

activate us, energize us;
to fulfill, replace, get reassurance for, prove
our denied selves;
sometimes to retaliate for our repressed selves,
all so we feel ourselves whole again.

24. *Guilt-ridden*, about ourselves, our bodies, our sexuality.

25. *Deformed*, gnarled. To conform, to get your approval, I deformed myself; to fit in, I tailored myself to your specifications. With foundations so diseased, it's a wonder anything can grow, much less a healthy human being.

26. *Crippled.* We can't systematically, intentionally cripple persons, then wonder why they can't walk, much less run.

27. *Not fully grown*, not into growing myself, stunted, substitutionally compulsive toward growing everything else bigger; immature.

28. *Pained*, hurting—from being squashed down inside.

29. *Resentful*, bitter, not my natural sweet self, rebellious.

30. *Angry*, hostile, rageful, aggressive, cruel, violent, militaristic.

31. *Top-heavy*, head-heavy. Our heads have developed disproportionately to the rest of us: our bodies, our emotional and moral development.

32. *Egotistic.* My ego is the sum of the faces of my repressed body.

33. *Super-intellectual*, cerebral, rigidly committed to intellect, arduously struggling to discover the true "meaning" of life (indicating I've not yet fully experienced life). "Meaning" is a head trip, resulting from my being too abstracted from my body, where life's to be found, experienced, appreciated. With my body repressed, I'll mistakenly locate my identity in my head, in ideology. Affiliation and affection become less important in my human relationships than agreement, ratifying my mistaken "identity."

34. *Low or without or negative in self esteem*, on account of being put down, not possessing and experiencing myself wholly, biologically, physiologically. Friend Lorenza Schmidt got some birthday cake powdered-sugar frosting down her windpipe, began choking. She found herself too low-self-regarding to ask for help until, her self-help efforts failing, she realized she'd die without help. Only then could she bring herself to ask. I awoke

tearful the morning of my 19th day on Maui with friend John, wondering why he'd choose to spend so much time with *me*.

Such low self esteem may lead to a distorted need for ratification from others, rewards from outside: gold stars, blue chip stamps, a pat on the back. Trying so hard to please and impress, I become oppressive, putting a burden on you to make me feel okay again (Dory Previn's "I Danced and Danced, Smiled and Smiled"). Needing to prove myself, make myself look/feel worthy again, I may attempt to put someone else beneath me to climb atop, to own, or to show off, to restore my sense of being "up" again. Competition may allow me to artifically reevaluate myself, so I jump whole-heartedly, blindly, compulsively into the rat race.

35. *Reversed about the natural relationship between being and having and doing.* Being is primary: to keep on *being*, I have to *have* (food and shelter); to *have* I have to *do* (to earn the wherewithal to have, in order to continue being). Instead, I've turned it all around: I repress my being, then compulsively search for substitute gratification in having and doing; they become primary, becoming ends *of* being, rather than means *for* being. Abstracted from, absent my own being, I search for my identity in wealth, money, property, an attractive spouse, high-achieving kids, authoritarian power, title, position, performance, artificial excitement, drugs inside myself, violence outside myself, susceptible to advertising, consumerism's "Buy this product, become beautiful, loveable, loved again."

Looking outside for aids to my lost natural beauty, I forget that beauty is skin deep. It's our interior beauty that counts, and my natural interior is beautiful. We're living a way of life that consumes, spends us humans, rather than nourishing, nurturing us humans. We've become dispensable, throw-aways, replaceable, with the dollar, the job, the corporation coming first, again having transposed our ends and means.

36. *Not into simple being*, which costs few dollars, though risks rejection. Instead, we're into having and doing, which cost money, use up our earth's physical, non-replaceable resources, and into the over-compensations of narcissism (preoccupation with self) or altruism (helping others at the expense of self).

37. *Jealous*: needing someone else to make me feel worthwhile, whole, because I've given up my natural wholeness. If I need to be the first if not only person in your life, it's likely

because I'm not being the first person in my life, not being sufficiently myself.

38. *Arrogant:* thinking I'm "too much", and overcompensating for having made too little of myself.

39. *Legalistic, formal, ritualistic.* Devaluing and distrusting my natural passion, feeling, loving, I "need" external sanction to make even my most involving human relationships legitimate. We need the external authority (church or state) to sanction them, rather than trusting our loving, living together.

40. *Out of touch with my natural being,* body, appetites, feelings. I'm conditioned to breathe shallowly to make my self safe. The deeper I breathe, the more I fuel my body, excite my feelings, feel my body. I'm always hungry for the energy which oxygen naturally provides my body. Absent that, I'm driven to eat excessively. Everyone I know well grew up starved, yet is hungry, especially for values and meaning.

I don't know when I'm naturally hungry, having lost my natural appetite. My family had set times for meals. Whenever I headed for the refrigerator in between, I was warded off with the instruction: "Don't eat now, you'll spoil your meal." (The worry was I'd spoil *her* meal, which provided her needed self-reassurance). I obeyed, betraying my natural appetite. During meals our family had the complementary instruction: "Eat all your food, clean your plate, remember (remember?) all the starving children in China (Africa, Biafra, the place varying with our times). Again I obeyed, betraying my natural appetite. Like a squirrel preparing for an unpredictable winter, I'd eat extra, knowing I couldn't eat again until they said it was time (what if they never did?). No wonder I lost my appetite!

Then I was sent to boarding school where meals were more stringently at prescribed times and, contrary to home, didn't taste especially good. Eating being essential, taste became irrelevant, then inoperable. No wonder I lost my (sense of) taste! Even today, I find it difficult not to "clean my plate"—no matter how much or tasteless the food is.

41. *Separated,* alienated from my own being, alienated from persons dear to me, from my social and physical environment, hostile toward them all, disrespectful, treating them badly as I treat myself.

42. *Feeling empty.* Too full of structures to feel my natural fullness.

43. *Lonely*—for the rest of, the missing parts of myself. Desperate for love, it often takes the form of inter-locking neuroses, unmet needs meshing. Desperate for community, communion, we become joiners, join cults, hoping to touch and be touched.

44. *Sad*—on account of the loss, death of part of my being.

45. *Depressed*—squashed down, flat, one-dimensional, without vision, numb, anesthetized against the pain of repression.

46. *Unhealthy physically.* Needing drugs to ease my pain, cure my disease, I seize feverishly on every fresh panacaea for my sickening lifestyle.

47. *Emotionally ill:* 25% of Americans seek psychological help during our lifetimes.

48. *Not inhabiting myself fully,* deficient, needy, needing my own space, becoming territorial.

49. *Neurotic,* compulsive, vulnerable.

50. *Needing to sleep a lot,* to replenish my energy dissipated in overcoming my resistance and repression—which also keeps me from fully, naturally taking in oxygen during my waking hours. Wasting energy holding up my masks and defenses. Not sleeping well because I'm afraid to trust my natural breathing process. No surprise, since I've not yet, on account of my repression, fully experienced its trustworthiness to sustain me automatically, even if I turn my mind off. Additionally, being asleep, I've turned off my conscious protective system, leaving me vulnerable to you, whom I don't trust that much.

51. *Intimidated,* timid, afraid to confront, challenge authority. Not knowing it's okay to be assertive, to take care of myself, building up pressure, becoming aggressive, violent, shy, afraid to speak out, even when I'm again being violated.

52. *Afraid of myself,* scared to freely, fully experience myself, fear-ridden, fear-driven. Afraid of you, putting on masks, putting up defenses, playing roles, concealing myself from myself and from you, so we rarely make significant, intimate human contact. Into the loop of mistrust, paranoia and defense: I'm afraid, get defensive, tense up my body into a fight posture, making me threatening to your perception, each frightening the other, containing ourselves, resulting in our relating together such that the sum of us together is less than the total of our individual selves.

53. *Constrained,* controlled, confining myself, then needing to

control you. To the extent I'm out of touch with my own substance, I'll be concerned about my form, appearance, and whether I look good, so I can fool you into believing I'm good, when all the time inside I "know" I'm evil.

54. *Edited*, lacking spontaneity, immediacy. The mask I've been conditioned, chosen to wear—to hide my evil nature— stifles my authentic being: I become inauthentic, closed, private, concealed, secret.

55. *Apathetic*, without energy, without passion. My energy and passion are contained, locked away inside myself, distracted from myself. We teach persons not to be expressive, assertive, then wonder why they grow up apathetic! Painfully conditioned early in life to be passive, to withhold my self for protection's sake, I watch from the sidelines of life where it's safe—no risk, no pain—become a spectator rather than a participant in life. I thus prefer to pass my time and my life observing other persons living and playing, rather than actively involved in my own being, in my own becoming, or in responding to my human brothers and sisters who are starving, unsheltered, ill, lonely.

56. *Unfeeling*, not fully feelingful, distrusting my natural feelings, susceptible to chemicals to move my energy and make me feel differently, alive.

57. *Breathless*. I lost my natural respiratory system and rhythm early in life, holding my breath whenever scared or hurt. Breathing shallowly, irregularly became my most effective means of mastering my emotions, suppressing my feelings. When my breathing doesn't supply me with sufficient oxygen, my organs function at a slower rate, my potential for sensory and emotional experience is reduced, rendering me "safer."

58. *Unable to cry freely* in appropriate situations, my natural crying mechanism blocked. Males, especially, are conditioned to believe "big boys don't cry; men don't cry." Rolfers (who guide a body-releasing growth process) report that often when they work deep into a male's jaw, they release some dike, and a long pent-up flood of tears pours forth.

59. *Uncaring*, lacking in compassion, without much feeling for my fellow humans. I'll do most anything to help anyone in my immediate blood family, no matter how badly s/he has done to date. Yet I fail to recognize, acknowledge members of my entire human family, little demonstrating sensitive response to my human brothers and sisters when they're hurting. I'm so quick

to judge and dismiss them, instead preoccupied with accumulating, showing off my possessions and skills. Unaware of my own depths, I'm unaware of our common human depths, and strikingly aware of our uncommon surface differences, and thereby become racist, sexist, etc.

60. *Unloving.* My spontaneous natural impulses of love, instead of freely expressing themselves, bump up against a thousand obstacles as they seek fulfillment. The knots, a form of "character armor" within me, divert my love impulses from their natural straight path, diverting me from the path of life—love.

61. *Amoral to immoral*—out of touch with my innate, moral, life-affirming valuing systems and capacities.

62. *Apolitical to anti-political.* Apathetic politically, I'm letting "George" or the government do it, and if they don't, complaining vociferously. When my life isn't working well, I'll likely look for someone to blame it on. Since I've been conditioned to expect the authority figure to make everything okay for me, I especially become resentful, attack government, our primary public authority figure, when *it* isn't making my life work for me. I suspect this attitude accounts in large part for our passage of Proposition 13.

63. *Mystified, ignorant, regarding myself,* especially my body. I'm not self-aware, therefore I can't know what I'm not being. I'm woefully ignorant about that which is closest and most central to my life, myself, my own insides. In fact so close, I couldn't have so overlooked myself by accident, it must have been deliberate. Rather than aware of my deep innate desire for self-determination and growth, I get more into self-termination. My human "machine" is repressed, turned off, virtually asleep, my energy at low levels, all making me susceptible to being intimidated, mystified and manipulated by others.

We maintain a remarkable commitment to ignorance, especially regarding ourselves, harboring and perpetuating distrust of information, facts, even the truth. The California Medical Association lobbied against a *study* on alternative birthing practices. Many legislators opposed my bill to expand our state's *knowledge* of developing human dimension educational programs—including moral and value development, self-awareness, self esteem, human relations, sexuality and spirituality.

64. *Distrustful of my self*, my own experiencing, intuition, judgment. From containing myself, I lost my natural wisdom, intuition, common sense, natural inclination toward life, outreach, expansion, growth, development, thus also losing my capacity to trust, risk, be assertive, passionate, valuing, responsible, responsible.

65. *Uncurious*, not fascinated with nor sensitive to myself—the one person from whom all my inclinations and actions emerge and proceed. How come we humans, who are naturally curious, have become so uncurious about the most curious of beings, ourselves? Why so much more fascinated with things than with persons? What attracts so much more of our energies to persons and times distant, remote, abstract, impersonal—than to those concrete, earthy, immediate, personal, alive? We've lost our sense of adventure and pluralism; we're more into the novelty of faddish things and ideas—than the novelty of persons. We choose usually to associate only with persons exactly like ourselves.

66. *Obsolescent*, like dinosaurs, at the end of our era, threatened with extinction. We are desperate, frantic and uproarious as we see our old world slipping away from us, not even recognizing the nature of the threat. Lumbering, cumbersome, clumsy, we can't see and even fight off efforts to help us see, save us. We're unlikely to survive unless we change ourselves to fit our changed and changing world.

67. *Repressed, and deluded about my repression.* I'm thus twice done in, placed in a double bind and doubly locked inside myself. Most insidiously our old vision repressed my capacity to be aware of, even to recognize that I'm repressed. Having little idea how repressed I am, what my potential truly is, I accept, even support the ideology of a ruling system that's killing me by denying my most basic human needs. Having lost my natural sense of inner-directedness, I become outer-directed, needing direction from without, especially susceptible to fascism. Repression is a grim trip I often don't try to free myself from, because I'm not aware of being a prisoner of it. I've become an accomplice in my own continuing victimization.

68. *Enslaved to culture:* the "civilized" person is born and dies a slave to culture. Imprisoned for life by institutions, I imprison myself with my culture's negative myths and taboos. I'm undermined, distorted, perverted by the very society we

devised to "save" us—too often from ourselves.

69. *Committed less to self*, more loyal and faithful to our old vision and its perpetuation, through our culture and institutions, even at the cost of myself. We bring up children in ways that almost assure they'll turn out the same way, fulfill our prophecy, keep it all going as it is. At dinner with Glenn Dumke, Chancellor of California's 19-campus, 300,000-student State University and Colleges, we discussed whether schools ought give grades. Glenn argued they must, since "the purpose of schooling is to prepare persons for living in our society, and life in our society is competitive and nasty. The purpose of grades is to help persons learn how to survive in our society, by becoming competitive and nasty." (He later denied including "nasty".) Note again how personal vision determines public-policy decision-making, how we operate our institutions off the basis of our personal belief, how they then in turn affect other persons.

70. *Undeveloped,* primitive (in the least sense of the term). I've been limited by these more visible, obvious effects and results of our old vision's treatment of us humans, all inter-connected, inter-operating within me. Our question after all that "living" within our old vision, absorbing its effects upon and within us, is "How much of my natural wholeness do I have extant? How much am I intact?"

Hopefully, my state of being is only temporary, interim. Hopefully I'm committed, despite it all, to outgrowing my conditioning, to liberating myself, to realizing myself fully.

Here's a personal anecdote that characterizes our old vision in its entirety: I have a dear friend, Christopher Leahy, now 11 years old. Chris is the youngest of four children of friends David and Joni. As the parents grew as individuals, each succeeding child received more support for her/his individuality. Chris' spontaneity and expressiveness were uncommon. Three weeks after he entered kindergarten, his teacher called Joni to come for a "parent conference."

Joni went and asked what the problem was regarding Chris. The teacher's first response was "Well, he's very tiny." Joni said "That's true. We expect he'll grow big enough in due time. We're not going to do anything special about it. Is that really a problem?" The teacher continued: "Well, the bigger problem is that Chris is a boy." Joni, becoming angry, asked "And what's that problem?" The teacher responded: "Boys don't behave themselves, like girls do. They don't sit quiet and docile in their seats." Joni responded: "Yes, Chris is a boy, and you better believe we're not going to do anything to change that! You'd better just get used to it. Is there anything further?"

The teacher responded: "Well, he's a lefty." Joni, more heated, asked: "And what problem is that?" The teacher claimed: "They do everything backwards, how they write, smear the ink..." Joni, now angry, said: "Yes, he's a lefty; we're not going to do anything to change that either. You'll have to accept our son as he is."

One morning a week later Chris came to his mother, Adidas in hand, asking "Will you tie my shoes for me?" Joni said, "Chris, what're you up to? You've been tying your own shoes for a year now." Chris responded, "Yeah, but I just found out my hands are on backwards and I don't know how to tie them anymore!"

That story is close to me for several reasons: First, I hate to see any person, especially a child, hurt that way. Second, Chris has been my dear friend since his birth. Third, I'm left-handed. In 1938, when I was in the first grade (no kindergarten then) my teacher began converting me to right-handed. I mentioned that at home at dinner. My father was the school principal. The next day he told the teacher to stop that. I was fortunate: Most kids don't have that kind of power going for them at school.

So I was rescued. Yet, now forty years later and despite much therapy and reading of psychology, I find myself super-conscious of my left-handedness. If I'm watching a movie and Robert Redford strikes a match for a cigarette, I see nothing but his left hand moving. If I'm driving and kids are playing football in the street, and there's a lefty quarterback, that's all I notice. Even from a distance, if someone is writing left-handed, I notice it immediately. I carry a scar from that early effort to change me from how I am.

Our traditional culture
operating on our cynical vision
labors so diligently
to take me away from my being,
condition me away from my nature,
causing me to surrender large parts of myself.

Necessarily that leaves me fractured, fragmented, less than
whole,
deficient, needy, needing
especially ratification—
then tries to sell me back
wholeness, happiness, beauty, satisfaction
via advertising, religion, drugs,
cosmetics, gadgets, trinkets
all (the while) offering, promising
absolution, salvation.

How delicate we human beings are!
we owe it to ourselves:
let's not tamper with our nature.

Our old vision has left us struggling amidst two remarkable
paradoxes.

One is our American political paradox. We have the finest
Constitution and Bill of Rights and system of government.
They're based upon a positive, idealistic belief about our human
nature and potential—that we humans have the innate capacity
to be free and responsibly self-determining. But that idealism
has never governed our country. Instead we've had a cynical
culture, believing precisely the opposite about our natural
capacity for self-governance. On that premise our culture
proceeded intentionally, methodically and effectively—to
convince us of our evilness and to condition us away from our
natural capacity for self-determination.

Our old vision disallows democratic character structure—in
which our intellects and emotions and bodies are equally valued,
liberated and integrated. It leaves us incapable of exercising our
natural capacity for living democratically. No wonder we're so
come-apart as individual persons and as a nation. No wonder
we're struggling. We're resolving our paradox. We're
outgrowing our culture's debilitation. We're developing our
capacity for self-determination. We're integrating ourselves,
toward realizing the promise of our governmental system. Our
American dream can't deliver on its promise until, unless we
resolve our American political paradox.

The other is our religious paradox. We have the finest
instruction from most of our religions: "love." Love our
neighbors, our parents, our enemies, ourselves, everyone. Yet

they impose upon us gross amounts of guilt and shame and fear, conditioning us away from our natural capacity for loving. No wonder we end up distrustful, hateful, hostile—anything but loving of our fellow humans or of ourselves. No wonder we're struggling. We're resolving our paradox. We're outgrowing our debilitation. We're developing our capacity for loving. We're integrating ourselves toward realizing the promise of our religions. Their goals, and ours—can't be attained until, unless we resolve our American religious paradox.

We can summarize: our old vision has truly done us in. It lives on, tenaciously, its scars powerfully operational within us all. I've not met a person whom I experience as free from its ravages.

A curious thing is happening as I'm writing this chapter. In my early drafts I referred to "*the* old vision." Later, wanting to write more personally, I found myself switching to "*our* old vision." My early feeling about our old vision was negative. As I then wrote "our old vision" over and over, I found myself beginning to hum the Nielsen tune "My Old Desk." He affectionately relates a tale of nostalgia for his old, now gone desk. I realized I was beginning to feel affectionate toward "our old vision." My negative feelings diminished significantly. I could recognize that our old vision did some good for me and was sincere. I no longer need be resentful. And I no longer need or want our old vision in my life.

If you see our old vision as I do, I invite you to participate in fully living our new vision. Persons still living by our old vision will most readily outgrow it when they experience acceptance and love. They'll then begin to feel better about themselves, become less dependent upon our old vision as they begin to love themselves more. We ought provide them that experience, through the character of our presence in their lives. We ought provide that continuously for each other.

If you don't see our old vision as I do, I invite you to think about it more. Perhaps you'll recognize (some parts of) yourself in my description of the effects of our old vision. If you do, I further invite you to wonder whether our old vision might be the reason for who and how you are today.

Even if you don't recognize yourself herein, I hope you'll recognize the significance of our old vision, as a shaping force in our lives and society.

III.
INSIGHT:
LIBERATING
OURSELVES

approaching 20-20: macroproblem sighted

> *"We have met the enemy and (s)he is us."*
> —Walt Kelly

With our new vision, we can recognize what's going and gone wrong, in our lives and society.

Any single answer risks oversimplification. Yet I begin with the assertion that it's our enculturation which lies at the root of our failures. Too much of the way things are is because we're like machines, programmed to act and not act in certain ways, rather than being natural life-affirming, life-responding human beings.

We can now better understand
how come so much failure in our society,
how come our American dream isn't working,
isn't delivering on its promises,
even why our problem-solving efforts
prove counter-productive rather than effective.

Analysis of our old vision
demonstrates our problems are systemic.

There's one central problem
underlying and accounting for the rest.
We've found our "macroproblem":
our culture compresses us
into one-dimensional persons.

Our system itself
is contrary to
our newfound vision of our human nature.
It's basically corrupt, corrupting and not correctible:
our old-vision *system*
is our problem!

We're still operating
our institutions, culture, society, problem-solving efforts
on our old vision,
based upon assumptions about our human nature
that we've long since, far outgrown.

Our society is sick
because it's sickening us humans,
conditioning us away from ourselves,
our natural humanness,
our natural health and wholeness,
leaving us fractured, crippled, paralyzed.

Our culture is dying
because it's deadly for humans.
It deadens us,
our natural life and humanness,
our energy, spontaneity, curiosity, expression.

Our personal and social failures occur
because we humans are growing up.
We're outgrowing
our traditional, narrow and negative image of ourselves,
our nature and potential,
upon which our culture and institutions
were conceptualized, designed and founded,
and upon which they're still largely being operated.
Our institutions are failing
because we've outgrown them:
The institutions that raised us;

are still being operated on "juvenile" assumptions about us.
They hold to a narrow and negative,
inaccurate and inadequate,
no longer sufficient nor fitting
vision of our selves and our potential.
They stifle us and
our growth and development as human beings.

We're like adolescents
who have suddenly shot up in size:
our parents don't want to recognize our growing up.
They're still trying to stuff us back
into our old infant clothes,
even our baby shoes.
No wonder our clothes, our appearances, are in tatters!

Our institutions aren't working,
are besieged and losing credibility
because they're not meeting
the expanding needs and wants
of our expanding persons.
It's not a breakdown of our society and institutions.
They're breaking up,
as we humans breakthrough, breakout of ourselves,
and our narrow institutional and personal molds.

All that's breaking down
are the too small, even tiny
images, cells, boxes, structures
within which we've been far too long,
unnecessarily and unheathily confined.
Traditional persons, institutions and culture
would still confine us thus.
We're saying, "No more!"

Our problem-solving efforts haven't worked because,
like our problems themselves,
they've been based upon
the wrong, even reverse assumptions about us.
It's our macroproblem again.

When we shift our viewpoint
about our own nature and potential,

we live differently.
Corrective efforts designed on our old vision
no longer work.
They become unavailing at best,
counterproductive at worst.
They get the opposite effect
from that intended and expected.
They aggravate rather than alleviate
our problems;
antagonize, even infuriate
persons living by our new vision.
They worsen our condition,
by reinforcing the roots of our problems.

When we radically change
ourselves and our vision,
our motivational processes
naturally change as well.
Processes chosen off our old vision,
absolutely contrary about our nature,
work precisely in reverse.

When I was in high school,
the fad was drinking alcohol.
Authorities used every possible fear tactic,
including threat of punishment and banishment,
to scare us from using it.
That largely worked with us in those days.

For persons now in high school
the fad is smoking marijuana.
The same efforts at deterrence
have little-to-none of the effect desired.
They're more likely to incur the reverse effect.

Our institutions are in trouble for several additional reasons:
- They're caught in the cross-fire between our competing visions.
- Persons at their top are the most edited epitomes of our old culture. They're least likely to have a vision for seeing what's wrong and how we can make it right.
- Institutions, laws, government are almost always sub-

stitutes for our failed efforts. They didn't create the problem in the first place, they usually can't solve it afterwards.
• We keep trying to solve problems intellectually, by words, cognitive education, therapy and development. Our problems are deeper within us, at an emotional, physiological, bodily level. We lack understanding and development of our deeper human motivations—unconscious until and unless we become more fully conscious.
• Our efforts are in the wrong direction. Our intellect analyzes, takes apart. We've analyzed our world to bits, virtually taken ourselves apart. Our emotions, our wholeness synthesizes, puts back together. We simply haven't developed that capacity of ours.

Our old vision is not our solution,
it is our problem.
We cannot solve our current problems
with our traditional vision.
We have to take ourselves
into another, new vision
befitting our new selves,
to understand our problems.
Our solution can only be discerned and discovered
if we get ourselves into our new vision.

Like our vision,
each of us is either part of
the solution or of the problem.

How do we get ourselves
into our new vision—
to make things right again
in our lives and society,
now and for our future?

Our answers are already emerging,
as we humans have begun
to solve the mystery of life,
the riddle of ourselves.

Let's look at our first transitional steps
from our old to our new vision.

Let's begin to develop an answer
to our monumental life-or-death question.

chapter 10

visible transition, dawning transformation

> *"Life must be understood backwards, but it must be lived forwards."*
>
> —Soren Kierkegaard

With our liberated vision, we can also understand how come our lives and society look so bad today—how come-apart we are, how weird we feel and act and look individually and as a society. We can understand why we're experiencing so much chaos and confusion, distrust and cynicism, greed and materialism, violence and blatant sexuality. We can understand how come we're experiencing so little certainty and responsibility, caring and sharing.

Life's very simple, we're very simple, naturally. We've so complicated life and ourselves that nothing's simple today. But we're on our way. We're in the throes of labor, giving birth to our new selves—an historic transition, beginning transformation.

According to our new vision, we're naturally okay, at root and by nature. According to our old vision, we're not. So they frightened us, repressed us, screwed us up, messed us up inside. Then they further scared us (a double bind) so we put on a nice cover, a veneer, over our internal mess. We walk around half-dead, trying our best to *look* nice—though our eyes, faces and bodies reveal our lack of vitality.

We have lifted ourselves and rebelled from our internalized repression, constraint, slavery. As we've been growing, our pressures inside have been building. We've outgrown our veneer, cracks begin to appear. We've blown their cover on us. We've lost our nice appearance. Our untidiness is full-showing. That's why we look so bad.

We're at the next stage of our evolution. From butterflies in our chrysallis, we're breaking out, trying our wings for the first time. We're no longer willing to be confined, yet not enough experienced in our newly-believed-in, newfound freedom and humanness. Hopefully we're moving on to realizing the full natural order and beauty which are our nature, potential and destiny.

We're experiencing difficulty especially because our effort is unprecedented in our human history. We have no models to refer to for guidance—for knowing ourselves, establishing our individuality, becoming our own persons, living horizontally, democratically, naturally.

We've lost our (old) way. We're in unprecedented, unexplored and uncharted waters. We're adrift, sailing without any map, chart or compass, and without any rudder, save our own, ourselves. We're unanchored. We've departed our old world and our new world's not yet clearly sighted. Everything seems out of control because everything is out of control. The center of everything, ourselves, is out of control. We're shifting the center of control from ourside to within us. We've not yet developed our internal rudder, our own radar.

We're not accustomed to sailing by ourselves, by our own sense of direction. We must discover and develop our capacity, depend upon and develop our own resourcefulness, become inner-directed, self-directing. We have lifted ourselves and rebelled from our internalized repression, constraint, slavery.

Our transition already shows in many ways. Our transformation is beginning to show as well. Let's look at some of our passages—(from) our past, (into) our present, and hopefully (onto) our future states of being:

•*From* denying and repressing ourselves on account of our old vision, *into* accepting and releasing ourselves as we are, including our repression, distortion, crippledness, deformity, brokenness, scars, resentment, rage. We're breaking out. What was beneath is now at our surface, fully visible. We've been living in a pressure cooker all these years, pent up, packed down inside. We're bursting forth with no sense of direction, reaching in every direction, experimenting, exploring our new found freedom, making up for lost times.

The first persons out of our pressure-packed-old-vision state often come out funny-looking and acting, exaggerated, even bizarre—in anger, conduct, dress and more: *some* women tough, *some* blacks enraged, *some* gays outrageous—all with reason.

With all our deformity, we are not pretty. We're confused, ugly, awkward, weird, ungainly. We're stretching, unsure—in an awkward, adolescent, rebellious stage in our personal growth, in our interpersonal relationships, in all of our society. We're releasing ourselves and our pent up passions. Better we release our caps slowly. Better yet never to have had caps put on us at all, but in our culture we just about all come with caps. There's great pressure within.

Hopefully *onto* becoming our free, innocent, beautiful, natural selves.

•*From* being largely repressed and unconscious, *into* becoming and being tremendously self-conscious, including conscious of our negative feelings, hopefully *onto* growing and becoming fully conscious, at which point we'll be un-self-conscious again.

•*From* being flat, one-dimensional persons, *into* opening up and exploring, showing our second distorted dimension, hopefully *onto* opening up and working through our distortion, to release, reveal and realize our wholeness, our full three-dimensional personhood, innocence, grace.

•*From* denying this life and ourselves, in order to gain the next life, *into* new-age living this life (karma) in order to live more the next life (a rationalization no less), hopefully *onto* simply living this life. Life is its own sufficient reason!

•*From* one common, superimposed, uniform culture, *into* separatism, retaliation, individual cultures, pluralism, diversity, hopefully *onto* our one common human nature, unacculturated.

We're moving along a continum of horizontalization:

•*From* vertical models of persons and institutions, *into* horizontal models of institutions; hopefully *onto* horizontal models of persons.

•*From* accepting our vertical establishments carte blanche, *into* rejecting, attacking and shattering our vertical models (We've not yet grown our underdeveloped beings enough to be/come able to live naturally, gracefully, horizontally, morally), *into* rejecting all that's gone before, resentful, having to isolate our selves to gain autonomy (Defining myself out of the mainstream is still being defined by the mainstream. Rejection and separatism are signs of my still being controlled by the mainstream, indicating I'm still not fully disengaged from what I'm struggling against), hopefully *onto* being free, autonomous, self-defined naturally. Returning to engage again is a sign I've gained enough maturity to be responsible, naturally.

•*From* following my imposed duty to be a certain way, fit myself into certain roles and expectations, subdue myself, my own person and desires, *into* rejecting roles and expectations, in favor of being myself, hopefully *onto* recovering my natural capacity for living, knowing what I want.

•*From* responsibility resulting from my being obedient and dutybound, forced and frightened at the risk of punishment, allowed no rights, dutifully performing and obeying out of fear, *into* being irresponsible (since my ingrafted, externally imposed sense of responsibility is gone and I've not yet discovered how to replace it, or how to develop my own natural responsibility; when allowed my rights for the first time, I tend to use them as license), hopefully *onto* recovering my natural capacity for responsiveness and my natural sense of responsibility.

•*From* growing up in a culture where I had to prove myself to you, *into* rebelling, now having to establish my identity by proving myself to myself, hopefully, *onto* not having to prove anything to anyone.

•*From* denying and not expressing my individuality and personhood, basing my life and society on self-denial, denying my natural innocence and worth, positing that worth is established by my doing and having, *into* outgrowing my self-denial, recognizing/resenting/resisting/rebelling against/ rejecting doing *your* thing, accepting and having to express and show my individuality in doing my own thing (a not surprising outgrowth of our old culture), hopefully *onto* recognizing that the truth is just in being, becoming *my own person*, in self-realization and self-fulfillment.

•*From* being self-denied, *into* being selfish, narcissistic, catching up on and with myself, making up for lost time, fascinated at my newfound discovery of myself, the "me" generation, hopefully *onto* knowing myself fully, no longer a curiosity, not so preoccupied with myself, more open to being fascinated with other persons.

•*From* I-didn't-know-who-I-was, mystified, ignorant about myself, not self-aware, *into* having to ask constantly "Who am I?"—because I've split, denied myself, don't know myself or who I am, hopefully *onto* becoming myself, thereby knowing who I am, no more separate "I."

•*From* not being myself, disowning myself, *into* reclaiming and repossessing myself, hopefully *onto* owning myself, being myself fully.

•*From* never speaking up, out, for myself, *into* growing enough to learn that I can speak for myself; learning my first word, saying "No" to someone else (in the 1960's our counter-culture persons were saying "Hell, no, we won't go;" in the 1970's our silent majority persons are saying "We're mad as hell, we aren't going to take it anymore)," hopefully, *onto* discovering I can say "Yes" to myself, then "Yes" for myself, then "Yes" to you and every other person.

•*From* being instructed, conditioned to be neat, clean, crew-cut, *into* breaking out and in over-compensation becoming unneat, dirty, long-haired, hopefully *onto* becoming naturally neat and clean, including my hairstyle.

I've been experiencing my own transition personally. It's been showing, occasionally to the chagrin of some persons. When first elected I was crew-cut, wouldn't appear on the Assembly floor without matching suit and tie. As I began my unwinding, letting myself out—much untidiness came forth. I gradually shifted to long hair brushed straight, then let it take its natural curl, then go haywire every which way, and long. I gradually switched to a sport coat with matching slacks and tie, then abandoned my tie, then my coat in favor of a light jacket or vest. Lately, as I've grown, I've also shed more of the untidiness within me, bared more of the natural neatness of my being. I'm back into being more neat: hair shorter, coat more often, even, on occasion, a necktie.

•*From* having been violated, becoming angry and suppressing my anger, *into* releasing my suppression and experiencing and expressing my anger, hopefully *onto* releasing my anger, at its roots, within me.

•*From* having my gentleness repressed, becoming violent, and containing my violence (violence has been favorably mythologized as an option in our culture—the Old West, war, cops and robbers, television, movies—as a way of solving our problems), *into* letting go and letting my violence out; preempting that cultural right to and for myself, embracing it as my individual right, participating more in our cultural life and norms; hopefully *onto* outgrowing, letting go of our culture, its violence, my own, and growing back into my gentle nature.

•*From* loving at the risk of punishment, because I'm supposed to, for fear of rejection, punishment or exclusion from rewards (earthly or heavenly) if I don't, or loving just within certain rules and roles, *into* not loving much or well, hopefully *onto* becoming naturally loving and caring, responsive to each other, to developing a natural fellow-feeling, empathy, compassion, learning to love and care for everyone, no matter whether blood-related (it's enough we're related by reason of our common human nature, our common ground of being, our common membership in our one human family).

•*From* sharing, denying myself things out of "should," compulsive, duty-bound, fear-induced, guilt-ridden altruism, *into* being resentful and hoarding, keeping things to and for myself, not sharing (materialism and greed result from my being self-denied, incapable of deriving satisfaction from my being, needing material things and money for "substitute gratification"), hopefully *onto* becoming naturally sharing, just because I want to.

•*From* being out of touch with myself, *into* rediscovering my sense of touch, my need for touch, hopefully *onto* getting back in touch with my natural self.

•*From* being competitive to survive, "doing" in order to have enough for "being," *into* being competitive to prove myself and my worth, hopefully *onto* becoming aware of my own worthiness, becoming cooperative.

•*From* regarding my body as negative and dirty, to be scorned, repressed, contained, guilt-ridden, shamed, tolerated at best, feared at worst, *into* opening up, letting out all my contortion and distortion, resentment and rage, leading me into bizarre forms of bodily expression and touching, sexual to violent, hopefully *onto* accepting, reclaiming and reinhabiting my body as positive, wonderful, vital to my living.

•*From* being separated from my body, anti-body, not even knowing it, *into* recognizing and affirming my body (explaining much of women's and gay liberation, the sexual revolution, body therapies (bioenergetics, Rolfing, Feldenkrais, Alexander), explicit sexuality in entertainment and advertising, sky-rocketing divorce rates, sex education, nudity, abortion, contraception, alternatives to the nuclear family), but still disidentifying with my body, trying new transpersonal psychologies and religions, perpetuating my disidentification with my body, my mind-body split, hopefully *onto* fully accepting my being my body.

•*From* my sexuality having been repressed, denied, *into* acknowledging my sexuality, being needy, hungry, compulsive, driven, preoccupied and outrageous about it, hopefully *onto* being fully, freely, naturally sexual, affirming of my natural sexuality.

•*From* being bound together by adversity, to cope with and conquer our physical environment, assure our survival; *into* relaxed affluence, because of our remarkably increased material productivity, allowing us to come apart, from each other and even with/in ourselves (though we're the most materially wealthy people in the most wealthy nation in our world, we can't seem to get ourselves together), hopefully *onto* getting ourselves together, individually and societally, coming together in our natural caring.

•*From* cynicism and distrust of ourselves and our human nature, conditioned away from our own natural trustworthiness, and our belief in our own trustworthiness, (Perhaps our most crucial issue: Our old culture's acculturation and socialization process has ground cynicism and distrust into our very being. We've been conditioned to be distrustful, especially of ourselves. We superimposed over this conditioned distrust of our human nature—a blind trust and awe, especially of persons in authority. We got used to operating our lives and society via mystification and vertical structures, on the basis of awe and blind trust), *into* a profound demystification process. (On account of our changing world and circumstances, we've outgrown our awe and blind trust. We're seeing through, challenging, and shedding our veneer of blind trust. When our blind trust is dispelled, we're left with only what's beneath its surface: our culturally imposed, conditioned-in distrust, of ourselves and of each other. No wonder we now so readily distrust each other. That's what we're operating out of now—no trust. We trust only where and when trust's been proved, by enough personal exposure and experience. We've got to earn trust, proving ourselves trustworthy in each other's experience.), hopefully *onto* working our way through our layer of distrust, to live our way through to real trust.

We're beginning to dispel the distrust of our culture,
to go deeper, beneath it, within ourselves;
opening to, getting down to, getting in touch with,
surfacing our innate trustworthiness.
Enough openness, exposure, experience with ourselves
would lead us to recognize our own natural trustworthiness.
Then we'll trust each other more readily, naturally,
trusting that each other is by nature
as trustworthy as I naturally am.
We'll then be expecting, recognizing, reaching for, evoking
trust from within each other, exposing ourselves enough to each
other, to earn and experience trust.

Additionally, as I grow more whole,
I'll grow less vulnerable,
enabling me to venture more trust with less sense of risk.

•*From* being awed, blindly trusting, believing that only
external authority is trustworthy; *into* learning we're more
trustworthy than that, authority is less trustworthy than that,
and therefore no more blind trust or awe of authority, position or
title, hopefully *onto* growing ourselves more whole, recognizing
our trustworthiness, getting to real trust and trustworthiness as
the basis for all our human relationships, with ourselves and
with each other.

(Trust is crucial, essential—in our political as well as in our
personal relationships. It's what enables a democracy to
survive, the people in it to come and function together. We've
been conditioned not to trust ourselves to solve our social
problems, not even to trust our experience of them. Politicians
keep telling us things are okay, to make us feel good—even
when we *know* different. We're accustomed to authority figures
making everything work for us. Things aren't working any more,
and we've not yet learned how to trust our capacities for making
things work for ourselves. We're now at a point in our transition
at which the risk of continuing, perpetuating our distrust, is far
greater than the risk of letting go and trusting—ourselves and
each other.

Overall, we've not yet discovered how to heal ourselves, make
ourselves whole, natural, innocent, gentle, serene, generous
again. We've not yet learned how to carry, dispose of our

overload, our scars resulting from our repression and deformity. We're discovering a new world, ourselves—a world heretofore largely undreamed of, unexplored, uncharted, the world within us. We're trying out something entirely new—ourselves!)

•*From* our traditional, vertical model—we've made great strides *into* and *onto* horizontalization, humanization—of our selves and our institutions. This enables us to more readily recognize the profound, foundation-shaking character of our liberating vision. We're questioning, challenging, shaking and changing the very foundation of our lives, within and beneath us, our culture and our institutions.

We humans are creating a powerful and profound earthquake. We're feeling "the earth move beneath our feet." We're losing our footing, our sense of security, we're frightened, scared, scrambling, grabbing, getting uptight, clinging tighter—all aggravating rather than alleviating our displacement.

Like an earthquake, our transformation is irresistible and irreversible, no temporary sidestep. It's a permanent shift, with more shifting forthcoming. The forces contributing to our pressure buildup and shift continue unabated. I can foresee no way our foundation won't keep on shaking and moving, unless we stop ourselves growing, which I can't imagine. We'll never get ourselves back onto solid foundations, solid ground—until we trust ourselves to move, to stand four-square on our new foundations.

A primary issue for each of us during our awkward time of transition is: How do I manage myself, my life and relationships, interpersonal and institutional—while I'm growing myself into my natural capacities for being human? My examination of the effects of our old vision (Chapter 8), and this chapter's examination of our being in transition are neither intended, nor serve as excuse for irresponsible behavior. Instead they're offered as grounds for understanding how come we are who we are, enabling us better to outgrow our conditions and transform ourselves. So understanding ourselves and our roots, we can take full responsibility for attending to improving our lives and society. We can then be/come hopeful about our current situation.

Our only hope, a great hope, is to open ourselves to our transition, caringly, carefully. Our task and challenge is to attend

to our continuing transformation. We must work our way
through ourselves as wisely, gently, expeditiously as possible.
We'll bare our real, natural, decent, life-affirming selves.

For directions to proceed in,
for directions on how to proceed—
let's consult our new liberating vision,
its content, intention and operations.

It enables us to understand what's right,
and how we can make more right,
in our lives and society,
now and for our future.

our liberating vision: innocence, trustworthiness & original grace

"We are all born with everything good in us."
—Galileo

In our troubled times,
we desperately need a new vision of
human nature and potential,
who we are and who we can be/come,
what it means to be a human being,
the possible human,
a fully-functioning human being.

We need a vision of being human—not as we humans now are, or have thought of ourselves—but as we might truly become. We need a vision not wholly a product of our fantasy, but one which might even be realized by us, in our lifetime.

Our liberating vision offers us an appropriate foundation for our efforts to attend to our lives and society—with profound implications and ramifications, personally and politically.

As its *content*, our new vision proposes a positive belief in our innate innocence, decency and capacity. We are not corrupt at base. *The wholly liberated, integrated human being is, at root and by nature—innocent*, gentle, caring, loving, trustworthy, life-affirming, responsible—for myself, to you and other human beings, to all of life and nature. Love is our normal, natural way of being. And loving works. Our new vision is fully faithful.

The genetic inheritance of the human is self-regulating, self-balancing, self-motivating, self-directing—inclined toward nurturance, growth, expansion, enrichment, self-realization and fulfillment. The most fundamental human life tendency is to fulfill itself, realize the ideal: itself, ourselves. Human beings are those unique beings who can self-consciously intend what we want to do, even how and what we want to be/come.

Consider the office plant of my former calendarperson Sherry Stansberry. It sat on the shelf outside the doorway between her office with no window and mine with two. However often she turned the pot, the plant always proceeded to turn itself toward the light and warmth available through my window. Is there reason to believe we're any different, by nature—any less needy, less innately wise about our own needs? Why should we expect less of ourselves than of a plant?

The rose provides a metaphor: early in its growth, it has a prickly stem. With proper nutrition, care, sun and water, a beautiful flower emerges. The potential always existed, only requiring the proper conditions for its growth and realization. We humans likewise carry within us the seed of perfection. We too require careful cultivation to reveal our latent beauty. If each day, as I walk by the rose, I pull off a leaf, if I don't water or sunlight it, but starve and darken it, what could I expect? Is there any reason to expect less of a human being?

And life is energetic, powerful, determined. Consider how a plant pushes its way up through the crusted pavement. Is there reason to believe we humans are less than that? Life is undeniable!

We humans are possessed of original grace rather than original sin. Consider the grace and sureness with which an animal moves. Contrast it with our clumsiness, self-consciousness. Is there any reason to believe we'd be less graceful and sure, if we developed naturally?

The original sin is believing in original sin, and inculcating that condition, perpetuating that belief in others—especially young, innocent, vulnerable human beings. Neither money nor human nature is the root of all evil: the root of all evil is our belief we're evil, and our resultant efforts—which serve to make us so.

Our liberating vision is really good news: we humans are okay, naturally. The unknown within us is more likely positive than negative. Self esteem is warranted, naturally. Our actual human potentiality is far greater along many more dimensions than we ordinarily recognize, much less realize.

How much we accept ourselves, how much we expect of ourselves—changes radically, dramatically. Persons can rise to much higher levels of functioning than usually seen in ordinary life. Our old vision's constraints have kept us from fulfilling ourselves and our basic needs. We've become fixated, stunted at lower levels of development. We can instead satisfy our needs, allow our growth toward self-actualization.

When we become self-aware and self-empowered, we become capable of otherwise seemingly impossible tasks. All of us humans have a common human nature, enormous human potential. Each of us can grow and attain far more than we have yet suspected.

Each of us humans is "the valuing animal" (Rollo May's *Psychology and the Human Dilemma*). The wholly liberated, integrated human being is naturally valuing. I know naturally what's good and bad for myself, what's best for my own growth and development and realization. The natural human being is free *and* responsibly self-determining. To be free is to be responsible—naturally.

Our new vision posits and promotes holism. There are no "parts" of me: mental, emotional, physical, spiritual, aesthetic, sexual. I am naturally one, organic, integral. There's only one me, I am only one.

All of me is valued,
no hierarchy within me,
no fragmentation within me,
no disidentification:
I am my mind,
I am my emotions,
I am my body,

I am myself,
I am!

How and where do I find, know and experience my identity
if I disidentify with any part on all of myself?
Why won't we humans just accept what is,
namely, ourselves?

We humans are also "less" than some would like to believe.
We're not disembodied angels, only rational and aesthetic. A
return to ourselves, our bodies, would undo both errors.

Our liberating vision's *intention* then is a radical concern
with and commitment to liberating and conserving our own
human nature, our natural capacity for being, growing,
becoming, loving.

The intention of our liberating vision is to nurture us humans—
so we might:
grow into recognizing our own innocence,
realizing our potential,
exercising our rights,
fulfilling our responsibilities,
developing our self-awareness and self esteem,
our self-realization and self-determination,
being ourselves, becoming ourselves.

We need to believe in, move and grow toward a new kind of
human being—unconditioned, natural, whole. Being—rather
than having and doing—must become our primary ethic.

Let's have faith in human self-perfectibility. Let's include the
expansion of our whole consciousness—personal, social,
emotional, intellectual, physical, sensual, sexual—to a fuller
level.

Let's believe in the inherent trustworthiness of our human
biological organism. We've never truly tried its freedom. It is
conditioning away from ourselves, our emotions and bodies and
sexuality—that alienates us. Let's call for true personal freedom
in a whole-person-affirming culture. Let's envision a perfectly
autonomous, fulfilled "I" for each and every human. Let's allow
our view of humanity and human history to be/come
fundamentally faithful and optimistic, owing to the ever-

growing certainty of our personally tested, otherwise unprovable faith—in ourselves!

Trust in ourselves, our own nature and decency, trust in each other—are deserving. Let's have faith in the inherent, profound trustworthiness, value, significance and potential of each human being.

Respect for the human person becomes natural, obligatory in our new vision efforts. Each human being is unique, previous, valuable, deserving of full life. The dignity of the human person is inviolable. Trust is at the base of it all.

Our liberating vision *operates* by acceptance, respect, trust, nurturance, love and touch. We ought trust the law proceeding from our own innocent human nature—contrary to the traditional natural law. Authorities tried to impose their natural law upon us from without, according to their view and vision of human nature. We have our own natural law: no one ought make us unnatural!

There is right and wrong, reality and morality. To be life-affirming is essentially moral. As I learn more, grow, expand my sense of myself, my insight and vision—I'll come to know better how to attend to the issue of making right and wrong choices in my life. And I'll come to know better how to make my life, my relationships and my society right.

Our liberating vision is well described by:
Sid Jourard's — *The Transparent Self, Disclosing Man To Himself;*
Carl Rogers' — *On Becoming A Person;*
Rollo May's — *Man's Search for Himself;*
Jim Bugental's — *The Search for Authenticity;*
Abe Maslow's — *Toward A Psychology of Being.*

Having examined our old and new visions, we're prepared to recognize the significance of the central event of our lives today: our human revolution—our conflict and transition between our old and new cultures.

chapter 12

our human revolution: polarized visions

> *"A little revolution now and then is a good thing."*
>
> —Thomas Paine

> *"Those who make evolution impossible make revolution inevitable."*
>
> —John Kennedy

Our perspectives (Chapter 5) help us understand how come we're experiencing so much chaos and conflict in our lives and society. We're in the throes of a full-scale revolution—a remarkable, unprecedented revolution, occurring at the very foundation of our lives. We're experiencing a massive effort, transforming our vision *and* ourselves from negative to positive. We're radically redefining what it means to be human.

Our old vision assumes our human nature is sinful, untrustworthy and guilty. Our new vision assumes we humans are, by nature, innocent, trustworthy and life-affirming. Each of us has the innate capacity for knowing what's best for ourselves, and for becoming truly self-determining—in a free and responsible way.

I have come to believe the vision I'm describing is *the* revolution. The true revolution is the revolution within ourselves. There's a revolution going on, we are the revolution! We're undergoing an historic, revolutionary transformation— about how to be/come more fully-developed, fully functioning human beings.

The central personal and sociopolitical event of our times is the emergence of a new model of humanness. That is our Human Revolution. We're revolving our vision of ourselves, and we're turning ourselves full around. We're proposing a new operational human model.

We are redefining ourselves in a way that fully recognizes the wholeness and inherent worth of each individual. Each human being has the inherent right to be/come her/his unique self.

In our human history we have made enormous discoveries, experienced enormous progress. In the end though, as in the beginning, our greatest question is "What or how is our human nature?"

We can find out only if we open ourselves and look inside. We're now doing that. For the first time we're turning our curiosity and powers of reason inward. We owe it to ourselves to get to the root of everything, ourselves. We really only have two ways to go: we can assume we're bad inside, never look in and maintain the pressure forever of avoiding ourselves; or we can wonder whether it's maybe good inside, take the risk, look in. Our human race, with our unquenchable curiosity, is eventually going to look inside, find out for sure what's in there. Let's go ahead and do it now—carefully and caringly.

So we're into a systematic exploration of the vast, deep, unexplored and uncharted universe of our own being. We're reaching beyond our surfaces, dipping into our repression, searching through it to liberate our innocence and natural wisdom. Our true perfect selves are erupting up, out and through the false faces and veneers we've unconsciously chosen to wear. We're New Age chicks, cracking open the brittle, stale shell of Our Old Egg. We're acknowledging our "anima" and "animus" (Jung). We're recognizing that every human naturally includes both feminine (pro-nature, receptive, nurturing, earthy, bodily) and masculine (intellectual, being in control, technological).

Our Human Revolution opens a new epoch in our human evolution. We are discovering that our inner space and personal universe are every bit as real, knowable, measurable and predictable as outer space and the astronomical universe. We are discovering that our descent into the "dark world" of ourselves is not evil. In fact, it is enlightening. Our Human Revolution is a revelation as well as a revolution—about who we truly are. It is the natural evolution of our human intelligence, curiosity and boldness. It is the necessary precondition for understanding and outgrowing the problems of our times.

At age eleven, my Godson Chris Weseloh told me he'd seen the movie "2001-Space Odyssey." At first he couldn't figure out the significance of the obelisk-like figure that kept appearing throughout the movie, at critical points in our human evolution. Recently he'd come up with the answer: "The obelisk represents the human being's unquenchable thirst to know." There's no better subject for knowing than myself!

The core of our Human Revolution is in where we place the source of power, where we look for authority, valuing and responsibility. That's the key to much of our conflict today.

Our revolution in values
derives primarily from how we value the human,
trusting the human's innate capacity for valuing wisely.
We're shifting the source of valuing
from outside, up there
to down here, inside, ourselves.
We're discovering that
the fully free human being
has a natural sense of valuing, is naturally responsible,
that the human being is, in fact, "the valuing animal."

Individuals and groups are engaging in a vast social movement—of redefinition *and* transformation. It includes our relationship to the institutions of our society *and* the nature of our participation in our society. The entire structure of our human consciousness is expanding. We're rediscovering our natural whole consciousness.

Our Human Revolution is an infectious, contagious epidemic. A glimpse of freedom is inviting. A taste of freedom is exhilarating. So is the vision of freedom. So is seeing a free person. Our Human Revolution is building energy. Signs of it are everywhere!

Let's not be afraid to use the word "revolution." The evidence is sufficient. That *is* what's happening. Revolutions are searches for new beliefs, symbols, rituals and institutions in which we can find life for ourselves. Revolutions are the discarding of beliefs which have ceased to provide us security, hope and fulfillment. We're revolving ourselves, the ultimate foundation for security, hope, and fulfillment.

Usually a revolution is superficially innovative, but substantially conservative—building its new order on the same old foundations. We get different persons in power, exercising power the same old way. Our revolution is radically different: it goes to the root of ourselves, changing our foundations, ourselves. We'll exercise our power differently.

A "revolution" is most simply defined as "changing the facts of life." We're redefining the *second most basic* fact of our lives: *how we envision our nature.* We are making a 180-degree turn in *our view* of ourselves: from fully negative to fully positive, guilty to innocent, untrustworthy to trustworthy. *How we envision ourselves* affects everything else in our lives and society.

And we're transforming the *most basic* fact of our lives: *our human nature.* We're making that same 180-degree turn in *ourselves*—changing from fully negative, guilty and untrustworthy to fully positive, innocent and trustworthy. *How we are* affects everything else in our lives and society. We're in a full-scale revolution—revolving everything!

We may as well recognize it, accept it, demystify it. We needn't be frightened by it. It's safe. We can participate in it. We can make it gentle.

And it's the most radical revolution. "Radical" is defined as "going to the root." That's precisely what we're doing, what we have to do. We are changing the root assumption about ourselves, on which we've constructed ourselves, our lives, our society and institutions. We are uprooting our old vision. We are exposing and growing our own roots, to become naturally strong. We are challenging our old institutions at the root of their belief, intentions and operations that would destroy our roots.

Our Human Revolution constitutes a total "paradigm" shift, a massive change in our "world view", our way of looking at everything. Like all paradigm shifts—at first only a few seemingly strange persons and events occur. They're scorned, shrugged off. Then many more occur, becoming almost commonplace. They're too many to be shrugged off, yet their implications are avoided. Then so many persons and events occur that a new shape begins to emerge. It must be dealt with. Then everything gets redefined in terms of it. The shift is on!

For the first time, we're actually aware our paradigm is shifting *and* that we can consciously be party to its changing. This profound transformation—from one age to the next— especially makes our times unique.

Our liberating vision and human revolution are also "subversive." To be subversive means "to undermine." Radically revolutionizing our root assumption undermines *everything* we are, and everything we do. Nothing could be more subversive—or wonderful—than our Human Revolution. The most revolutionary, radical, subversive idea is that *I am, in fact and by nature, okay!*

Our revolution is rightfully characterized as "human," because it's a revolution *of* us humans, about our very nature. It's a revolution *for* us humans: offering us a wholly, wonderfully different way of understanding ourselves and our lives. It's a revolution *by* us humans: we humans are saying "Yes" to ourselves; we're saying "No" to those conditions, events, processes and institutions which have been saying "NO" to our human nature. It's our new Declaration of Independence. We're declaring ourselves independent human beings!

We humans need to explore whether our human nature is open to transformation, and whether our moral, emotional and human climate can enable that transformation. A major challenge for all of us is whether we're ready, able and willing to envision a new model of humanness. Are we willing to recognize and respond to the new persons emerging in our society—even to the new persons emerging within ourselves?

Our Human Revolution has profound effects upon us personally. Our new vision posits and promotes our self esteem—contrary to our old vision. It changes my experience of myself. It enables me to make a different person of myself.

Our Human Revolution has profound effects upon us institutionally. Post-secondary education provides an example: it seems caught between our old and new cultures. Many of the persons who pay for our institutions (including universities) are primarily of our old vision. They're not willing to pay if our insitutions cater to the perceived needs, wants and goals of our new vision persons (such as holistic, humanistic, self-awareness, self-improvement, affective domain development, touching, feeling). Yet, if our institutions fail to respond to our new vision persons, those persons will not be content, and they'll abandon the institutions. We experience conflict between persons operating institutions off our old cultural model, and persons being served by them, who are into our new cultural model. Our institutions, including our universities and our democracy/republic, are in danger of being destroyed in the collision of our two visions.

Such stupendous changing in our conception of humanity, our nature and ourselves is bound to have the most profound social and political ramifications, to produce the most stupendous political and social changes.

Let's explore the connection between our psychology and our politics, our character structure and our social structure. Our liberating vision provides a basis for a new, more human political critique, program and strategy. How we see and do politics depends upon our vision of ourselves as human. Our vision determines our attitudes about politics, power, self-determination, participation and political process. Our new greater vision of humanness is politically revolutionary. It sees human beings as naturally responsible, and therefore deserving of empowerment. It challenges our traditional vertical politics.

There is an inherent connection
between my personal vision
and my public-policy decision-making.
making.
Who I am determines what I do.
The experience I have of myself, as human
provides me the vision I carry into all my relationships,
interpersonal and institutional—including political.
The politics I do is who I am!

The major crisis of our times is de-humanization. We can no longer afford to perpetuate the myth of "man's inhumanity to man." We can hope for more than containing our "beastliness." We can and will discover "how to grow healthy human beings."

In our search for answers, we come right back to the issue of our underlying vision. Our liberating vision proposes that our old vision is the basis of our problems. It is our macroproblem. Our only solution is the implementation of our new liberating vision. There's no solution within our old vision, but only without it. It only reinforces the problems it's created, the more we operate from it. Our liberating vision empowers us to outgrow and overcome our macroproblem.

Again, that's revolutionary. We're throwing off our old vision's constraints. We're redesigning ourselves and our institutions—according to our new vision. The central personal and sociopolitical event of our times—our Human Revolution—directly addresses the central personal and sociopolitical issue of our times—"how to grow a healthy human being." No wonder our turmoil!

Our Human Revolution is timely. We live in pivotal times. We're standing at a fork in the road. One way leads down to the demise of everything we cherish, the other leads up toward realizing our dreams. We either give up to our dehumanization and become an ever more mechanistic, materialistic, militaristic world, or we surrender to our humanness, and become more open and loving and peaceful—thus making our world more human.

We're at the end of an era, choosing to abandon a sick and dying society which has been sickening and killing us human beings. We're at the beginning of a new era, choosing to create a healthy society for nurturing human beings. What happens tomorrow will result from how we believe, live, work, play, think and feel today. The sweep of evolution reflects our personal lives. We participate in it as we make our daily choices about how to be with ourselves, with each other, with our social order and with our earth.

Our answer doesn't lie in apathy, acquiescence in evil, political disengagement, or dropping out. It's to be found and formed in personal, human, even heroic action—applying our truth to our own conditioning, and to the conditions of our society.

Let's recognize we live in one world. We are one human family, with one common human nature. We humans must discover how we can live together—more peacefully, gently and intelligently—or we will likely perish from our earth. Discovering that our common human nature is good mightily improves our prospects!

Each of our prior revolutions has been difficult. We had to reconstruct our entire society and culture, all our institutions— to match our new recognition. This time it's the most difficult. We must again reconstruct everything *outside* ourselves, and we must as well reconstruct *ourselves*. This is also the most promising of our revolutions. It's the most we can do for ourselves.

Alex Haley popularized the search for our historical roots, how we came to be who we are. Now it's time we popularize the search for our internal roots—how we can be/come more than we are now. We need a politics for growing healthy human beings. We need a healthy politics of our bodies, if we're to have a healthy body politic. Our sexual revolution is vital to our political liberation. We must become whole!

From time to time we hear cries that we Americans have lost our sense of national purpose. We hear calls for a debate to get clear about our national goals. Yet we *know* our goals and purpose: we'd all like a peaceful, orderly, safe, free nation—with liberty and justice for all.

I suggest we need a more basic dialogue—an engagement about our national *faith*, our human faith, our faith in human nature and potential. On that faith our visions differ absolutely. And on that faith we respectively choose the processes for achieving our national purpose. Since we lack consensus about the nature of humans, we utterly disagree on the processes needed to get ourselves from where we are to where we want to be! We're living in a period of remarkable and radical differences in our most basic beliefs, assumptions and values. We live amidst diametrically opposed assumptions upon which we translate our statements of purpose into our programs for action.

An illustration: I participated as guest speaker at an evening community meeting for searching out goals for public schools. After two hours discussion, an older woman spoke: "All this talk about goals is fine, except you're not talking about what's more basic: the nature of the children we have to work with. We've got to recognize they're inherently sinful and adapt our processes to that recognition.''

Again, this dispute speaks directly to the central issues of our times: inhumanity and dehumanization. We find ourselves in between, in transition, between those opposite visions. No wonder so much polarization and conflict today! We have a double ''holy war'' on our hands: against our traditional culture's negative assumption about our human nature—and against our traditional science's solely objective/intellectual model of humanness. Both put us at war against ourselves.

Now we're instead into waging peace, for ourselves, against those visions that no longer fit us.

These are the tensions we're experiencing throughout our society. This conflict between contrary assumptions is present in all our institutions, private and public. It's in all our public-policy decision-making, and within many of our people. The conflicts on our campuses, in our streets, cities and ghettoes—are now moving into our public-policy-decision-making places. They are conflicts of differing experiences, perceptions and values. They are conflicts from experiencing more or less conflict in life.

Today's world is the arena in which two contrary personal creeds vie for dominance: the idealistic/humanistic/holistic and the cynical/negativistic/behavioristic; the humanizing and the dehumanizing. Their successes and failures relate directly and profoundly to our individual lives. The present and coming struggle is between these two groups of contrary believers—struggling over our lives.

One group consists of persons whose vision is cynical—including traditional religionists, other traditionalists, Skinnerians, and others. They believe we humans are by nature evil, untrustworthy and violent. They expect sinfulness, divisiveness, prejudice and war. They believe that at best, we can *contain* our evil inclinations. They propose that we human beings have tried freedom and dignity—can't handle the former and don't deserve the latter. According to this view, our best (if not only) future hope lies in our discovering more and better ways of controlling ourselves and each other. They logically choose repressive institutions. I was once a member of our traditional group. When I was, I characterized our new vision group as hopelessly naive.

The other group of believers are those of the humanistic vision—Carl Rogers, Abe Maslow, Sid Jourard, Wilhelm Reich, and others. We're more positive about our nature and potential. We claim some greater sense of what we humans are and may become. We expect the best of us: that we're innocent, trustworthy, life-affirming and gentle.

We believe that our old vision causes and explains our failures. It's so deeply rooted in our old cultural norms, our traditional religion, philosophy, education, science and art—it's easy to understand why we find ourselves in a state of personal, social and global crisis.

We propose that we humans have never truly *tried* freedom, that our future lies rather in our discovering more and better ways of loving, nurturing, releasing and liberating ourselves and each other. We as logically propose liberating institutions. We oppose "behavior modification" because its positive reinforcement continues to put the source of power, right and wrong, outside us. At best, it may prove valuable in enabling us to change our behaviors, resulting from scars of earlier behavior modification efforts. But the scars linger. We characterize our traditional group of believers as hopefully-not-hopelessly cynical.

Fiction writers have posited how persons of our old vision might react to our liberating vision and human revolution. Arthur Clarke's *Childhood's End* fantasizes a new generation of humans so conscious—the Gods had to come from the sky to evacuate them from the earth, lest the older generation, in their fear, exterminate them.

Thomas P. MacMahon, in *The Hubschmann Effect*, fantasizes about six humans born as the first children in a Florida town after a birth control pill experiment. All were born utterly innocent, without fear. Older generation persons were so threatened—they exterminated the youngsters. Older generation law then prosecuted the birth control experimenters—for having performed acts harmful to the well-being of minors.

We're living fact, not fiction. Friend Mary Sweeney's son came in one day bleeding, having not fought back when neighbor kids beat him up. She consoled him: "Tell them you're a lover, not a fighter." "How come?" he asked. She responded, "Because I raised you that way." He then asked: "Why'd you do that?"

We do the same thing as in the fiction, but less obviously and less extremely. We kill the innocence of our newly arriving humans, making them instead guilty and afraid, especially of themselves.

There's plenty of resistance to our revolution. Our new vision challenges the roots of many persons' belief systems. Since they've often given over their natural identity to our old system, they find their identity in its ideology. They're scared, threatened by our new vision. They move to more rigidity and authority. That in turn provokes our resistance. More of us become defectors, refugees.

Our future lies precisely in this struggle between persons believing, living and promoting these two contrary belief systems about our human nature. The character of 1984 will be determined by whether Skinnerian or humanistic psychology becomes the public policy of our society.

We have a responsibility to ask ourselves a question: How do we manage ourselves during these times of revolution? How can we human revolutionaries survive and remain within—even be paid by—the system and institutions against which we are proposing revolution? We can remain there in good faith— because we believe all humans will be better served by our humanized institutions. We can survive by attending to our own further personal growth and with the help of healthy human relationships.

We have a responsibility to assure our revolution is nonviolent. Violence has no place in our Human Revolution. It doesn't fit our vision, it's against what our Human Revolution is all about. And it won't work, anyway. Only love works. We simply have to be present with our old vision persons in loving, gentle ways. We need to model our vision, especially taking personal responsibility for outgrowing any violence within ourselves. We must make our revolution, ourselves, gentle.

We need not spend our energy tearing down the oppressive institutional structures which confine us. They're already crumbling. They'll fall of their own dead weight. Instead, we ought apply ourselves, our focus and our energy to building up the human alternatives, new institutions to match and fit our expanding selves.

From thirteen years of struggling, I'm well aware that the process of our revolution is evolutionary. There's no magic, instant change or cure. Overall, we're a schizophrenic society. Our differences are basic, foundational, profound, all but irreconcilable. Discovering how to bridge this gap between contrary cultures is a life-or-death (ad)venture for us human beings.

We ought not be naive. It's impossible to adapt our new vision to our traditional vision. Our new vision is an indivisible whole. It can't be edited to make it palatable for persons clinging to our old vision. Our old vision simply must be outgrown. Whatever its origins, its successes, its values for us in our past—it no longer fits us, no longer serves us well.

We can't reconcile our visions. Our only hope is to reconcile ourselves. That's not easy. Our differences are not the simpler ones of different *thinking*. They're the most complex, subtle ones of different *feelings*, *visions* and *values*. And we're all too threatened by the challenge to be gracious. We're not yet whole enough to realize that affection and affiliation—rather than agreement—are the basis for the most healthy human realtions and efforts.

We need something more basic than a dialogue about beliefs. We need in-person engagement among ourselves. We ought respect each other's integrity. Persons of opposite conviction can be equally sincere. We can be encouraged that we're now discussing basic questions.

We've simply got to summon up enough faith—in our own durability and in each other's decency—to engage each other about the root of our differences. We can recognize the real difference between us: our assumptions about our nature. We can recognize that, beneath our surface differences, we humans have no difference, we share a common human nature. We humans are the same. That's a hopeful beginning.

With our liberated vision, and our Liberating Vision—
we can begin to see
how we can make things right,
personally and politically,
in our lives and society,
now and for our future.

Before we explore that,
let's undertake a vision check.

IV.
VISION:
AN
INESCAPABLE
CHOICE

chapter 13

visions beyond dreams

> "*Every person should expend his chief thought and attention to the consideration of his first principles: are they or are they not rightfully laid down? And when he has sifted them, all the rest will follow.*"
>
> —Plato

Our revolution makes evident the deep significance of the vision each of us chooses to use in living our lives. Upon it we choose and create ourselves, decide how to relate with each other, and constitute and operate our institutions and society.

The most basic fact of our lives is our own human nature. The second most basic fact of our lives is our vision about our human nature. Our vision is central, it's foundational. The choice of our vision is an appropriate place to begin—in our effort to discover how we can make things right.

Each of us humans possesses an ideology, either consciously or unconsciously. Each of us lives by our individually chosen belief system—a religion, philosophy, whatever. A belief system is basically a way of looking at, envisioning our world, especially ourselves, our human nature and potential. For a human being, there's no such thing as not having such a vision. Although it may not be formally organized in my consciousness, the way I choose to live, the actions I undertake—derive from some root sense of what it means to be human—to survive, grow, satisfy, fulfill myself.

My personal vision/belief system/ideology has profound effects upon my life. It determines how I choose to believe in, create and operate myself and my life. It determines how I conceptualize, design and operate my institutions—since we create institutions for dealing with, between and among people.

If I envision human nature as guilty rather than innocent, untrustworty rather than trustworthy, I'll logically choose institutions that repress our human nature. If I envision human nature as innately innocent and trustworthy, I'll as logically choose institutions that nurture and liberate our human nature. Our difference becomes an enormous difference. If you and I differ in our basic vision, what we believe is appropriate for us to do will be markedly different.

In turn, our institutions profoundly affect, if not determine, the character of our being—especially the character of new persons coming into our society. Will they grow up—or will "bringing up" the child consist of bringing down the person?

By so determining whether my human nature is repressed or liberated, our institutions will in turn particularly affect my vision. They'll determine whether and how I actually see and perceive. If repressed (closed down), I'll look at and see the persons and events around me very differently than if liberated (opened up). In the former, I've so constricted myself, I have tunnel vision. In the latter, the more expanded I get personally, the more clearly I'll see, the more fully I'll perceive, the more I'll envision.

The more I get myself together, the better my vision gets, the more I recognize connections, cause and effect relations and solutions. My further liberating myself expands myself, which in turn expands my vision, which in turn leads me to further liberating myself. I've found this true in my experience. This ever-widening circle of liberation goes on and on, hopefully to fulfillment!

If my vision of human nature matches the reality of human

nature, I'll act appropriately and live at little, if any risk. If my vision of human nature is contrary to the reality of human nature, I live at risk—either way. If human nature is guilty and I envision it innocent, I open myself to danger, for sure. If human nature is innocent and I envision it guilty, I endanger myself as well—less obviously but no less dangerously, and far more profoundly. My every effort will produce the opposite of my intention.

If I'm underassessing human nature, I'll act in ways that will bring it down, tarnish its innocence. If I'm overassessing our human nature, perhaps my actions will enhance human behavior, perhaps my loving will evoke better behavior. In either event, might I not be living a self-fulfilling prophecy? As I believe and act, isn't my effect to pull our human nature down or up, to elevate or depress it?

Choosing my own vision and belief system is a pragmatic matter, an enormous, awesome responsibility, for several reasons. It determines the actions I choose and undertake. It's an operating reality in any event. In fact, I'm already acting on a choice, the choice is there. There's no way to ignore, avoid, hide, escape from making a choice, decision. I've already chosen a vision, whether I think so or not. I better think about it.

Upon my choice of vision as foundation, I'll choose and create my own life and being. Upon it I'll choose how I'll regard, approach, treat you—my fellow human being, all human beings, interpersonally and institutionally.

Certainly our choosing is a matter of *philosophy*. It regards the very nature of our being. But it's no abstract, luxurious, philosophical debate. Our issue, our controversy, is very down-to-earth. The philosophy we hold largely determines who we are and become, how we live. We need to redefine our philosophical basis, on which we design ourselves and our institutions.

Likewise it's a matter of *theology*—regarding the very meaning and purpose of our human existence—and the quality of our own nature, wherein lies our salvation.

Our choice is *psychological* as well—since it concerns how we human beings grow and develop, function and relate. It becomes far more than a frivolous, titillating hobby or diversion, a toy of affluence, a psychological game we're playing. It becomes a matter of life or death!

Less obviously, our choice is ultimately *moral* as well. The processes I choose for relating with you, interpersonally and institutionally (love or hate, inclusion or exclusion, welcome or rejection, encouragement or discouragement, liberation or repression) will profoundly affect you, your life, your growth and development. How I am present with you profoundly affects the most subtle environment in which you live and breathe. I'm affecting not just your physical environment, but your emotional environment, your subtle human environment. I will either affirm or disaffirm your life and living, your growing and development, your self-esteem and your self-realization. I'll either occasion, enhance, facilitate your further human growth and development, or I'll do the contrary. It's immoral to destroy, even to cripple life and human beings. It's moral to support and nurture life and human beings. How we relate with each other, interpersonally and institutionally, is a moral issue!

Let's quit ignoring and rejecting our responsibility for affecting each other's experience and existence. The central moral issue at hand demands that each of us choose wisely. The era we're entering needs fuller realization of the values we have previously most commonly called "religious": truth, honesty, responsibility, trust and love. We so much cherish *talk* about the importance of these in our personal lives. Now it's incumbent upon each of us to make them central, present and *operational* in our personal—and our public and political—lives. We need to become moral enough to handle our world, to deal humanly with our other developed powers.

Our choice is *political*. You and I have power over each other, subtly in our interpersonal relationships, explicitly in our institutional roles and relationships. My every belief, act and statement is political. Our most important public policy is our personal policy, vision, belief, value system—regarding human beings and our own nature. It underlies *all* our other public policies. How we humans most healthily grow and develop is the central political issue of our times. Upon the belief system I choose, upon the vision I carry—I'll choose the processes I believe most conducive to realizing our goals, personal and political, individual and societal. Thereby I'll determine our future, our lives and our society.

It's essential that we recognize our society rests on a belief system, too often not explicit or examined. Our vision *must* be examined for—examined or not, explicit or not—it's always there, always operating, to do us in or to lead us out. A pessimistic attitude toward human life—accepting its supposedly inherent sinfulness and propensity toward evil—concludes that our condition, while deplorable, is irredeemable. Call it religious pessimism, cynicism. If we believe we are by nature untrustworthy, the best we can hope for is bleak: containment of our evilness. Even worse, the processes we choose may instead contain the *best* in our nature, fulfill our expectations.

We can instead choose an essentially optimistic, faithful view of life and human nature, in terms of its innate possibilities for good. From that we'll proceed to formulate a doctrine of progress and redemption in society, make it the basis of a millenial quest for love and peace.

Our choice of vision is more than a nicety, it's a necessity, a matter of profound significance, even of our survival as a human race. It's the place where philosophy, psychology, theology, politics and morality converge, merge, become one. How we use our political power becomes a moral issue—nothing less! As our times are developing—what's moral, what's expedient, what's self-interest-serving and what's socially sound—all are converging.

I'm not proposing something new: the interrelationship of personal vision and philosophy, psychology, theology, morality and politics. It's already a fact of our lives. I'm just calling attention to that fact—so we might better attend to empowering ourselves to do something creative and human about changing ourselves and our institutions.

Life is short, matters are bad, we've no time to waste. Now is the time for taking responsibility, for choosing explicitly. Each of us must choose. Let's choose for our future, choose for life, choose for ourselves.

How do I choose? At root, every belief system choice is a matter of faith: believing that which we do not know, for which we have neither experience nor *rational* proof. Each of us simply believes. No one of us knows for sure, there's no concluding evidence, no final proof. There's little point in arguing, one way or the other. I don't merely choose what appeals to my head. My belief comes from much deeper within me. Each of us must make the choice, take the chance for ourselves.

As for me, I simply don't like our traditional vision—that my human nature is guilty and untrustworthy. I don't like what it expects of me (the worst), requires of me (containment to repression), makes of me (an irresponsible cynic).

It logically requires I repress myself. That hurts! Consequently I constantly do battle with myself. No wonder we so readily war against our neighbors at home, next door, around our entire world. It makes me crippled if not paralyzed, crazed if not insane, contained if not exploding from the pressure built up inside me. It alienates me from myself, makes me lonely for myself, destroys my innocence and passion, puts the responsibility outside myself—someone else will fix me, save me, make me okay. It says I'm not responsible, it makes me irresponsible. By the methods it chooses to use on me, it produces a self-fulfilling prophecy.

I prefer and choose to believe and live our new liberating vision. I believe in my own natural human innocence—with all its risks, whatever its risks. To me it's equally *logical* with the contrary belief, and it more readily matches my own *experience*, especially of myself, as well with others. My experience of myself most profoundly provides me the vision I choose, then carry into all my relationships, interpersonal and institutional.

I prefer our new vision for the faithfulness, hope, challenge and responsibility it accords me. I prefer it because of what it expects of me (the best), how it treats me (kindly), what it makes me (an idealist) and what it requires of me (it makes me responsible for who I am and be/come).

Just having such a liberating vision isn't enough. Inherent in such a vision is the impulse and impetus that prompts action toward further liberating myself. I become responsible for further reclaiming myself and my innocence.

I'd rather be an idealist than a cynic. At least then I'll have the basis for faith, hope and love. I'll try to make our lives and society and world better. Even if I fail, I'll at least have tried.

I've chosen my vision, our new Liberating Vision. It serves me well, personally. It also serves to enable me to see and synthesize what's happening in our lives and society. It helps me understand what's gone wrong and how I can make it right. It provides me a theoretical *and* practical basis, a plan of action for my life—personal and political.

I've indicated my preference and choice. Now it's your turn.

First, admit you have a vision—one way or the other—by which you have determined who you are. Second, ask yourself: which vision do you hold? Which do you prefer, choose to believe and live by, for yourself? Third, ask yourself: how do you experience yourself? Innocent or guilty, trustworthy or not, by nature? Do you find yourself a "sinner" or an "innocent" *at heart?*

Let yourself dream. Do you know a better vision, more comprehensive and hopeful (I trust you prefer hope to despair) than our Liberating Vison? If not, why not let your idealism surface, let yourself fantasize. Wouldn't it be nice if life could be this way? Couldn't it all be a self-fulfilling prophecy? Wouldn't you like to let go, trust more, find kindred persons, participate in building a more human society, be more in love, and...???

Take full responsibility for your choice—your belief, vision and experience of yourself. Choose your vision, for yourself, for your life. Why not choose the best?

chapter 14

"shadow-boxing" the skeletons in our closets

> *"The way of life is fundamentally different, more difficult, more dangerous, more honest and more hopeful."*
>
> —Wilhelm Reich

The choice each of us must make is profound, its responsibility awesome. I have confronted my own reservations about embracing our liberating vision. I suspect they're commonplace. Perhaps how I'm resolving them for myself will assist you in your choosing for yourself.

Is our new vision narcissistic and self-indulgent? It can appear that way. But they are only stages in our growth. Like all life, we humans seek our own fulfillment. We're in transition from a culture which denies us ourselves—to one which supports us in being ourselves. We're looking inside ourselves, examining our own beliefs and being—freeing ourselves. As we break loose, we're naturally fascinated by ourselves. Talking about ourselves becomes our new pastime. We belong to our times. We'll not be this way forever. Already we're outgrowing it.

*Will we be scorned—for being anti-intellectual, too much into
that "touchy-feely" stuff?* Our vision isn't anti-intellectual, it's
supra- (not super-) intellectual. I cherish my intellect. I want it to
operate at its best. It needs the best and most accurate
information—which comes from our bodies, senses and
emotions. I want to elevate them to its level, to fully develop and
integrate all of myself—my body and emotions, senses and
intellect.

For some time people have been labeling me "the
touchy-feely legislator." It's usually an effort to put me down,
dismiss me. I used to be self-conscious, and defensive. Recently
I've grown more secure within myself. I now understand that
persons calling me that are revealing themselves—reflecting
their own fears about emotions and physical contact.

If we were all into feeling more deeply,
touching more naturally—
we'd all be better off
individually and as a society.

I'll be a proud and pleased Assemblyperson if I can inspire
more human touching and feeling in our world.

Is our vision too "Pollyannish"? Idealism is a belief—the
natural by-product of our liberating vision—in our inherent
goodness. Let's proudly be idealists. In today's world only
idealism is pragmatic. What's been thought "realistic" no
longer works. "Cynicism" (defined by Webster as a "negative
belief about human nature") is itself our problem. It's the root of
our problems.

I'm tired of cynicism. It's a dead and deadening perspective.
Cynicism is no more than the projection of our distrust of
ourselves and our nature. We owe ourselves more than that.

Cynicism is the belief state of persons who've earlier been
hurt, and don't trust ourselves to reach out again. It's often used
as an excuse for not reaching, risking or taking responsibility. "I
needn't do anything, it wouldn't matter anyway." I don't act, it
doesn't get better, then I say "I told you so!" Cynics perpetuate
their own belief. That saves their having to reevaluate, perhaps
surrender, their cynicism.

I must recognize my personal responsibility for my own

cynicism, for perpetuating it until now. I am responsible for confronting and outgrowing it, from now on.

I'm innocent rather than naive, faithful rather than Pollyanna-ish. I'm a pragmatic dreamer. I want to "dream the impossible dream," awake into my life. I live in the gap between how life is and how it could be.

I refuse to be bound by history or its interpretation. I don't want to relive and repeat past history, I want to bend future history. My personal history, living my vision, bears out my idealism. I know persons can change a lot, experience profound growth. I've perceived that in my friends, I've experienced it in myself.

I don't underestimate the difficulty of what I'm proposing: breaking out from centuries of accumulated belief and tradition, from layers of accumulated conditioning and repression. But already many persons are undertaking marvelous efforts. A short while ago our vision seemed only a fantasy, incredible. Now it's seeped into the very atmosphere in which we live and breathe. It's become credible.

I'll do my best to make my vision visible, credible, legitimate and attractive. But it's not my responsibility to convert you to being an idealist. *You're* responsible for your faith, for choosing how and who you want to be and believe. I won't produce all the evidence I can to demonstrate my faith. I don't especially enjoy arguing about my vision. I often find myself—when arguing with a cynic—feeling frustrated, poisoned and demoralized. I just want to put my vision before you, the best I can, for your consideration.

It's time for the many of us who are "closet idealists" to come out! I'd rather be utopian. Let's not allow the cynics to impede us.

Is our analysis of our current situation unduly alarming, pessimistic—reciting all that's (going) wrong, all the failures of our society?

I'm not being Cassandra-ish. That perpetuates our old style and expectation. Still I do want to look at raw reality, tell it like it really is. I can only effectively cope with reality, correct and improve it—if I fully acknowledge precisely what our circumstances are.

Is looking at our faults unpatriotic? In August, 1968 I went to San Francisco's Jack Tar Hotel to speak a brief welcome at an elegant Portuguese commemorative dinner (my father's Portuguese). I found the place surrounded: police cars outside, police at the door. I had to "talk my way in." I only then found out the guest speaker was Spiro Agnew, nominated the week before for Vice-President.

In my brief comments I acknowledged our Portuguese successes. I added my hope that as we were dressed up, eating steak in a rich setting, we'd not forget our fellow Americans without food, clothes or shelter that evening. Spiro spoke next, said "What a nice young man"—then added he was "tired of hearing people say what's wrong with America, I want to say what's right with America."

My way is the opposite. I know what's right. I needn't talk about it—unless I'm trying to reassure myself, ease my doubts. To improve our situation, I need instead to acknowledge our problems. If I do that, we'll more likely solve them.

The truth is that our lives and society and institutions aren't working. Our American dream isn't delivering on its promise. To raise questions about America is to raise questions about ourselves, our possibilities. Patriotism doesn't demand blind loyalty, but *active loving engagement*—including criticism. My best friend is my most valuable critic: only s/he knows me well enough to recognize the ways I'm not realizing my full potential (as a person, state or nation); only s/he cares about me deeply enough to risk calling it to my attention. I care deeply. I love America too much to leave it as it is. I'm wanting to improve it. I'm unwilling to be silent!

Will our Liberating Vision appear revolutionary, radical, subversive? Those are uneasy labels in our political climate today. But let's be forthright: it will appear so—for in fact it is all three.

But the embarrassment and apology isn't ours. We'd have no need for revolution if our society were already healthy for growing human beings. We'd have no need to be radical if our society were healthy at its root. We'd not need to be subversive if our society were completely well. We owe it to ourselves to be revolutionary, radical *and* subversive. Our times demand that. We have *no* choice. To be other is to perpetuate the inhumanity and dehumanization that plague us all!

Is our vision an upper-middle-class luxury and hedonism—with no sociopolitical relevance, especially for laboring and third world persons? I've thought a lot about this. I consulted my friend Lorenza Calvillo Schmidt about it. She's a Chicana, oldest of nine children of a California farm worker family, now a counselor at the University of California, Irvine, and a member of our State Board of Education. She reassures me: persons saying that are more revealing their haughtiness or misunderstanding about working and minority persons—than accurately describing them.

We all aspire to human dignity, love and a more caring society. The persons most oppressed are the ones who most need our vision's implementation—for their sustenance *and* for our growing to care and share more with our fellow humans. It's no luxury, it's a necessity. We must grow ourselves into a further human and moral dimension—to be/come able to cope with our extraordinary, astonishing and frightening scientific and technological powers and situations. If we don't develop our moral powers, we live in peril of extinguishing ourselves. And our capacity for such growth depends precisely upon our personal belief system—about our human nature and potential.

Are we being presumptuous or arrogant? Who are *we* to be proposing all this?

My worry about that derives from my upbringing which taught me I ought not think too highly of myself. I was brought up to believe I'm a "sinner." I won't accept that viewpoint of myself any longer.

I don't claim my thesis and critique are original. Many before have proposed this. Today it seems more timely: more persons are ready for it, our situation is ripe for it. Nor am I claiming special credit for what's happening. I'm reporting what many of us humans are doing, just focusing our attention and energy on it.

I'm not claiming I have all the answers. I'm only claiming I know the right question: "How do we grow healthy human beings?" Together we will discover the answer as we grow, as we discover ourselves together.

I encounter one paradox:
I believe my way is the only way.
Yet it in no way intrudes on you.

My way is that
you are the way, your way.
You are your answer—even as I am my answer.
The answer is buried deep inside each of us, in our nature.
It's up to us to bring ourselves forth, discover our own answer.

I don't claim to have more natural capacity than anyone else. I don't feel I'm better than anyone else. Our vision proclaims we're all, by nature, the same. I have nothing to tell you that you don't already know, deep down inside yourself. I'm simply proposing to call it to your consciousness, bring it to your attention. Will you listen—deeply—to yourself?

Rollo May theorizes it's the persons most scarred (by culture?) who have the most need and drivenness—to plough ahead, discover and open up new territory for all of us. They experience the most pent up pressure. Such emotive powers once unleashed compel, propel them forward. They often spring forward the furthest. All in all, a mixed blessing! I had to grow—because I hurt so much. I had to undertake extreme measures for my recovery. I've evolved by setting myself faithful standards, living what I believe.

I find it impossible to believe I'm different by *nature* from you. I trust I'm not a random, freakish example of human development. Perhaps you've developed yourself in response to the same forces that have molded me, with the same potential, the same need to grow that I have. Perhaps we can share our stories, and our lives.

I'm not telling anyone what to do...that's up to you. You'll do what you want, anyway. I'm simply declaring myself, telling my story—what's right and true for me. I'm telling you the conclusions my life has brought me to. I'm not trying to impose them on you, just awaken them within you. I'm hoping you'll be interested enough to consider them for yourself. And, of course, you're free—to reject it all. My vision leaves the final choice up to you!

By so revealing myself, will I risk seeming too different or strange? Am I risking my personal relationships, or my political life? I'm into being my own person, showing all of myself—and supporting you in your doing the same. I recall my father instructing me: "Just because someone else is a certain way is no reason for you to be that way."

Even though I'm an "insider," in life and in politics—I often experience myself as an "outsider." An illustrative anecdote: A fringe benefit of being a legislator is that you provide me an American automobile of my choice. In my first term I chose a white Mustang convertible with red side racing stripes. I got a special license plate—"A 24"—identifying my Assembly district.

During our 1967 fall break I drove it to Palm Springs. On my return I received a letter from J.B. Lawrence, Judge of the San Bernardino Municipal Court: "Dear Assemblyman Vasconcellos: I don't mean to be intrusive, but rather to be helpful. Last Tuesday driving on the San Bernardino Freeway, I was passed by a white Mustang convertible, top-down, being driven by a swarthy young man. If your car has been stolen, let me know and I'll provide whatever assistance I can."

I responded: "Dear Judge—I appreciate your concern. I simply want to inform you that I am a swarthy young man."

As I'm concluding this writing, the risks of public involvement and/or speaking out and/or being different are current and compelling. On November 22, 1978 I took off time from writing this to attend the funeral of my friend and former colleague (to whose chairmanship I succeeded in the Assembly), Congressman Leo Ryan (he'd once told me I was more like him than any other legislator). Next to me at that ceremony sat friend and former colleague, San Francisco Mayor George Moscone. Eight days later I sat in another church for George's funeral.

Those experiences reminded me of my own two death threats. On election eve, 1970, a threatening note was forced under my office door. My friends took the next day off to be with me and assure my safety. On the night George Wallace was shot, a phone call to my apartment warned that I'd be next.

The worst that ever *happened* to me was at a Phi Beta Kappa dinner at the University of California, Davis. In my banquet speech I urged the honorees to add to their well-developed intellects by living lives of utter openness and authenticity and deep feeling. Afterwards a professor, father of an honoree, approached me and insisted I couldn't have meant what I said about "utter openness." I assured him I meant exactly what I said. He slapped me across my face.

On July 4th, 1978 I lost my staff coordinator Harry Horoho to drowning. I knew assassinated San Francisco Supervisor Harvey Milk. I recently almost lost my long-time friend and Administrative Assistant Joni Leahy to breast cancer. I expect to live only once, I'm going to let myself live, as fully as possible, now.

Because I believe in living at the very edge of my limits, seeking to continue my expansion as a person, I will not let my "role" in life get in the way of my life. Attending to my continuing growth is irresistible and irreversible. I expect I'll never stop growing. As I continue my growing, how I experience and perceive and value life continually changes. I may always be "different!"

Life is a dynamic process—like riding the crest of a wave. I have to ride it leaning forward a little, like on a surfboard. If I stand there flat-footed, I'll crash and drown. (My single try at surfing broke my neck.) I've learned to lean into life.

And I've come to trust my sense of timing—in letting go and revealing myself publicly—how much, how far, how fast I can go without jeopardy—personal or political. And I'm increasingly willing to be unorthodox publicly—as orthodoxy increasingly fails publicly. What I know and have to say is important. I'm willing to risk. I prefer living precariously to vicariously.

And I trust you!

May we—by our coming together—empower each other to take the risks and make our choices—for ourselves and for life.

Each of us must choose. It's your turn!

chapter 15

humanizing politics

I include this interview, by psychologist/writer friend Ken Dychtwald, because it gives you a perspective of me that I can't provide myself. An edited version was originally published in NEW AGE *magazine, October, 1978. The chapter is copyrighted © 1978 by Ken Dychtwald, and is reprinted here, with minor editorial changes, by permission of the author.*

I have been fortunate enough to know John Vasconcellos for several years, during which time we have become fellow explorers and good friends. Now a sixth-term Assemblyman in the California Legislature, he is a lawyer by training, and is presently chairman of the Subcommittee on Postsecondary Education, and of the Ways and Means Subcommittee on Education. He is also a member of the full committees on Education and Ways and Means, and of the Subcommittee on Educational Reform. He is a Democrat.

John has focused his legislative efforts on issues affecting human growth and devlopment, human values and relationships. He has pioneered legislation toward alternative birthing practices, opening and humanizing education, methadone treatment, and drug abuse prevention, and is currently initiating statewide efforts toward "positive parenting." John is co-founder of SELF DETERMINATION: A Personal/Political Network, and was recently voted to the Board of the Association for Humanistic Psychology.

Years ago when I first became aware of John he was referred to as "the politician who is into personal growth." When John first began to speak out regarding the relationship between human potential and political vision he was called "too idealistic" and was affectionately written about as the "touchy-feely legislator." Yet, as the years have passed and John has repeatedly seen his visions actualized on the floor of the Assembly as well as in the spirits of the thousands of people who have heard him lecture throughout the country, many people have begun to take a much more serious look at the issues and notions about human experience that John has thought through so deeply. In a political world that all too often seems devoid of honesty and humanistic values, John has almost single-handedly launched a campaign to create a strong bond between those people involved in personal growth and holistic health and the world of politics and public policy making. John is an impressive man in his straightforward style, his candid sharing about his own personal journey, his honest concern for people and his relentless desire to humanize politics.

Dychtwald: Before we explore some of your ideas regarding the relationship between personal growth and political power, why don't we begin with some more basic issues. What do you see as being the purpose of government?

Vasconcellos: As I see it, the proper role of government should be to foster healthy human growth and development, and to help create environments where people are able to realize themselves and develop in moral, caring, sensitive, non-arrogant, non-cynical, gentle, non-violent ways.

Dychtwald: It seems as though different people have different notions as to what is best for themselves and others and so create political/social priorities based on those beliefs. What do you see as being the priorities of the present American political/social system and how do they relate to the founding principles of our government?

Vasconcellos: Different people and groups attend to a variety of assumptions about human nature and human potential. If they believe the worst about our nature, then they will design institutions to fix, edit and repress. What our government ought be about and theoretically is about, is the development of political systems which are based on a belief in the innate goodness of people.

The striking thing about our political system is that it was founded upon the rights of the individual which assumes a capacity for self-governance and self-determination as well as a motivating interest in life, liberty and the pursuit of happiness. In fact, all of the founding principles and documents of the American political system are quite profound and deeply idealistic.

Dychtwald: Are they idealistic in ways that you agree with? Are they appropriate to our times?

Vasconcellos: The structures of American government were created out of an extremely faithful and humanistic vision, yet I think that we are caught within a remarkable paradox right now because we have a political system that is based upon a belief in the innate human capacity for honesty, wise-decision making and self-determination; yet the culture in which we have all grown up assumes the contrary about human nature...that we are flawed, sinful, untrustworthy and don't know what's good for ourselves.

For example, the whole child-rearing process is mostly about teaching a child to distrust his or her own experience, body and feelings, and that someone else's interpretations are always more correct than our own.

Dychtwald: What you are saying then, is that it is the values and beliefs that people have about themselves and each other that determines the nature of their political ideology and governmental style and that at this time who we are doesn't quite match who we need to be for our government to work most effectively and fairly.

Vasconcellos: Exactly! One way to more clearly understand this paradox is to realize that, in the extreme, there are two basic contrary beliefs about human nature out of which people design cultures and institutions, out of which people develop theories as to how to best grow healthy, alive responsible citizens.

One theory comes from our traditional negative belief system which assumes that human nature is perverse and not innocent, and therefore you make people responsible by scaring them, intimidating them, repressing them and rigidly controlling their lives. I came out of a background like this, one that was very traditional, intellectual and Catholic, with a mind that worked well, and not a lot else.

The other theory is the one I prefer; it is close to that which is emerging from the humanistic psychology and holistic health fields. It assumes that human nature is benign, life-affirming and trustworthy and therefore the more acceptance, love, touch and nurturance that people receive, the more they will develop into healthy and responsible social animals.

Presently we have these two opposing value systems vying for dominance and we all live right in the middle of this conflict. There are obviously many people who are deeply bound to the traditional repressive system and there also seems to be a growing number of people who have made extraordinary efforts to liberate themselves from that...to live out of a new paradigm. I suppose that most of us fit someplace in between.

I would also like to point out what is evident but not often acknowledged publicly; the old repressive authoritarian paradigm not only doesn't work, but in fact, is counterproductive to a democratic way of life. It cripples people's natural capacity for self-governance.

We talk about a democratic society and we all long for that. Most people would agree that the goals of this society would be for us all to be free...free from unreasonable external constraints as well as free from inappropriate internal constraints. We would all like to have a society where we could walk the streets and not be afraid of being in danger...We would like to have the most opportunity and enough money to get good education, health care and housing...We want our kids to be able to be loving and loved, and to have relationships that are supportive and productive as well as active in the community... and to have the whole thing hold together and work.

Dychtwald: What kind of person might you expect to emerge from this new type of culture?

Vasconcellos: I don't think that we have much idea about who we might become. We are still very primitive as humans and we have little idea about what kinds of capacities and potentials we are available to develop. But, I expect that this person would be intuitive, honest, insightful, immediate, sensitive, unafraid, relaxed, assertive, responsible, loving, healthy and trusting. In a way, I guess that these are also the qualities that I am working toward in my own life.

I strongly believe that a true democratic society would be a function and result of people who can live democratically. This is where Abe Maslow's term "democratic character structure" relates. It relates to that person in whom the body, mind and emotions are equally possessed, inhabited, cherished, connected and integrated and in fact, become *one*. My sense is that we will only have a truly democratic society when we have enough people who are able to be open to develop themselves democratically. We must become more of a free, unobstructed, unstructured people. This is precisely where politics and personal growth deeply connect.

Truly, politics is about people and consciousness and growth and fulfillment and our capacities to relate in society and make our lives more decent. In reality, politics and government are simply *us* acting collectively.

Dychtwald: If the government is *us*, why is it that many people feel unempowered to interact with governmental officials and agencies and why does it seem as though our political leaders are uninterested in honestly communicating with us? How can we enact a democratic government if we do not feel involved?

Vasconcellos: From my own experience, I think that there are two major reasons why people and governments aren't more actively and responsibly involved with each other: lack of trust and an absence of responsibility...and it's reciprocal. First, as I have previously mentioned, we are not encouraged to develop a great deal of trust either in ourselves or in others. Although a democracy depends largely on trust, credibility and communication between its various parts and groups, it's clear that this

Interaction takes place only to a very limited degree. The people or citizenry have to be able to trust the leaders to run the government fairly or it doesn't work. Also, the leaders have to trust the citizenry or the government won't work.

Dychtwald: Could you elaborate a bit on the issue of trust with regard to both of these sides?

Vasconcellos: On the latter side, what comes to mind is Nixon and his capers and the Watergate papers...all the secrecy and all of the deceit that politicians put on people. All this says is that politicians don't believe that they can trust their fellow citizens with all the information regarding important matters. There is the attitude "We know what is best for you and we will take care of you, so simply do as you're told and don't ask too many questions." In a sense, this attitude is reflective of the authoritarian style of leadership. I think that we are outgrowing this kind of relationship. That is why there is so much unrest and so much resentment toward the actions of the government and its agencies. A main reason why the government isn't working today, or the family, or most of the rest of the institutions of our culture, is because they are still usually run by people whose basic assumptions about human nature are negative and narrow. As more and more people outgrow these oppressive beliefs and work seriously toward their own humanistic growth and liberation, they demand involvement in their government and expect to be trusted and have more participation and power.

In terms of how the citizenry doesn't trust the government, the best example is the fact that half of the people don't bother to vote. In not voting they are saying that they don't trust that their vote has any meaning or worth and also that they don't trust the governmental leaders and agencies to be sensitive to their needs. People are redefining what they want from government and government still offers what they used to want or thought they needed.

Yet, in many ways, people are just as responsible for creating the discrepancy between themselves and their political leaders, for they blindly defer too much power to outside authority and often hide behind the myth that only government and politics are messed up in our society. In my own experience, public officials are not any less or more bright, caring, honest or diligent than the rest of us. Yet, people expect much more of a politician and look for a hero. There is this great hero mythology alive in America...probably in all cultures for that matter...We wanted John Kennedy to come along on a white horse and bring Camelot. But of course this won't happen because politicians are mortals like us who are simply trying to live their own lives while also attempting to help create institutions and rules that will support the culture's needs. When people fall into this hero worship situation, they usually sit back and wait for the politicial leader to make things better without actively doing anything to help. This is where we see the "I deserve this and you better do something about it" attitude. Then, when politicians prove to be no more or less than human, there is this great flurry of anger, disappointment and resentment.

Dychtwald: So then, the lack of trust that exists throughout our culture is not just something that is experienced by a few isolated individuals, but instead reflects a collusion in which a great many people in and out of leadership roles are consciously or unconsciously participating. Politicians assume a role where they take too much responsibility for everyone else, hoard great power, keep valuable information to themselves, and try to regulate the citizenry with intimidation, fear, and rigid controls. On the other hand, the citizens assume too little responsibility for themselves and each other and look for authoritarian figures to give their power away to and then to blame their failures and dissatisfactions on.

Vasconcellos: Exactly. But recognize that such lack of trust is endemic to our culture (if not all cultures)...which cynically distrusts, and teaches us to distrust, human nature.

Dychtwald: The solution, then, would lie in...

Vasconcellos: Maturation on both sides. The government is not going to solve all of the problems of society nor was it designed to do so. People must individually and collectively take more responsibility for improving the well-being of themselves, their family, community and planet. There is child abuse, crime, family breakdown, alienation, loneliness, stress and unhappiness that are not products of government at all. These are rather

the results of individuals who are unable or unwilling to adjust
and relate and it is irresponsible and immature for us to expect
that the government can unilaterally change this. No
government could! All government can do is to try and be
sensitive to the needs of its people and then try to put some
ideas into place. It is then up to the people who operate the
programs and participate in the culture to make these ideas
work or suggest other ideas to make it all work better.

Seen from this perspective, the government is not the
absolute source of power, but instead acts as an intermediary or
facilitator, serving the purpose of responding to the needs of its
people with appropriate and effective guidance, sensitivity and
support.

Dychtwald: Do you think that liberals are more trusting people
than conservatives?

Vasconcellos: Not necessarily. Both liberals and conservatives
are basically cynical and untrusting regarding human nature
(although most liberals would probably not agree). Liberals are
into a lot of government design work that takes care of people,
and have not done this in ways that have allowed people to
outgrow the need to be taken care of. They do not actively attend
to providing systems that are in themselves liberating and the
dependency is maintained. Conservatives attempt to generate a
great many external constraints whereas liberals encourage the
development of a great many internal constraints. Both ways
serve to limit and restrict people.

The best definition of a leader is a person who enables other
persons to recognize and realize their own capacities and their
own ability to become their own leaders. This is what
government and political leaders should be about.

Dychtwald: Which I suppose takes us to your second reason why
people aren't more actively involved in their governmental
activities: *responsibility*.......Why do you think that we are so
unaccustomed to taking responsibility for our lives and for the
well-being of our communities, culture and planet?

Vasconcellos: I think that it is largely on account of the fact that
early in life we are taught not to be too expressive, not to be too

assertive, and not to take too much responsibility. For example, in most school systems, it is believed that you won't influence kids unless you shape them up and teach them how to be uniform, conforming, docile, afraid and ultimately subject to authority. Certainly this type of learning process will not generate self-aware, self-responsible human beings! The best intentioned parents, churches and schools assume that the newly arriving infant has no natural decency, capacity or wisdom, and then whenever it expresses itself it is poked, pushed or paddled in some way. When this takes place the individual learns to contain and repress self rather than be authentically expressive or self-responsible. As a result, we grow up to be out of touch with our own natural wisdom and therefore vulnerable to someone else who professes to have that which we feel we lack. Wilhelm Reich talked about the fascist and authoritarian personality and the roots of it early on being the home, the church and the school. What we need to do then is to find ways within ourselves to become more whole, authentic, alive and responsible so that we will defer less of our energy and power to authority figures and begin to take greater control of our own lives and facilitate our fellow citizens doing the same.

It is also important that we remember that the politics we do is who we are. As people, we evaluate and support ideas and issues that are reflective of each of our own personal value systems. Our sense of ourselves, our possession of ourselves and our integratedness as human beings directly determines what we do politically. In fact, how we experience ourselves provides us the vision that we carry into all our relationships... interpersonal as well as institutional and political.

For example, last year during a debate on the Assembly floor about capital punishment, one person from Southern California got up and said, "Let's face it...we are all sinful to the core and we need capital punishment in order to repress ourselves and be able to live in peace." This is precisely where personal growth and vision and political growth and vision cross. If you are a politician who believes that you are sinful to the core, no good and untrustworthy, then you will create and support political structures and relationships that overcontrol and repress you and everyone else.

However, those persons who have spent more time exploring and developing what I call a positive self-image, are those who more trust themselves and others and are usually more willing to give people personal freedom (like in health, drug and sex laws). These are the ones who begin to abolish corporal punishment and to share material wealth because from my understanding of Norman O. Brown's writing, those who are self-possessed and are not repressed sexually are much less inclined to need authoritarian power and material things to get themselves off on, up on, or completed by.

It becomes very clear that the politics that happen in the legislature, on school boards, on hospital boards, in stores and communes or in personal relationships are really an expression of the people themselves who are there. When we acknowledge this, we must also realize the importance of having people in leadership roles who are open to a more humanistic/holistic vision of human nature and human relationships.

The people who are least self-aware are the most dangerous because they will least likely understand what is truly a healthy environment for other people and what human needs and wants truly are, who we are and can be/come. Those politicians who are into ego-trips, power trips and competition, party "baloney" and all the rest are not likely to pass laws or appropriate funds in ways that truly enhance a person's opportunities for growth, health, self-determination and self fulfillment.

Dychtwald: What you are suggesting is that if we want our politics to change or work better, we as people must take responsibility for becoming more trusting, caring, sensitive and aware enough to facilitate the emergence of healthy and humanistic life styles and systems.

Vasconcellos: Absolutely! You could change all the political leaders and the rules and institutions tomorrow, but if we did not in fact change ourselves and we kept on carrying all our fears, self-denials and self-repressions in our bodies and minds, then we would live no differently than we do today...We could live no more caringly, lovingly or healthfully! And we'd probably recreate precisely those same authoritarian and repressive leaders, institutions and rules.

It is crucially important that people recognize that the government is *us* and it is as we choose it to be. We elect people to serve as leaders who are close to where we are in terms of vision. I think that we have all been so conditioned not to understand or take responsibility, we don't know how to do it. We are still caught in a terrible era of blaming and scapegoating, which doesn't get us anywhere...it certainly doesn't get us what we want. We need to be willing to attend to our own growth enough, in a responsible way, to see to it that our institutions, the government being one of these, become peopled by persons who share our struggle and vision about this human transformation. The real challenge of this society is to discover how we can transform ourselves into whole human beings. Only then can we see through and break out of our double bind: our irresponsibility *and* our present incapacity to recognize our irresponsibility.

Dychtwald: Your notion of political change and revolution is intriguing, for you are obviously not suggesting a violent revolution fueled by hatred and bloodshed but instead you seem to be proposing a much deeper kind of revolutionary event, one that would take place...or perhaps is already taking place... *within* many of us. Could you say a bit more about this revolution and the context for such an event here in America?

Vasconcellos: I define a revolution as "changing the facts of life." The most basic facts of our lives are those questions and assumptions about our own nature out of which we choose how we will live. When we begin to examine the values and beliefs that underlie our ways of being, then we are entering into a highly significant revolutionary/evolutionary process.

In the last fifteen years, we have been witnessing a liberation revolution. The major public and political issue that is emerging is our struggle for liberation from psychological bondage: from internalized conditioning, towards owning our own body, mind, feelings and being and becoming ourselves. This means not passively surrendering ourselves and our power to some authority figure or institution who thinks they know better than we do who we ought to be. Rather it means liberating ourselves from such conditioning, and surrendering *to* ourselves.

The groundwork for this new revolution has been laid by a variety of efforts: black, brown, women, gay, grey, kids, parents, healers and whatever else. There are literally millions of persons beginning to speak out and say "It's O.K. to be who I am. There is more to me than I thought. I want to experience myself more positively, with less shame, guilt and fear. I want to be who I am and I want to be whole.''

In California we've recently seen an interesting variation on this theme with the passage of Proposition 13. People who have stayed silent because they always thought that they should stay quiet and take instructions from whatever was going on, have finally started to speak. I think that student outcries in the sixties have taught a lesson to the silent majority who are now themselves challenging the popular mythology.

Dychtwald: Is there a trend to these various liberation events that you perceive?

Vasconcellos: Yes, I believe there is, and that there is a way of seeing the revolutionary developments of our last two decades in terms of where we might be heading. As best I can discern, there have been five major steps that have expressed themselves so far. They are: 1) A demystification of authority...where we've begun to move away from the model that somebody other than us had all the power and authority such as the parents, the principal, the priest, the President or the Pope; 2) A breaking out of vertical authority models and a real effort being made toward horizontal models in sharing of power, influence and responsibilities; 3) A movement toward individualization where we are trying to change from a situation where we fix individuals to fit institutions, to organizing institutions whose function is to fit themselves to individuals; 4) The emergence of a personalization or humanizing ethic in which the whole person has become the focus of attention and energy in public and political policy-making; 5) A movement towards ''empowerment''...a real effort to support, encourage and evoke *persons*, in order to empower individual human beings to become healthy, whole, self-aware persons who are able to live horizontally, without mystification, fear and guilt.

The truly revolutionary political act is to fully take responsibility for defining and declaring who I am, and enabling someone else to see and do the same, for themselves.

There is a great movement on, and I think it's irreversible and unstoppable. When I add together all the persons in our country who in their own ways are attempting to become more aware and whole and to free up their bodies, minds and spirits, I realize there are millions of people involved in this new revolutionary struggle. However, what we've yet to see is a clear enough statement or theory or vision about this event so that more people can understand its significance and help it along in creative and effective ways.

I feel that the last decade of my own life has been one of numerous revolutionary self-realizations as I have begun to see more clearly who I am and to more deeply open myself and take charge of my life and to repossess my own body, emotions, feelings and mind. And this is where politics today really is... recognizing the vast resources of human potential that live within all of us so that we can become open, alive and expressive.

Dychtwald: To what extent do you think that people can really change and evolve themselves into more happy, healthy beings?

Vasconcellos: To extents beyond what we can now imagine. I know many people who have done much changing and growing in themselves, but the most profound evidence is always my own experience. I've spent the last twelve years, concurrent with my involvement in politics, attempting to recover parts of me that were so long lost. Through numerous workshops at Esalen, a period of time in Rogerian therapy, and several years in Bioenergetic therapy I have been struggling to grow and change myself. I am certain that I am much different now as a person. I also know that I've got a lot more to go. I've also noted that as I have grown personally I have become a much more effective legislator. On account of my changing, I think that I am a more wise, influential and healthy public official. The work I do in politics is done more insightfully and humanely and powerfully than when I first got in office.

The old myth about human growth is that we have minimal wisdom or capacity to effect and determine our own beings. My sense is that we form our own character and personality just as we form our own bodies...out of our experience. As we have formed ourselves, so can we reform or recreate ourselves. Actually I believe that this is exactly what you talk about so effectively in BODYMIND. I'm sure you understand how revolutionary the notions of self-determination and self-creation are.

Dychtwald: Definitely! Actually I've realized that while there is enormous resistance to the idea that we are responsible for ourselves, there is simultaneously a great deal of enthusiasm and support for this notion for it suggests that we have choice as to who we are and we can become.

John...there has been a great deal of talk lately about people overdoing personal growth. Do you feel that when people spend time working with themselves and attempting to improve themselves that they become too self-indulgent or narcissistic?

Vasconcellos: While there are certainly people who are unconcerned about anyone other than themselves, my sense is that the person who has really grown to become self-aware takes responsibility not only for him or her self, but also is more immediately *responsive* to other people. This is true in every way. The whole person is naturally inclined to be present and overflowing with other people. In my own life I've found that I have become much more responsible naturally, rather than being responsible on account of being afraid not to be.

Dychtwald: It's obvious that in the last two decades we've witnessed the emergence of numerous liberation movements. We've seen the drug revolution, the sexual revolution, the sensitivity revolution, the spiritual revolution and revolutions in life style and family structure. Do you have a sense that there is some core or basis to the revolutionary/evolutionary journey that we are presently involved in and are moving toward?

Vasconcellos: Yes, for sure. It's the human *body*.

Dychtwald: How so?

Vasconcellos: One way of describing this trend toward the body and health is to realize that we were raised in a culture based upon Descartes' "I think, therefore I am," The rest of our being was demeaned and diminished. The sixties witnessed an explosion of emotion and feeling...a revolution toward "I feel, therefore I am." Now we are witnessing a new phase to this movement from "I think and feel, therefore I am," to "I am my body"...or simply "I am" and my body is vitally, inherently me. The whole body awareness and liberation fields which include countless techniques and processes...holistic health, yoga, meditation, massage, Bioenergetics, Rolfing, Feldenkrais, dance, jogging...are all involved. All the material emerging about touching and tenderness, contact, sexuality and energetic expression are the next state of that recovery of our wholeness that is profoundly upon us. An example: research now indicates that infants who are kept close to their mothers and are bonded in this fashion develop twenty points higher on I.Q.'s than those who don't. In California we're trying to gather support for a wide range of body, human-oriented issues such as gentle birthing, nutrition education, humanizing the work place, humanizing education, holistic approaches to services for the elderly, death with dignity (as reflected in the hospice movement), and a real examination of alternative healing practices.

It is my feeling that the liberation of the body might very well be the most difficult of all the liberation movements. It's the most deeply challenging because of the degree to which we have internalized a fear and resistance of acknowledging our bodies and their needs as ourselves. It's the most controversial because of the profound taboos on touch and sexuality. My personal bias, after being involved in Bioenergetic therapy and continuing to spend upwards of an hour each day doing energetic body work, is to believe that inhabiting and possessing my body is the basis for my being able to be open, authentic, tender, present and supportive. If I recognize myself in that whole way and identify with myself entirely and responsibly, I will in the same way respect and cherish you and be responsive to your needs.

I deeply believe that much of what is wrong with our society is on account of our being so dispossessed of our selves, especially of our bodies. My hunch is that self-esteem isn't really a matter of getting gold stars or a higher salary or a good-looking spouse, but at the root, self-esteem is a function of how we inhabit and possess our bodies. I also suspect that self-awareness isn't just a matter of therapy, encounter groups or drugs but of truly opening our bodies at a deep muscular level. When we have repossessed ourselves at a very deep energetic level, we will all be more alive, healthy, responsible and democratic, and more naturally inclined toward a democratic society. When the bodymind is seen as one totality and we begin to be with each other in caring sensitive ways, all of the stereotypes and either-ors begin to fall away; male-female, black-white, rich-poor, straight-gay or whatever else.

Dychtwald: What is your sense of how we all might get more involved in facilitating this movement toward a healthy and humanistic political vision?

Vasconcellos: First, everyone must recognize that government and politics are about people, and the different political parties and philosophies are really just expressing their differing beliefs about human nature and human potential, growth and development. Second, it's absolutely essential that persons with a faithful humanistic vision activate themselves in the political process by campaigning, lobbying, publishing, meeting with political representatives, writing letters, holding town meetings, speaking out, holding conferences, even becoming candidates, and numerous other ways to be sure that the humanistic vision is made explicit and legitimate, and is taken seriously, and has a chance to spread throughout America. Third, as we develop and promote a specifically human agenda, each of us must recognize ourselves and our own continuing growth as a person, as the first item on that agenda.

In summation, if all of the sensitive, honest and aware people were to take a more active role in local and national politics and policy-making, we would quickly see a great change in the political and institutional priorities in our country. The best politics are those politics which are the product of human beings who are in love with each other. And that's up to you and me!

Ken Dychtwald, Ph.D., a psychologist, is co-founder of the SAGE Project Holistic Health Center, and Founding President of the Association for Humanistic Gerontology, both of Berkeley, California. In addition, he serves as a consultant to government and industry, and an adjunct instructor in psychology at several universities. His publications include *BODYMIND* (Jove, 1978), *HUMAN POTENTIAL: GLIMPSES INTO THE 21st CENTURY* (with Dr. A. Villodo), (J.P. Tarcher, Inc., 1979), and numerous articles on issues of health, aging, and life design.

chapter 16

will you declare
your independence?

Not to decide is to decide.　　　　　　—Harvey Cox

(The following is a 4th of July—1976—"sermon" I delivered
at the invitation of a monsignor friend, at St. Francis de Sales
Cathedral, Oakland, California.)

I'm feeling some anxiety.
This isn't my natural habitat.

It's strange—
　　after so many years being down there, being talked at—
　　being up here, doing the talking.

I feel some trepidation—
　　thinking how much the things I want to say, standing up
　　　　here,
　　are contrary to all I used to hear, sitting down there,
I feel some delight, impish delight—
　　thinking that, being up here—
　　I can go ahead and say it all anyway.

I'm anxious also—
    coming before you several hundred persons—
      all strangers to me—
    wondering what I can do and say—in a few minutes—
      that will make our time together worthwhile;
    recognizing especially that words are so hollow—
    that what most needs transmitting—spirit—
      is so difficult to transmit.

Yet I want to try—with my words—
    to reach for our common human spirit!

I want to explore with you the "Spirit of 1776"—
    the spirit that moved our founding fathers
    to make their magnificent Declaration of Independence—
    for that spirit needs to be born anew—
I want to explore with you the "Spirit of now"—
    the spirit arising within so very many persons in our
      nation—
    for that spirit needs to be nourished—

I find three striking similarities between then and now:

First—now, as then, we Americans are into a very new
    world.
    Now, by reason of automation and technology
      and universal education and mass media and
        affluence—
    our scene is a world as different from before
    as was the world of 13 colonies from Eurpoe.

Second—now, as then, we Americans experience
    tremendous frustration—
    as we perceive that our needs and our wants,
      our will and our ideals—
    seem thwarted by the powers that be.

Third—now, as then—that frustration seems to emerge

from the rising aspirations made possible by the new
world.

But I find two striking differences as well:

First—now, unlike then—our new world, with its new
possibilities
results precisely from the efforts and ingenuity and
sacrifice
and generosity of those older world persons—
(for which we might well give them credit).

Second—then the source of frustration lay without;
now our source of frustration lies within;
then the source was in a foreign land;
now the source is in our own land,
perhaps even within ourselves!

What, then, *is* the spirit of our times?

Where is our *own* spirit?

How do we rediscover—get in touch with—rekindle—
the Spirit of 1776—for our lives now?

Let us return to the Declaration of Independence
and explore its promise(s) and its meanings—
for us and for our nation today.

Its most basic declaration is
"all men are created equal"—

We *know* that in our nation
we have not lived up to that promise!

We've practiced "equal—if"—
we've practiced "equal—but"—
we've not practiced "equal—period".

It's time we recognize that simply by reason of being
human,
each and all men are equal in *value*;
to be human is to be valuable, and equal in *value*—no
matter what else;
whether black or red or brown or yellow or white—
whether male or female—whether old or young—

whether rich or poor—whether straight or gay—
    whether bright or dumb—
the *value* of each human being is equal!
And—if we are to survive as a nation—
we must each of us give ourselves fully—
to make that promise a living reality within our nation.

The Declaration of Independence speaks next of
"certain unalienable rights"—

I find myself flashing to the remarkable alienation
pervasive throughout our nation today.

I find myself suspecting that the troubles in our land
exist mostly because the assumptions and official
    policies—
of our government, of our culture, and of our major
    institutions—
are *inherently* alienating!

For they assume that:
something's *inherently* faulty with us human beings;
we aren't basically trustworthy;
we don't know what's best for ourselves;
we haven't the capacity to be responsible for ourselves
    (even that we need protection against ourselves);
we must be split in half—mind from body;
we must be denied and separated from
    large parts of our own being and experience
    (especially our bodies, and our feelings);
we must be controlled and conditioned;
we may be manipulated and used.

No wonder—we are alienated—
    from ourselves—and from each other!
But let us look further—
and examine those "certain unalienable rights"—
as we perceive and experience them—
    practiced and available in our nation today.

First—what about our national commitment to *"life"*?

I find our nation committed to death—rather than to life!

I see us committed to war, rather than to peace;
  —to violence, rather than to peaceful means;
I see how we fail to value human life—
    so clearly demonstrated in common attitudes
    to black and brown and yellow and red life,
    to criminal life (death penalty) and to fetal life (abortion);
I see how we fail to trust human life—
    so clearly demonstrated by
    the ways in which our institutions
    stifle individuality and freedom and spontaneity and
      authenticity;
I note how we scorn those who say—"make love, not
    war"—
    how we encourage movies exalting the destruction of
      human bodies,
    even while we discourage movies portraying the
      enjoyment of human bodies
I note our taboos on tenderness, and touching, and
    intimacy, and feeling, and sexuality and play, and
    pleasure, and loving.

"Life" *is* an unalienable human right—
it's time we recommitted ourselves
    to cherishing and affirming and valuing and trusting
      human life!

Second—what about our national commitment to
    "liberty"?

I find our nation committed to bondage—rather than to
    liberty!

I see us hung up on laws and institutions and rules and
    roles—
rather than on personal liberty and freedom
    (with its inherent responsibility).

When I think of "liberty"—
    I flash on "liberation"—
    black liberation, women's liberation, gay liberation,
    Chicano liberation, senior citizens' liberation,
    even children's liberation—
and I recognize our deep common yearning—

so greatly unrecognized and unrealized—
for personal/human liberation/
to be ourselves!

For too long our nation has interpreted "liberty" to mean
only
"economic liberty"—the right to put property before
persons,
the right of wealth to be protected by government,
the right to "con" consumers,
the right to pollute our environment.

Ironically—we show our cultural bias in
exalting "free enterprise"—
while scorning "free love".

For too long—
we have considered man as primarily an economic being;
it's time we recognize man as primarily a human being!

It's long past time we redefined "liberty"—
to mean that ultimate human right—
"the right to be one's self"!

And "the right to be myself" includes:
the right to my own head (intellect), and to question, and
to dissent;
the right to my own feelings;
the right to my own body and sexuality;
the right to believe in myself as basically trustworthy;
the right to be free of fear of myself;
the right to feel innocent (rather than guilty)—and
the right to feel proud (rather than ashamed)—
just to be myself;
the right to feel my own worth, to my own self-esteem
the right to be (come) a whole person—
all conditioned *only*
by the same rights
of each and every other human being!

Third—what about our national commitment to "the
pursuit of happiness"?

I find our nation failing here in two respects:

in "where we look for happiness"—and
in "who gets to say how I pursue happiness".

Obviously we have looked for happiness in material goods,
    and things,
        rather than in persons;
and in so many ways, our culture operates on the premise
    that
        someone else gets to determine where and when and
            how
        I get to pursue happiness!

It's time we recognize that—
    neither the pursuit nor the capture of happiness,
        lies without us;
    but rather that happiness is to be found
        within and between ourselves—
            in the search for and discovery of ourselves and each
                other—
            in becoming a whole person—
            body and feelings and mind!

It's time we recognize that—
    no one else has the right to do that for me,
    for no one else *can* accomplish that for me;
rather, each of us must have the right to determine
    our own pursuit of happiness,
        for *only* each of us can effectively do that for ourselves!

Recognizing, then, our nation's failed commitment
    to "life, liberty and pursuit of happiness"—
it comes as no surprise
    that there is now a *new declaration of (human)
        independence*
    shimmering and quickening and growing and emerging
    (from) within the hearts and bodies and minds and
        feelings
        of many human beings.

And so should it be!

For whether you call it
    the American dream,—or
    the human potential movement,—or

the Judeo-Christian message—
man's unalienable rights
    to equality and life and liberty and the pursuit of
       happiness—
must be recognized and affirmed and responded to—
if our nation is to survive,
    even if it is to *deserve* to survive!

So here we find ourselves—asking ourselves—
    where and when and how shall we proceed?

I caution you—
    to ponder that no government, no laws,
       probably no institution (not even a church)—
    can do that for you—
for only you in your life—and I in mine—
    can do that for ourselves.

Nor can words—no matter how fancy or sound or true;
    Nor can symbols—flags and parades.

Rather each of us—you and I—
    must search out our own spirit—
    discover our own ways,
    chart our own journey—
    so as to assure ourselves life and liberty
       and perhaps even more than the *pursuit* of happiness.

Father Dan Berrigan—in "The Geography of Faith"—
    proposes where (how) we should live—
       not at the comfortable center of our times and society,
       but at the furthest frontier—
       dreaming, daring, risking—
       living an outfront, authentic, caring human life—
only out of which human progress and fulfillment is
    possible.

Not surprisingly—in our culture's flight from ourselves—
we have commonly placed that search geographically in
    outer space.

Not surprisingly, vastly increasing number of persons
    are recognizing that outer space is not the place to
    search—

For the best geography, the true frontier
  is only within ourselves;
It is only in exploring and experiencing our inner space
  that we may truly discover
  our own life and our own liberty,
  our own happiness and fulfillment.

St. Iraneus wrote:
  "The glory of God is man fully alive."

So—just as our forefathers freed themselves from external
  bondage,
  each of us—you and I—
  must declare our own independence—and
  free ourselves from internal bondage—by
  taking seriously our own responsibility
  for liberating and integrating and healing ourselves!

For only then will our spirit be released—
  And the power of our loving,
    flow forth to be fully felt!

We have come into a new world;
We are coming into a new age—
  for America, for all of mankind, for ourselves.

Whether we realize its potential—
  whether we realize our own—
Depends so very much upon you, and upon me,
  and upon the willingness of each of us as human beings
To bring *all* of ourselves
  to each other
  in our common search and struggle!

Whether America lives up to its promise(s)
  depends simply upon whether and how
  you (and I) live the answer
    to a simple invitation—

      "Will you declare your independence?"

V.
ACTION:
FOR
GROWING HUMANS

chapter 17

a new human
bill of rights:
let our sun shine out

"A human being is...a single being, unique and unrepeatable!
—John Paul II

"Each person is a unique being of flesh and blood: each person represents a unique and valuable experiment on the part of nature: the very special and always significant and remarkable point at which the world intersects, only once this way and never again. That is why every person, as long as s/he lives, is wondrous and worthy of every consideration. Each person represents a gamble on the part of nature in the creation of a human!

—Herman Hesse

I hope you begin to share my excitement about the human possibilities which come with our liberating vision. Now I want to share with you my sense of what it means—its ramifications for us, individually and societally.

Generally, it proposes how we can make things right, in our lives and society, now and for our future. Specifically, it proposes that we can and must do that by beginning at the only proper beginning, the true foundation—ourselves. What are the effects of our new vision upon myself, my own being, my identity, my life?

Our new vision gives deeper, personal meaning (again demonstrating the inherent connection between personal and political) to the first section of the California Constitution: "All persons are *by nature* free and independent." "All persons" includes "this person,"—me—I!

Shifting our vision logically leads to profound changes in how we look at ourselves, at our nature, at what we expect from (within) ourselves. If I have that genetic inheritance, I am naturally innocent. I have the natural capacity to be/come human and whole. Having that, as naturally I have certain rights: humanly, psychologically, biologically, morally, politically, societally. I submit that I—and you—each have at least the following rights—a New Human Bill of Rights:

1. *To live*—rather than to die. Life is about increasing energy, heightening awareness, maximizing experience, realizing potential, raising consciousness, becoming free, living in the moment, actualizing ourselves.

2. *To breathe*—freely, naturally, deeply, wholly; to gain for myself the oxygen basis of a harmonious body and being, necessary to produce enough energy to invigorate my body and being. How shallowly, stingily most of us breathe—like the owner of a nine-room house living only in the closet!

3. *To be natural*—rather than unnatural, artificial.

4. *To original grace*—rather than original sin. To be natural is to be graceful, nature is grace, I am nature's grace personified.

5. *To my innocence*—rather than to be made to feel guilty. "Guilt's the worst damned thing in the world. What a waste!" (Barbara Stern)

6. *To be/come whole*—rather than in pieces, fractured, fragmented; to unite my mind and body—rather than having them separated, split; to bring my mind and body back into my natural oneness.

7. *To be myself*—rather than as you—or anyone else—would have me be; not to surrender myself to you, but to let go, surrender entirely to myself.

8. *To know myself*, all about myself—rather than to be mystified, either within/about myself or from without; to follow our oldest educational dictate: "Know thyself;" to be told the truth about myself, always, in all circumstances. The truth will make me free, the truth about myself will free me to be/come fully self-aware.

9. *To be fully conscious naturally*—rather than unconscious; to not need to seek altered states of consciousness (especially via drugs) which only unalter my already culturally-altered state. Consciousness is a matter of clear, natural energy flow within me; it's essential I not structure myself, my body—so as to limit my natural flow.

10. *To trust myself*—rather than distrust myself.

11. *To fully trust my experiencing*—rather than distrusting or fearing it.

12. *To experience myself freely and fully*, in three dimensions. Once, working with Stanley Keleman, he had me lying on my back, lifting my arms, palms pressing against his, resisting his pressing down. For several minutes I experienced myself *pushing* against his hands. Suddenly I had a flash that I was gone away, by myself, onto my own desert island. Then I came back. I became aware of something different happening: I experienced my hands *reaching* toward his hands. I realized I was experiencing my hands differently. It wasn't my usual only surface awareness—front and back. Instead, now, I experienced my hands in three dimensions. I *felt* what's in between. My mind flashed on two words: "gifting" (I was giving myself, my hands, to Stanley) and "golden" (I was golden). The feeling extended as far as my wrists. I tried with all my mind and might to extend it up my arms—to no avail. I've never again had that experience. Yet I believe it natural, available to us all, beneath our layers of mystification and constraint of ourselves.

13. *To think for myself*—rather than to be brain-washed, indoctrinated; to own my mind. I am my mind.

14. *To freely express verbally what I think*—freedom of speech; to dissent—rather than to be forced or frightened into agreeing.

15. *To feel fully and freely,* to fully experience and trust my own natural emotions—rather than only having conceptual feelings; to own my feelings; to be passionate—rather than apathetic. I have as much right to feel freely as I have to think freely. I am my feelings.

16. *To fully express my natural emotions/feelings* [*so long as I don't harm you by doing so*]—rather than suppress, contain my feelings.

17. *To own, inhabit, experience my body fully and freely,* without fear, shame or guilt—rather than to be bodily repressed; to have a sound mind and a sound body, a sound bodymind; to relax my muscles; to nudity in appropriate places; to own my body. I am my body. My body (through my senses) informs my intellect and (through my energy flow) forms my character. Self esteem is a function of how I experience myself physiologically. My freedom to do as I wish with my body is as important as my freedom to speak. Freedom of bodily expression is a critical basic freedom—usually denied us all, from our earliest days. As children—having little perspective— we accept prohibitions on our bodies and sexuality. I'm told a lie detector works partly because its sodium pentathol relaxes all a person's muscles. To tell a lie requires tensing up my muscles. So much of our child-raising consists of instructions to tighten up. Are we intending to produce lying adults?

18. *To experience and express my own natural energy* (*flow*)—rather than being blocked, blocking its natural flow.

19. *To freely express nonverbally what I feel*—nonverbal freedom of speech, including touch and dance.

20. *To move*—rather than to be made to sit, stand still (absent

reason). Especially for a child, to move is as basic a need as to eat or sleep: my physical and intellectual development depends on it. We suggest a human who uses only a few words is mentally deficient. Mòst of us use only a few of the more than 2000 movements we're naturally capable of. We ought recognize our physical deficiency.

21. *To touch and be touched,* to experience the joys of touch as I choose—rather than as proscribed by others, individually and/or through government. Touching is vital to my health.

22. *To own and experience fully and freely my sexuality*— rather than to be repressed, ashamed, guilty, afraid of my sexuality.

23. *To express myself sexually,* to let myself go and be sexual—rather than hiding, containing my sexuality. Sexual relations are a matter of persons touching certain parts of our bodies together. Why does anybody care who touches· whom where, so long as we're adults, consenting and discrete?

24. *To be my own person*—rather than to be conditioned by you, as the price of your approval, acceptance, inclusion.

25. *To personal liberation*—rather than repression.

26. *To be unafraid, especially of myself*—rather than afraid.

27. *To accept myself*—rather than reject myself.

28. *To be different*—rather than to conform, be uniform.

29. *To love myself*—rather than hate myself.

30. *To be open, disclosing, revealing*—rather than closed, concealed.

31. *To be self esteeming*—rather than self-demeaning; to feel good about myself.

32. *To be truthful at all times, in all places.* Each time I tell the

truth, I release energy. Each time I withhold the truth, I waste energy, withholding myself.

33. *To be honest, authentic always*—rather than editing, dissembling myself; to say what I mean, to mean what I say. To be false is not to be (free to be) myself.

34. *To self-realization, self-actualization*—rather than self-destruction.

35. *To self-gratification, self-fulfillment, self-satisfaction*— rather than self-denial.

36. *To self-determination, autonomy, independence, inner-directedness*—rather than outer-directedness, dependency, chauvinism (someone else "knowing," choosing what's best for me); to march to my own drummer; to have a say in my own life, decisions, destiny.

37. *To be deemed innately responsible, to take responsibility, to be responsible*—rather than being deemed and being irresponsible.

38. *To be spontaneous, immediate*—rather than withheld, delayed. To be cautious and contained is not honest or healthy for me personally.

39. *To relate openly, authentically, intimately*—rather than at a distance.

40. *To be deemed valuable*—rather than of no inherent value; to have my entire being (intellect, emotions, body, intuition, impulses, senses, sexuality) valued and accepted by you, wherever I am.

41. *To be trusted* (at least until I prove untrustworthy)—rather than distrusted.

42. *To value according to my own innate valuing system*—rather than forced to adopt and operate off your system—or anyone else's system—of values.

43. *To be/come moral*—rather than immoral.

44. *To be/come political,* to involve myself in the public-policy decision-making that affects my life and being and future—rather than to be turned off to politics.

45. *To dream*—rather than to give up or give in. Robert Heinlein's *Stranger In A Strange Land* is a wonderful fantasy. *A Liberating Vision* began as a dream!

46. *To grow*—rather than be stunted. To grow is so natural, why do we doubt and deny it? My most basic, ultimate human right is to be/come myself, fully human, a fully-functioning human being.

47. *To explore, experience, expand myself*—rather than not. I want to be/come utterly free, open, guiltless, authentic, clear, whole, simple, perceptive, intuitive, loving.

48. *To be utterly free*—rather than confined. Let's not get stuck arguing ''how free ultimately can we (afford to) be; are we *totally* innocent?'' You and I might disagree, argue incessantly and unprofitably. Let's focus on the operational issue, on which we agree: we can be/come *more* free than we have been, now are. We ought attend to that. As we do, as we get freer—we can reassess whether we can afford to get further free. The more freedom I have, the more free I become—the more I know I can handle more freedom responsibly, the more freedom I want.

My New Human Bill of Rights is epitomized by friend Jim Mathis' comment on reading St. Exupery's *The Little Prince*: ''I like it a lot, except for the part about being tamed. I'm an animal. I don't want to be caged or tamed. To be tamed is to be domesticated. To be domesticated is to be made useful. I don't want to be used. I want to be experienced and loved.''

When Alex Haley went to Africa searching out his ''roots,'' he found a wonderful ancient tribal custom. Upon a child's birth the father went off into the jungle for four days of meditation, his mission to select the child's name. On his return the tribe gathered for the celebration of the child. In the first ritual the mother handed the infant to the father. He brought the infant's ear to his mouth and into the child's ear whispered—the first time spoken—the child's name. Their theory: The child ought always be the first person to know who s/he was.

I claim that as my right: to always be the first person to know who I am!

I am deeply committed to our New Human Bill of Rights—for myself, for you, for every human being. I regularly, faithfully, exercise my rights under it—especially my right to grow, to be/come a fully functioning human being.

But—important as these rights are—they're only part of our picture of ourselves, the new humans.

reflections:
a new human bill
of responsibilities —
for and to myself

"The glory of God is...(persons)...fully alive."

—Saint Iraneus

*"To be nobody but yourself
in a world which is doing its best night and day
to make you everybody else
means to fight the hardest battle
which any human can fight
and never stop fighting."*

—e.e. cummings

Having the capacities proposed by our new vision of my human nature,
having the rights therefrom derived,
just as certainly, naturally, I have responsibilities,
on account of our new vision of my human nature.
With plenty of rights comes plenty of responsibilities.
They are fourfold in character:

First, I am responsible *for myself*;
Second, I am responsible *to myself*;
Third, I am responsible *to you individually* in our interpersonal relationship;
Fourth, I am responsible *to you all* in our institutional relationships.

I'll explore the first and second here, the third in Chapters 19 and 20, the fourth in Chapter 21.

Our liberating vision provides me a whole new theory of responsibility. I am primarily responsible *for* myself. I'm responsible for my becoming responsible, for outgrowing my current irresponsibility, for developing my sense of my own responsibility, even for developing a positive attitude toward responsibility.

Too often I interpret my suffering and failures as caused by the nature of things ("that's the way life is," "that's human nature") or as someone else's doing. I'm responsible for recognizing my part in it all. I'm especially responsible for my complicity in my own continuing cynicism, mystification and victimization. I'm responsible for regaining my ideals, my vision and my autonomy. I am responsible for myself and for my life.

I shouldn't be naive, carrying my theory of responsibility to an over-compensating extreme. I shouldn't ignore or underestimate the present effects of the actualities of my life up til now. Past events in my life's experiencing provide reason (not excuse) for who and how I am today. I may have had little choice when they happened or, if I did, they are *now* accomplished fact. Example: how my parents and teachers treated me when I was a near defenseless child had its effect on me, still has. I'm not fully, solely responsible for all the actualities happening in my life now. Example: I didn't choose, I'm not responsible for being born when, who, where and how I was (I'm not into reincarnation and karma).

I am responsible, though, for—
how I experience and perceive the events in my life,
how I feel regarding them,
how I manage and respond to them,   and
for doing something about changing, improving my life situation.
As our external environment grows more out of control and unpredictable,
I'm more responsible to take charge, make sense of it all, especially my part of it.

Since under our new vision I'm primarily responsible *for*

myself, I'm also primarily responsible *to* myself. I propose at least the following responsibilities I owe myself. (Will you accept them *for* and *to* yourself as well?)

For easier reading of this long bill of responsibilities to and for myself, I'm dividing them into several sections: Self-Responsibility, Self-Awareness, Self-Expansion, Self-Healing, Self-Exploration, Self-Repossession, and Self-Involvement. Bear in mind that the distinctions are artificial—accounting for some overlapping. It's the best way I yet know to describe a holistic process (which I'm still going through)—in written words.

SELF-RESPONSIBILITY

1. *To take full responsibility for myself.* Self-help is the essence of our new vision.

2. *To be/come fully responsible*, able to responsibly exercise all my rights as a human being.

SELF-AWARENESS

3. *To recognize we humans are redefining who we are and can be/come.* We little experience, know, sense or even imagine the extent of ourselves, how much of us there truly is. We have learned enough about ourselves to know there's far more to us humans than we've believed. Who knows what lies beyond our wildest imaginings about ourselves—intellectually, emotionally, psychically, sexually, spiritually, physically, tenderly, mystically, parapsychologically? We're in the age of discovery of humanness.

Some experts estimate we humans are realizing and utilizing only 10% of our potential. I suspect it's less than that. We are primitive. We need to realize, develop and use all of our human potential.

Consider the facts and implications of recent research indicating:
> —The sufficiency of touching a baby immediately after birth (called "bonding") affects later intellectual development—"I.Q."—by twenty points. (Marshall

Klaus, Cleveland);
— Up to age six, if a human's fingertip is cut off, it'll natu-
rally regenerate itself (Howard Schneiderman, University of California, Irvine);
— The different and complementary operations of our left
and right brains;
— Our brain operates on a "hologram" model (Karl
Pribram, Stanford);
— Rats whose brain function had been temporarily blocked
by amphetamines, fully remember—in their bodies—
where in a maze they experienced an electric shock
(Jim McGaugh, University of California, Irvine);
— The molecular structure of morphine (the active,
addicting ingredient in heroin) precisely conversely
matches the bodily cellular structure of addicts (Avram
Goldstein, Addiction Research Institute, Stanford, CA);
— Causal relationships between the character (positive to
negative) of touching received by infants, cultural
attitudes toward premarital sexuality, and violence (Jim
Prescott, Washington, D.C.).

For the latest, reliable information on human development
discoveries see Marilyn Ferguson's *Brain/Mind Bulletin*, P.O.
Box 42211, Los Angeles, CA 90042, the *Behavior Today*
newsletter, 2315 Broadway, New York, NY 10024, and the
Journal of Alternative Human Services, 1172 Morena Blvd., San
Diego, CA 92101.

Consider the fact and implications of all the personal human
explorations now going on—including physical and psychological and parapsychological activity. Jogging, dance, body-
work, out-of-body experiences, telekinesis are growing enormously in popularity.

What I'd most like to figure out for myself now is:
— Wherein is self-esteem based, derived, lost, regained? And
— What's the nature of the chemistry, electricity, or physics
(vibrations) that occurs occasionally in my experiencing
another person?

I have far more to know, to learn about myself. I have far more
to experience of myself. I am far more than I have thought and
believed.

4. *To choose my own vision of myself*, of my own nature and
potential.

5. *To recognize, acknowledge and examine closely my own vision about myself,* my nature and potential; determine how much my personal vision actually measures up to, matches our liberating vision. This serves as a needed basis for my personal faith, hope and action. My goal is liberation from the unquestioned, unexamined life. I want to constantly challenge my taken-for-granted views of myself, life, personal relationships, social institutions, religion, politics, everything.

I've done this much, often and increasingly. I began at the opposite pole, with my negative vision. I've closed that gap. I've got my head, mind and vision in close, faithful accord with our new vision.

6. *To become self-aware enough to recognize clues about the vision of myself* I hold. The clues used to be obvious: whenever anyone complimented me, I heard myself denying what they said. As I grew, the clues grew more subtle; I sensed myself feeling uncomfortable in hearing a compliment. The most subtle clue I've picked up (with friend Jim Mathis) is catching myself shaking my head from side-to-side, indicating disbelief—at the precise moment I'm experiencing myself and declaring my life more positively. I suspect my side-to-side head-shaking serves to block my energy from flowing naturally from my body into my head. If my sense of myself matched my positive vision, I'd be shaking my head up-and-down. That indicates belief, acceptance, "yes", affirming, acknowledging, accepting, and going with my good experience. That frees up my natural flow of energy from my body into my head.

7. *To redefine my image of myself;* to shift myself from our old vision's negative model to our new vision's positive model of humanness, human nature and potential, human growth and development; to take responsibility for (developing) my own faith; to discover and adopt a new faith which stops distrusting myself and everyone, life and nature; to stop perpetuating that distrust; to challenge and overcome my own cynicism, to be/come faithful instead; to look no more with jaundiced eyes, to look with eyes of hope; to become a visionary.

8. *To undertake the more difficult and challenging task: to examine myself and my life*—to see whether and how faithfully

I'm living our new vision; to recognize wherein I'm not yet my whole, natural self—in keeping with our new vision. A belief system (religious or otherwise) must be practiced, not merely contemplated, to be authentically in my existence; otherwise I'm a hypocrite.

Many awake experiences provide me assurance that I'm living this vision, including writing this book. My dreams provide me special assurance:

—having a ferris wheel in the pit of my stomach, with its cars each time digging deeper and digging up more dirt;

—winding my way down a series of staircases, until I came to the very bottom one and found a door with the legend "The Answer";

—being in an amusement park, playing with mechanical animals, which suddenly turned on me, threatening me with death; I realized I was dreaming, recalled reading that a person never dies in his/her own dreams, and simply trusted and relaxed; whereupon the animals turned very gentle and loving.

9. *To accept responsibility for knowing myself better than anyone else can or does.* Otherwise I'll seek authority elsewhere, outside myself—in a parent, teacher, clergyperson, politician, guru, treatment, drug, whatever.

10. *To know myself fully.* It's no wonder I hardly know myself: I've been taught not to, conditioned to be afraid to. I've barely *been* myself. It's difficult to know what I haven't experienced!

11. *To learn to accurately see myself,* to observe my own being and behavior honestly, stripping away my usual social justifications; to candidly assess how I am, being and doing; to do what I can to mitigate or avoid self-deception, by constant, totally honest self-examination.

12. *To learn to observe myself caringly*—not with guilt but with curiosity and wonder—for symptoms and signs of our old vision still operational with me.

13. *To wonder about myself,* why I still have, enact, display those scars of our old vision; to come to understand all that's

happened before in my life, all my earlier experiencing. That provides me no justification for remaining how I am now, no excuse for my stopping here. It enables me to better understand why I am who and how I now am—so I can more readily outgrow my present self.

14. *To forgive myself for giving my self away*; to not feel guilty about feeling guilty.

15. *To wonder how I can outgrow, shed and liberate myself from those scars*; to recognize how I best outgrow the worst parts of me. It's not by being naive (pretending I don't have them), nor by ignoring, denying or driving them in deeper, reinforcing their roots within me. It is by being honest with myself, honoring those sad facts regarding myself, acknowledging them, then wondering how I can outgrow them.

16. *To recognize that as a human I tend to do things to protect and further my own self-interest*, as I perceive it; to transform my *self* such that my perception of my self-interest shifts from the negative, cynical, distrusting, competitive, either/or, win/lose model—to a positive, faithful, trusting, loving, cooperative, both/and, win/win model.

SELF-EXPANSION

17. *To undertake the most difficult and challenging task: to change myself and my life*, so I'm faithfully living our liberating vision; to change myself into positive living. It's not enough to shift my vision intellectually. I'm such a cerebral being, I've so much conditioned myself to live through my head, it's no wonder I first figure out intellectually that I can—and even *how* I can—become a more human being. Then I have to struggle for years afterwards to develop the rest of myself, in keeping with my expanding intellectual recognition. It's only by opening myself, attending to my own growing—that I begin to get in touch with my wholeness.

18. *To wonder about myself, my nature and potential, who I am and who I can be/come.* I've done much of this, found it

conducive to, valuable for, my ongoing discovery, insight and growth.

19. *To recognize I'm using only part of my innate human potential.*

20. *To develop and realize all my as yet untapped innate human potential.*

21. *To trust my own human nature and potential;* to not underestimate myself; to trust my innate innocence and essential goodness, my own human being and becoming; to be/come faithful, have great faith, trust my own faithfulness; to make a leap of faith, greater than that proposed by our traditional culture (into some external infinite being); to make a gigantic leap of faith into myself, from within myself, into believing in my own nature and potential; to assume I'm capable of developing my own goodness; to recognize I am special, my own hero/ine, guru, leader. To imagine I can be/come more than I now am; to grapple with the potentialities as well as the reality of the "I."

22. *To recognize I'm sitting on a gold mine, myself;* within me, I am golden; to initiate the mining—rather than the undermining—of myself; to quit looking for the missing link, recognizing *I'm* the missing link, that I've got plenty of links missing within myself, I need be about reconnecting myself, getting myself together.

23. *To have courage to explore and experiment with my humanness*—not in remote laboratories, but in the immediate laboratory that is my daily life and relationships; to not be timid in this endeavor; to recognize I'm a Daniel Boone, plowing through the wilderness of myself, a toddler in the world of persons. I'm just beginning to scratch my surfaces, see what's beneath, become familiar with it, and like myself.

Our new vision offers me a new, contrary promise and hope: the more I open, disclose, shed all my layers, masks, defenses, roles—the more natural and whole I'll be/come. The unknown inside me is more positive than negative, is more a source of celebration than consternation. I should have the courage to live—by taking risks—in order to grow myself.

This is not a time for being cautious or intimidated. It's a time to be bold pioneers at the edge of life ourselves, risking always on the side of innocence and freedom. It takes getting used to—living life as one gigantic, never-ending risk, plumbing the unknown of ourselves—especially after being conditioned to fear what's inside. It's sure worth it!

24. *To live at the edge of my own being,* consciousness, expansion—the "geography of living" (Robert Coles and Daniel Berrigan's *The Geography of Faith*); to risk living—not at the comfortable center of our times and society, but at its furthest frontier, at its edge, letting go and trusting, living at the edge of my own unconsciousness, my own expanding consciousness, all the time, in every moment. Only if I live continuously at the edge of my own growth—dreaming, daring, risking—living an outfront, authentic, caring, human life—can I see ahead, sense where I'm going and what's coming, even as I'm growing.

I can't yet know my final destination, but I can surely call my current direction.

I try to live at my edge, becoming aware of my edges, reaching for my edges, massaging my edges—which turn out to be only the edges of my resistance. As I gradually release my resistances, my next edge exposes itself (See Michael Murphy's *Jacob Atabet*).

25. *To not wait for a leader;* to recognize we're into a new process: there are no outside leaders; to recognize I'm the actor, it's up to me, no one else will, or can, do this for me. I simply have to recognize that *I am the way,* the path for myself. I have to take responsibility, act now, initiate action myself. "Life is trying to fit the next piece into a gigantic puzzle I've not seen the picture of before." Perhaps I can do something as simple—and as profound—as solve the puzzle of my own existence.

Thus, I become an explorer of humankind; realizing that the new frontier is here within me. We humans are the new frontier. The biggest bittersweet mystery of life in our times is our own being, our insides, our human nature and potential; to unravel the "sweet mystery of life."

26. *To not wait for "the time to come";* to recognize we're in a

new time: there are no (other) experts. Each of us can go ahead, try ourselves, become our own experts about ourselves. I can come to be the person who knows the most about myself, better than anyone else can and does. Who could possibly know more about me than I do? After all, no one else has an inside position, gets an inside "look"; to accept responsibility to know myself, the best.

27. *To recognize that as I'm the new frontier, pioneer and experimenter—I am both the subject and the object of today's primary, unprecedented, human exploration: ourselves.*

28. *To trust that I can grow and change profoundly.* I know and trust this from perceiving persons closest to me personally, and especially from experiencing myself. I've changed enough, I can even note my changing. I can clearly detect the turn-around periods in my life, recognizable from my differing internal feelings and external actions:

—In high school, competing for a college scholarship, I was asked what I wanted to be and why. I answered: "I want to be a lawyer, to help rich people be sure they don't get taken advantage of by the government in their taxes." Though still concerned about persons getting ripped off by government, I'm *more* concerned about sound government action to help needy persons;

—I ardently opposed the Catholic Church's changing its ritual language from Latin to local; later I led a group demonstrating the new ritual. My contrary responses on successive readings of Sid Jourard's *The Transparent Self* (if you're not finding my book touching you, you might put it on your shelf, for future reference. Reach for it a year from now);

—On my May 11th, 1966 birthday, friend Barbara Nicoara gave me Herman Hesse's *Siddartha*. Feeling dutybound, I read it. It touched nothing in me. A rereading a year later hit me like dynamite;

—On January 22, 1966 I went to the San Jose Jaycees annual banquet where they present "The Outstanding Young Man of the Year" award. I was widely rumored as the favorite. I expected, wanted, "needed" to receive it. I didn't. I was crushed, devastated. Two years later I received the award: though pleased, I experienced no marked feeling.

29. *To recognize it's never too late to grow, to change.* No matter what my age, I can open the traps that have imprisoned my inner life, releasing and revealing the free, beautiful, well-made, natural individual I was meant to be/come. It's never too late to free myself from the programming of my past, to assume responsibility for my own being, and to discover possibilities, potentialities I don't even yet suspect.

30. *To recognize that once I've begun my growth process, there's no turning back, there's no returning.* Once I start growing, truly growing, I can't close myself in again. I can only keep on, go on growing, unfolding, bringing me into closer touch with the university of life—of which I'm a vital part.

31. *To recognize the two major steps in growing myself;*
—opening myself fully to my current state of being, letting myself fully experience myself as I now am, with all my feelings, exactly as they are;
—going deeper, working to further open my body, changing who I am and how I experience myself, in the same situations as before.

32. *To recognize the precious moments, events and experiences that keynote my growth:*
—When I am accepted, loved so deeply, well and much that it powerfully contradicts my current negative sense of myself, my lacking self esteem. That challenges the self-image I'm carrying, requiring me to surrender it, change my mind about myself, and undertake efforts to grow myself;
—When my growth efforts bring me to the point that my natural life force outstrips, outbalances my remaining repression and resistance. After that it's full speed ahead. I have no choice but to keep on growing.

Loving myself and being loved are the keys to my human growth.

After long years of therapy and growth efforts, I'm only beginning to know my own goodness from within, at my gut level. From my experience, I come to know that whatever I carry within me will lead me far more wisely and surely to my goal—than will any outside source. The fundamental guidance of my life can and must only be internal. It can in no wise be external, arising from the will of other persons.

33. *To take responsibility for my continuing evolution toward my full self-actualization.*

34. *To empower myself to act upon my vision that we humans are naturally, decently, responsibily, self-determining,* capable of wise choices for ourselves; to replace my powerlessness and passivity with my personal power and self-regard and ability to act, to grow and change myself.

SELF-HEALING

35. *To undertake to heal and grow myself;* to grow not out of fear or guilt, but out of my natural impulse to want wholeness.

36. *To be/come myself*—wholly, naturally; to become a person (see Carl Rogers' *On Becoming A Person*); to be/come my own person, to be/come a full-fledged, fully-functioning human being; to become the first person to know who I am; to be/come autonomous and self-determining. The highest form of creativity of which we humans are capable is the development of a free, inner-directed, autonomous being, out of a helpless, outer-directed, other-directed slave. That's my ultimate *responsibility*, as it is my ultimate *right!*

37. *To attend daily to my changing, growing, developing myself*—fully, wholly, naturally. I'm responsible for my choices, for who I am from now on, despite the perils and scars of my upbringing; to realize that I'm my own primary goal, as well as my own primary obstacle; to break myself out, simply because it's my nature to recognize and realize and fulfill myself; to take responsibility for my own self-expansion; to be always stretching myself, toward becoming a fully-functioning human.

38. *To deeply want to heal and grow myself.* No progress or growth is likely, lacking strong personal desire.

SELF-EXPLORATION

39. *To start with myself—with who and how and where I am, here and now.* I can't proceed, get anywhere, without beginning at the proper beginning: myself, here and now. I'm beginning to recognize that I am the beginning.

40. *To recognize my chrysallis state,* that as a person I'm an adolescent, even a toddler. I'm awkward, gangly, ungainly, funny-looking, confused, struggling—on account of my state; to recognize I'm about to be/come beautiful; to watch myself grow beautiful, like a butterfly.

41. *To not be alarmed or discouraged by my rawness, roughness, confusion, missteps, failures*—as I turn myself toward growing; to recognize how difficult it is, and why; to recognize that the problem, my condition, is the result of my conditioning; to not be discouraged by the pain and difficulty of it all; to take heart and go, grow on, go on. I don't know what lies within or ahead of me. But I want to explore, searching for a new world, within and without—trusting the unknown within me is more likely positive than negative.

42. *To cope with and overcome the feelings of inadequacy, failure and guilt that afflict me* upon stripping away the usual social justifications, observing my own behavior honestly.

43. *To attend to reading, in search of myself.* I've found some books especially helpful:
Sid Jourard's—*The Transparent Self* and *Disclosing Man To Himself*;
Carl Rogers'—*On Becoming A Person*;
Abe Maslow's—*Toward A Psychology of Being;*
Victor Frankl's—*Man's Search For Meaning;*
Rollo May's—*Man's Search For Himself* and *Psychology and the Human Dilemma;*
Jim Bugental's—*The Search For Authenticity;*
Hugh Prather's—*Notes To Myself;*
Colin Wilson's—*An Introduction To the New Existentialism.*

44. *To look for other persons of my "carass"* (*energy family*) *who will facilitate my growth*; to locate persons enough self-assured and personally powerful to feel safe and free in

challenging and criticizing me, so I can grow further in their presence, on account of our relationship. My best friend is my best critic; to locate persons in whose presence I feel safe enough to trust myself more, let go to myself, let myself go to the edge of who I am becoming, let myself show with all my rough edges, let myself become vulnerable.

45. *To be willing, unafraid, unashamed, unembarrassed to ask for help in my search*, my efforts to heal and grow myself; to be willing to try therapy, making my unconscious conscious again, especially through uncovering therapies; to struggle to overcome my entrapment: when I'm feeling worst, the most down and depressed, I have the hardest time asking for help, even accepting offers of help. I then feel least loveable, least worthy of your caring, your affirmation, your help.

46. *To cope creatively with the fear I'll initially experience when I let go of everything else*, and depend solely upon my unaccustomed self, my inner being; especially to tolerate the basic terror I'll face when my belief system is breaking down and I encounter the naked void, "the experience of nothingness." (Michael Novak).

47. *To recognize my special vulnerability at that moment;* to be wary of grasping at passing straws, in search of *The Answer*; to beware of false prophets, often those into false profits. If anyone claims to have *The Answer*, "the truth," "the path to enlightenment," "the path to make you free"—I should examine carefully. There are giveaway clues to their likely inauthenticity, their *not* having *The Truth*:
—If they charge more money for it than necessary for their survival;
—If they have ranks and hierarchies within their operation;
—If they have to proselytize, talk a lot about it, rush you;
—If they have proscriptions or prescriptions, rules beyond "Be yourself";
—If they have to keep it secret, mystical—rather than utterly open;
—If they're at all exclusive—rather than all inclusive;
—If they have a "magic" jargon, "canned phrases" for every situation. (See Michael Rossman's *New Age Blues*, especially

his "spiritual crap detector.")

The truth will make me free—to be myself. I'll naturally be overflowing, wanting, willing to share, spread it and myself freely and openly, with all other persons. Gurus, groups and cults too often offer only the illusion of freedom. The price I pay is often myself.

48. *To look inside myself for my own innate answers*; to become my own guru—rather than searching for the answer outside, in other gurus, mysticism, religion, politics, liberation movements, the counterculture, transpersonalism, meditation, pornography, fast cars, sky diving, whatever; to recognize, in becoming my own master and guru, that I need no other master or guru; to be/come my own primary model by which I live.

49. *To recognize I can learn and grow through my pain;* to not avoid my pain (though not be masochistic); to let myself fully experience myself, with all my scars, pain, emptiness, loneliness. While witnessing the play "Equus" and Bergman's movie "Face to Face," I early on found myself crying lightly, later profusely, afterwards for a half hour weeping. Those experiences provided me insight into the roots of my own pain, repression and constraint. Suffering can be a valuable precondition for personal transformation—though never a sufficient one. Indispensable other factors include exposure to a credible alternative means of believing, acting and being in life—and love.

For several years, in quiet moments, I found coming to mind a snapshot of me as a child, in overalls and beanie, standing on the porch of a house we then lived in. I couldn't relate it to anything. At one point in time, as I progressed deeper into myself via my body work, I experienced a slight pain low in my back, just above my right hip. As I kept on with my body work, my pain grew to the point I almost couldn't sleep at night. Not knowing what else to do, I tolerated my pain, kept on with my body work, focusing my attention and breathing into my pain.

Finally one night as I was deep into my body work and my pain, that picture came again to mind. I suddenly flashed on a painful incident that occurred on that porch. I recalled my father, in response to my calling nasty names at persons passing by, spanking me severely (I don't recall his ever otherwise hitting me).

I recognized the connection, breathed more deeply, let myself go more fully into my pain, began letting go of my pain, releasing it. It alleviated slightly, then gradually and entirely in the next few days of working. I've never experienced that pain again.

50. *To take responsibility for being the grounds of my own hope,* to grow my own hopefulness; to not give up and fall into apathy, cynicism, despair.

If I'm solely intellectual, I'm almost bound to be cynical. It means I haven't access to the rest of myself, I don't know my own goodness. Additionally, my intellect primarily takes apart and analyzes things. It hasn't capacity for seeing and making whole, putting back together—which is the grounds of real hope.

SELF-REPOSSESSION

51. *To accept myself,* thereby liberating myself from the performance demand to prove myself worthy, to myself and to others; to celebrate myself. In my favorite fiction, Tom Robbins' *Even Cowgirls Get the Blues,* heroine "Sissy Hankshaw" turned her remarkable difference—a gigantic thumb—into an acclaimed speciality, hitchhiking. In so doing she celebrated life and endeared herself to everyone. Rather than transcending myself—my humanness, my body, my natural self—into some alleged transpersonal range, to be into growing myself wholly, transcending the transpersonal.

52. *To let myself be myself;* to learn to be myself; to relax, let go to myself, utterly surrender to myself, let myself experience my wholeness, my own natural being, my innocence.

53. *To fully explore, experience, expand myself.*

54. *To trust myself, and how I'll grow, naturally;* to have no expectations of what will finally be born—just trusting, letting go, letting myself be/come; to take my cues from nature, where growth happens most healthily with love, space, light, warmth

and respect; to have faith, to nurture my nature, to expect and trust I'll grow properly, properly attended to. Why should I expect less of myself than of Sherry's plant, leaning toward light and warmth for self-fulfillment? To trust my growth urge is innate; to trust that urge.

55. *To live fully here and now.* I live only once. Commitments to the past in this life, to past lives, to the after life, to the next life, or to life ever after—are often avoidances, substitutions for fully living my life now.

56. *To develop my ability to yield fully to the present moment,* not holding myself back on account of past scars or future fears; to simply and utterly let myself go, to myself and reality; to be/come like the water in Bradford Shank's *Fragments*—always meeting life precisely where it is, neither abstracting from nor pushing on it. "Don't push the river!"

57. *To breathe—in order to live fully.* Breathing needn't be taught, it needs liberating. It's imperfect because it's blocked; to correct my breathing, to breathe fully, deeply, naturally rather than by force; to let my body rediscover its own, my own natural personal respiratory rhythm, to attend to my breathing naturally, to let go of my constraints upon my breathing, so I fully inspire, energize myself.

58. *To always, in all times, places and circumstances—be true to myself and truthful;* not to need to be "consistent" with my previous statements on a given subject, my previous actions in a given situation; to be consistent with truth as it presents itself to me in this moment. That results in my growing, from truth to truth, ever more truthful.

59. *To live my truth.* The fact other persons don't share my viewpoint doesn't make them right and me wrong, them sane and me insane, them realistic and me unrealistic. I should outgrow my still-remaining conditioned-in-resistance to going ahead and acting, truthfully.

60. *To have the courage to be/come authentic,* to live authentically, to liberate myself from the authority figures

implanted in me—so I can be/come the author of my actions and my life.

61. *To become natural rather than artificial, edited, structured;* to choose to reveal rather than conceal myself, to be open and self-disclosing, for my own self-knowledge and emotional wellbeing; to drop all my shells, masks, disguises, poses, defenses, roles; to act no longer "as if," but instead to be; to let my natural self, even scarred and scared, fractured, needy and vulnerable—out, for me (and you) to see.

62. *To reestablish my identity*—by reidentifying with, unifying all my being. Freud suggested my identity is rooted in how I experience myself physiologically, biologically; to regain my self esteem, best done by liberating and recovering my body— whose repression largely accounts for my loss of my natural self esteem; to retake full ownership of myself, my being, naturally.

63. *To recognize the triple bind I'm in,* on account of my acculturation: afraid, therefore unable to see myself, therefore unable to recognize my repression, therefore unable to liberate myself.

64. *To free myself from my fear, to outgrow my intimidation;* to recognize, confront and outgrow my fear of myself, so I can go inside and uncover, rediscover and recover the rest of, all of myself. There's lots of myself I don't have access to. There's a reason for that (my repression). That's the reason for our problems (personal and social).

65. *To undo my second bind, to demystify myself;* to free myself from our collective hallucination, the unconscious; to attend to my own seeing, to see for myself, clearly and thoroughly, to regain my awareness that I'm repressed. I've blown their cover on, within myself. Awakening from my unconscious sleep begins the process of my personal transformation.

As I become more united and simple—I more fully experience my own wholeness, interrelatedness, interconnectedness. I find my vision, my sense of the interrelatedness of everything—you, me and nature—becoming much more one of unity, wholeness, oneness. My intuition sees connections better and quicker.

66. *To struggle toward demythologizing, demystifying, liberating, understanding, developing all of myself,* my every part, my every human capacity; to go into and let myself experience myself—my mind, body and emotions, fully and freely; to recognize the thrill, excitement, wonder of turning my attention and curiosity into myself, into making myself and my life more open, deep and loving.

67. *To uncover, rediscover, recover and live from my third, noetic, all-wise and all-knowing whole self.*

68. *To discover myself*—not only from the outside, but from my inside as well. I read of a person who has no mirrors in her house—to facilitate *internal* self-discovery.

69. *To raise, expand, deepen, heighten my own consciousness;* to be/come fully conscious; to grow into a wholly new dimension of humanness, a fully-dimensional human being. Awareness is a combination of experiencing, observing, thinking, and assessing—overall an astute recognition of how things truly are, and even a hunch about how they could be/come.

70. *To undo my third bind, to cure, heal myself, to make myself right.* We talk so much today about our need to clean up our polluted external environment. I need as much to clean up my own *internal* polluted environment, from all those blocks and structures I've taken into myself. What's wrong is that our old vision assumed I was evil, then subjected me to processes that made me wrong. It's up to me to make myself right again; to outgrow my conditioning, wounds, scars, to make myself whole again; to undo the learning done unto and into me; to take responsibility for my own rehabilitation; to liberate myself from all my repression; to end my victimization, to refuse to continue being an accomplice in my own repression. Inward freedom is the origin of all the other freedoms.

71. *To be/come unself-conscious—by liberating myself from my inhibitions.*

72. *To outgrow my defensiveness.* Defensiveness derives from my not sufficiently trusting my natural being. To be defensive is

unnatural.

73. *To be/come intelligent, clear-thinking, thinking for myself;* to be/come analytical, competent, skillful. Intellectual liberation is essential.

74. *To wonder about and challenge the origins, appropriateness, sensibility, and ramifications of the mind-body split which underlies our culture.* I'm not intending to separate out or downgrade my intellect. I'm intending rather to heal my earlier separation, to elevate my body and emotions to their proper natural place as coequal partners of and in my whole human being. I'll improve my intellect and thinking—by improving the operations of the rest of me, upon whose information my intellect acts.

75. *To resolve my mind/body split;* to abandon my from-the-top-down traditional model of character structure; to overcome my separateness, the divisions within me, such that I be/come more simple; to resurrect my body, reunite it with my mind, so I am body and mind; finally, on to a felt, experienced realization that my body and mind are one, which is me, "I," bodymind; to cease the civil war within me, between my own parts; to bring my parts into peaceful coexistence; to be at peace with myself. This is the true peace-making effort, out of which all others proceed. To reinhabit, unify and make whole all of me again.

76. *To go beyond, transcend our traditional culture's either/or, body/mind, masculine/feminine, personal/political, black/white, tough/tender, winner/loser dichotomies;* to recognize there's only me, I am one. My capacity to recognize my oneness is related to how much I've regained consciousness of my own wholeness, my own oneness; to recognize and transform myself instead into a oneness model, a oneness state of being; to go on to recognize my own oneness, my oneness with you, each other person, with our entire world.

77. *To build myself a conceptual base from which to launch my voyage of self-discovery and self-recovery,* especially if I'm an intellectual.
    Since I've been conditioned to be intellectual, it's necessary I

appeal to and through my mind. I had to start my growing rehabilitation by reading extensively, to turn my head around, persuade it, justify to it—that it could let go, let the rest of me protrude, emerge, proceed, let my emotions and body function more freely, fully. If my intellect lets go, my other elements function better and, in turn their better functioning enables my intellect to function better. Liberation of the rest of me enhances the operations of my rational powers. If I improve the speed and precision of my nerve commands between my muscles and brain, I'll improve the functioning of my brain. If my feeling system is bad, blocked, distrusted, crooked—I can't think straight.

78. *To recognize, challenge and overcome the irrationality of my singular commitment to reason, rationality, my intellect;* to turn my rational powers inward, pay attention to the rest of myself; to open and explore, uncover and rediscover and recover, repossess and reinhabit, unite all the rest of myself; to look at myself, into myself, at and into my own life. I'll find a nice, natural me, beneath the distorted me I'll find on first looking within.

79. *To come to trust my instincts, impulses, intuition, insight.* In our culture our development of our heads and minds has far outstripped development of our emotional, intuitive capacities for seeing how things fit back together. I'm now needing my intuition with its primary function—seeing how things connect, fit back together again. I act on account of my instincts, impulses, intuition, on account of my feelings. Then I make up reasons—at best rationalizations, at worst excuses—to justify my actions; to become utterly subjective and objective at the same time.

80. *To recognize the significance of my emotions.* There's enormous power in my energy and emotions. If I deny them their natural course of flowing, their natural operations—they act funny. They'll have their way, one way or another, if not naturally then unnaturally. "It's only with the heart that one sees rightly," observed *The Little Prince*; to recognize the superiority of an expansive, sentient and rational person over a dichotomized, diminished facsimile. My belief isn't anti-

intellectual, but anti-intellectualizing. I want to elevate the rest of myself, my emotions and body, to *coequal* status and stature in my whole human beingness. Liberation of my emotions is essential to my moral development (see #101 below).

81. *To develop my emotional maturity;* to become a naturally, fully feeling person; to pay attention to, recognize, explore, discover, understand, repossess my emotions; to let myself fully, deeply experience my feelings—rather than rushing to put them into words, diminishing and sanitizing them, making them and me "safer" by reducing my excitement; to overcome the way I tense up to constrain my feeling, vitality, excitement, consciousness.

82. *To learn to listen to, recognize, discern, "read" my own feelings—directly and immediately;* until I do, to utilize ways to discover my feelings indirectly. If I can't discern internally how I want to choose in a particular dilemma, I'll flip a coin or ask you the question, then I'll carefully observe myself for feelings of delight or chagrin with the answer I hear proposed. I'll come to know my feelings more clearly.

83. *To explore, discover and develop, become familiar and comfortable with, my sense of touch and touching.* As I've done this, I find that at times, my hands have a remarkable sense of touch, a life and knowing of their own beyond my rational knowledge; especially they're able to search out, discover, touch and provide some relief and release for tight, constrained places in another's body.

84. *To recognize the full significance of my embodiedness;* to admit I have a body, I am my body; to recognize that everything comes down to my body; to become familiar, comfortable, competent with body talk, body language, nonverbal communication; to become aware of the relationship between the whole that is my body, and the whole that is the universe. To assume and exercise my own power over life, over my own life, I must first of all take cognizance of my body. It is only from within my own living mobile body that I can find comfort and the possibility of my happiness and fulfillment.

The more my body is a stranger to me, the more I remain a stranger to life. To deepen my knowledge of my body, its desires and possibilities; to experience it from within, not just perceive it from without. I can't love myself until I become aware of the bound-and-gagged body I now think I have to deny or defy. I can never get myself together if I keep denying "I am my body."

We humans are just beginning to understand the significance of our bodies and of the effects they have upon our personality and character formation. We choose and form our character as we choose and form our bodies. We humans are only beginning to scratch our own surfaces, and get a glimpse of the subtlety and profundity that is our body:

—My body is the basis for my being and experiencing;

—My body is the basis for my identity and self esteem. This *doesn't* mean that if I'm crippled or have some disease, I have no hope of being or becoming okay. It's the way I possess and inhabit the body I have, rather than its shape or formation, that accounts for my self esteem;

—My body is the basis for the working of my intellect. My intellect gets its information from my body and senses. The more open and clear my body and senses are in observing and reporting reality inward, for and to my intellect, the more realistically, accurately, truly my intellect will operate.

We humans are just beginning to recognize the depths of our rejection and repression of our bodies. They are the realm beyond, within—with untold mysteries to be plumbed, discovered, experienced and enjoyed.

85. *To acknowledge that my body is good, innocent, okay, clean;* to regard myself and my body as an indispensable sacred whole, I am a corporal *and* moral unity; to view my body as a totality, a whole work.

86. *To trust my body.* If I surrender to my body, I'll discover it will act to reestablish its natural unity, seeming to know better than I what it has to do. My body will direct me to satisfy its desire for (my) well being. My body is a work of art. I should sculpt and shape my body, according to its natural desires.

87. *To be/come comfortable with my body.* The animal and the human exist in one body, are one person, are one. When the

animal's desires are about to be fulfilled, the human ought not
be disgusted with the animal's appetites, but rejoice and enjoy
their fulfillment; to get comfortable touching my body, looking
at my body. In fact, the animal and the human are one, the
human is an animal.

88. *To take responsibility for the state of my body;* to be a body
first of all, be a body at last, to be; to feel within my body who I
am, that I am; to feel that I exist in space; to attend to the
recovery, resurrection, and repossession of my body, to
be/come my body, to reincorporate myself; to own and inhabit
and experience my body fully, freely; to open, demystify,
loosen, relax my body; to let it be; to explore fully the realm of
my body; to work with my body and what it can yield.

All this will move me toward my wholeness—not just my body
at the expense of the rest of myself, but to the advancement of
the rest of myself. I will restore myself to my wholeness, restore
my wholeness to myself.

We humans may be the first animals with mind enough to
liberate ourselves—not from our bodies, but to liberate our
bodies, thereby liberating and integrating our entire being. Just
as I am for political mobilization, I am for the mobilization—the
putting into place—of all the parts of each body of every human
being.

I work daily
in/with/in my body,
stretching and twisting myself
subtly, gradually, cumulatively—
liberating my body,
releasing it again
to its natural unity and wholeness.

Sometimes the interior configurations of my body
become as tangible to me
as the outside surfaces of my body.

The more I work with my body,
the more relaxed, open I become.
The more difficult I find it to dissemble,
the more perceptive I become of other persons, their
dissembling.

The thought of that is eerie:
there's no more hiding, no more secrets.
In actuality, its experiencing proves engaging, delightful, reassuring.

Especially when I get working and open deep in my body,
I recognize how much freer I am than ever before in my life.
I simultaneously recognize the tightness I still carry,
seemingly more than before.
One day Stanley Keleman agreed: I'm 80% freer than I used to be,
80% more aware wherein I'm not yet free.
How much more I have yet to go!

That helps me recognize how difficult liberation is, how long a path.
That also gives me grounds for great hope for my future:
With the body work and breathing I do each day,
I each day become freer, more whole.
I have this to look forward to
for the rest of my life:
Each day I will be/come freer, more whole.
How awesome. How wonderful!

I've found the following books helpful in my body liberation efforts:
* Therese Bertherat's *The Body Has Its Reasons*;
* Don Johnson's *The Protean Body*;
* Stanley Keleman's *The Human Ground: Sexuality, Self and Survival*;
* Orson Beane's *Me and the Orgone*;
* Ken Dychtwald's *BodyMind Approaches to Living*;
* Michael Murphy's *Jacob Atabet*;
* Alexander Lowen's *Bioenergetics* and *Pleasure*.

89. *To recognize I always have my body with me, I am always in my body.* I am always my body—hence my sexuality is always present with/in/to me, I am always sexual.

90. *To recognize the significance of my sexuality*; to realize how simple my sexuality is, how silly to fear it. Sexuality is simply energy moving in to certain parts of my body. Sexual liberation

is simply the ability to feel my energy, to respond to my feelings
about myself, and to respond sensually in a free way, without
guilt or shame or fear. Sexual liberation is an opening up: an
attempt to live a life filled with persons, generosity, and joy.
Fully experiencing myself sexually is more immediate and
pleasurable than substitute sexuality. It provides a profound,
empowering lesson in trusting my natural feelings, my not
needing (to put) any brake on my natural feelings.

The muscles I use to constrain, repress my sexuality connect
directly with the muscles in my chest. I suspect they produce a
corresponding effect there, constraining my capacity for
breathing, perhaps my capacity for loving.

91. *To take full responsibility for my human sexuality, naturally;*
to become a consciously, proudly sexual human being; to open
up my body to my sexuality, so I can get it out of my head,
especially beyond my eyes; to grow from compressed genitality
to reeroticizing my entire body; to recognize that sexuality can't
be localized: its center is the entirety of my body; to relax and let
myself fully experience my sexuality. See Lonnie Barbach's
lovely *For Yourself: The Fulfillment of Female Sexuality* (which
is nearly as valuable for males); Jackie and Jeff Harrigan's
demystifying, amusing *Loving Free*; Mary Jane Scherfey's *The
Nature and Evolution of Female Sexuality*.

92. *To recognize the political significance of my human
sexuality.* We can't divorce the sexual suppression in us from
childhood from the political repression in our culture. The
politics of position in the family bedroom usually project, reflect
themselves in the politics of position in the corporate boardroom
(Ruth Glick). Sexual freedom is an absolute rock-bottom
personal key to human freedom, happiness and political
freedom.

To discover that a taboo is invalid, by experiencing that fact,
is to open a major, never-again-closeable wedge in the door of
authoritarianism. Since our greatest taboos and repressions
center on our sexuality, the sexual revolution may be the most
profound of all: demystifying, reclaiming and reexperiencing
our bodies; ceasing giving away our energy, power, sense of
ourselves, our inner-directedness. Sexual liberation is a key to

human liberation. I should promote and promulgate that everything healthy with respect to the body and sexuality is natural and good.

Sexual liberation and political liberation come hand-in-hand. Spreading information about love, talking about it, is one avenue toward sexual liberation. Another way is to trust my feelings to be sexual—as long as it's all voluntary and no one is hurt.

93. *To reinstate the true natural law*—rather than betraying my nature by conforming it to our old vision's unnatural "natural law."

94. *To give up, outgrow being pompous, arrogant, chauvinistic, paternalistic, maternalistic, mechanistic, materialistic, militaristic*—all of which I'll do by becoming truly self-esteeming.

95. *To recognize the inadequacy of money, wealth, prestige, role, title, technology, the sciences*—to fulfill my inner needs; to outgrow my need for things, drugs, alcohol, power.

96. *To take responsibility for outgrowing my own violence.* If I'm not a warm loving human being, I am the most dangerous, destructive living being on the face of our earth.

97. *To outgrow my need for competition, including with myself.* When I compete with myself, it's my well-being that's the loser. When I compete with you, one of us must lose. The more competing, the more losing, the more we magnify our problems. Loving and such competition are contrary, contradictory.

SELF-INVOLVEMENT

98. *To be/come a loving person, a lover.* Loving is in me naturally, it's my inherent capacity. I ought be able to love any, every person. Instead of the suspicious, guarded, cruel, plotting, plodding creatures familiar to us, we humans ought become aglow with love for one another. The source of our transformation should be our human nature itself. We ought be inspired to place ourselves in harmony with its, our capacity for loving.

99. *To bear in mind that I am always my body, a partner in full loving.* What is friendship, if it isn't love, if it isn't complete love, completely being in love, completely being loved? Where should I draw the line—head, neck, hand, heart, waist, organs, front, back, where?

100. *To challenge "the myth of the quantifiability of love."* I can love more than one person at a time—truly, deeply, sincerely, fully loving in every sense of the word. Love isn't a pie, whose cutting and giving away leaves no more. Love is an artesian pool: no matter how many cups of water I take out, I'm not going to lower the level of my pool. It constantly recharges itself, refills. There's always more I can give away. Love may be even more than that: the more I love, the more I open myself to giving love away, the more love comes bubbling up within me; my supply grows, rather than diminishes. My capacity develops.

101. *To become moral.* I need to grow my inner moral power to match—and to become able to wisely use—our remarkably developed other powers: intellectual, technological, scientific, whatever. Consciousness generates conscience. Conscience resides in consciousness, which resides in my body. Jose Vasconcelos, founder of Mexico's public school system, proposes a theory of epistemology and morality: my body collects the data through my senses; my intellect orders the data; then my emotions do the valuing, choosing what's good and bad, right and wrong for me. Only if every part of me is liberated, fully free and possessed by me, fully-functioning, will I be/come properly valuing, responsible and moral.

102. *To be/come faithful that we can again recognize our reality, face our future, mobilizing ourselves and our enormous talent and good will*—to deal effectively with our social problems; to maintain a sense of optimism about the possibilities of effecting significant social change.

103. *To understand and make sense of my world, to live in it, act on it, creatively, humanly.* Our new vision proposes I am naturally responsible. Naturally I'm responsible for what's happening in our society, for what's gone wrong, for righting it. I'm responsible to recognize and take my proper responsibility for—involve myself with—our world, to protect my interests, my well being, my right to be myself. Responsibility implies activism, acting out my feelings to make all our lives more decent; to believe I am capable of getting what I want, what I seek.

104. *To be/come political, to activate myself, to involve myself in politics;* to be *liberal* about *conserving* my own roots, my human nature; to see to it that our government and institutions become supportive and nurturing of my own further healthy human growth and development.

105. *To develop my own durability system and process.* I need faith and patience and friends—to endure. It's a long time between seed planting and the first sign of growth breaking through the ground, showing.

106. *To become a seed person, a new person, a new consciousness person, a new age person,* a person of tomorrow, a person on the way toward becoming more of a person; to become a full-fledged, fully-conscious, fully-functioning human lover—of myself, of life, of other persons, of our earth.

107. *To recognize that all of my above responsibilities fit together as all my parts fit together;* to recognize, believe, honor and realize the fact that I have the natural capacity, right and responsibility to become one whole, healthy, fully-functioning, compassionate, responsive, active human being. Recall my godson Chris' insight: it's my right and responsibility to direct my unquenchable thirst for knowing inward upon myself, toward knowing myself.

Authentic self-realization of the human being cannot be an isolated enterprise. It must be lived as if every moment, every act—were a moment and act of the absolute—for they are. I'm responsible for taking responsibility for my own hope and faith, innocence and passion, involvement and participation. I simply want to be/come an authentic, growing, passionate human being, fully and appropriately responsive to what's happening in my life and times, society and world, here and now, in this present moment.

108. *To be ready to take on ever new and increasing responsibilities.* As I demystify, heal and grow myself, I'll

recognize further responsibilities to myself.

109. *To recognize that fulfilling my responsibility to grow myself best fulfills my other responsibilities.* My personal searching isn't just a hobby or luxury, some sort of side show or exercise, or just selfish or narcissistic. It's my primary, absolute responsibility. It's the antidote to our macroproblem, the basis for righting things again in our society. It's the frontier at which we humans are. It's the precondition for our survival on our planet. It's how we become able to meet, match and overcome our overwhelming, seemingly intractable social problems.

The survival of our society and the fulfillment and survival of each of us personally aren't inconsistent. They are complementary; they are one and the same. What's good for me is as well good for you. My exercising and fulfilling these responsibilities to myself will work as well to your advantage, serve you well. I'm not (proposing) dropping or copping out. I'm becoming more responsible, more able to be with you and everyone in our society, in a far more caring, healthier way.

All of this naturally leads to my becoming more responsive, taking more responsibility for seeing to it, socially and politically, that such opportunity is provided for all human beings. My taking responsibility for who I am and be/come, my individual struggle for growth and self-fulfillment is my most important contribution to the dynamics of our society, interpersonally and institutionally. The most I have to give is all of myself, all of me, the most fully-developed human being I can grow into. The persistent drive for self-discovery makes people into major thinkers, writers, actors, leaders, driving forces in their age. Our age needs such persons in our midst today. Our society should encourage rather than discourage personal human growth and development.

110. *To recognize that persons and institutions and culture are inextricably interrelated.* Each affects the other, powerfully and profoundly. They constitute a circle, vicious or virtuous, repressive or liberating. The most easily accessed entry point in that circle is in the individual, myself. Neither the government nor any other institution or person can keep me from growing myself more whole. I will start the circle turning, toward myself, toward life, for us all!

projections:
a new human bill
of responsibilities —
to you

> "In a world in which life so perfectly responds to life,
> where flowers mingle with flowers in the wind's eye,
> where the swan is the familiar of all swans, (hu)man
> alone builds his (her) isolation. What a space
> between...(humans)...their spiritual natures create.
> Why should we hate one another? We all live in the
> same cave, we are borne through life on the same
> planet, form the crew of the same ship."
>
> —Antoine de Saint Exupery

The second great ramification and application of our new vision is in respect to you, my fellow human being.

You're primarily responsible for yourself—just as I am primarily responsible for myself. Therefore I'm not primarily responsible *for* you. Yet I do have a significant responsibility *to* you. What have you a right to expect from me?

Since you and I share a common human nature, you have the same human rights I do. I have a responsibility correlative to your rights: I'm responsible to exercise my rights in a manner that doesn't harm you, nor adversely affect your exercising your rights. Naturally you have the same responsibility to me, correlative to my rights.

Our traditional culture instructs us in this regard with "The Golden Rule": "Do unto others as you would have others do unto you." That's appropriate advice. But it's hollow—unless I discover *how* to develop myself to be/come able to live that way toward you. Until now we humans have been more living "Do unto others."

Another traditional culture instruction is more helpful: "Love thy neighbor as thyself." That's my basic responsibility to you—to love you. Since I can only love you insofar as I love myself, that takes me back to my responsibility to myself: to love myself. Only insofar as I *am* myself, will I be/come able to love you.

In fact we're already living that instruction. Currently we love our neighbors the way we love ourselves. Our problem is that we don't love ourselves well. Hence we don't love our neighbors well either. Growing myself into a loving person isn't narcissistic. It's rather the precise precondition for my carrying out my basic responsibility to you. My father taught me: "I can't give what I haven't got." My experience of myself provides me the vision of human nature and potential I carry into all my relationships with you—interpersonal and institutional. My self-respect naturally brings me to respect you, your person and your rights. The more grown I am, the more of me there is to be present with and for you, in a healthy, supportive and liberating, rather than a dependency-maintaining way.

As noted earlier, a belief system must be practiced—not merely preached—to be authentically mine; otherwise I'm a hypocrite. If I preach "love my neighbor," then compete with you, stand by fat while you are starving, observe from my warmed house while you are homeless in our cold streets—I'm not fulfilling my responsibility to you. I'm then responsible to ask myself: "how come?" And I'm responsible to attend to closing the gap between my theory and my practice toward you, my fellow human being.

My actions are the expression of my values,
which come out of my awareness,
which is me—I.
They are the projection and expression of who I am.
I must take responsibility for who I am,
as a way of changing my awareness,

as the way to change my values,
to enable me to act more responsibly toward you.

Specifically, I believe I have at least the following responsibilities to you personally:

1. *To faithfully carry and live my liberating vision into the entirety of my relationship with you.*

2. *To recognize you are my brother/sister,* a fellow member of our human family; to be your friend, in weather foul or fair.

3. *To recognize we share a common human nature;* to assume your natural ways, desires, impulses, needs, wants, fears, hopes and aspirations—are the same as mine.

4. *To tell you who I am;* to disclose to you my basic vision, beliefs and values; to disclose myself to you, let you know me fully. When I know myself wholly, I'll refuse *not* to be known by you. Only then will I seek to know you fully.

5. *To look you in the eye, to let you see me, to let myself be seen by you.*

6. *To listen to you tell me who you are;* to hear you—a function of my capacity to listen to and hear myself; to listen to and observe you carefully and caringly, giving you my attention while we're together; to listen attentively, rather than using the time you're talking for thinking up what I'm going to say when it's my turn to talk.

7. *To be with you in a way that invites, occasions your opening, discovering and disclosing more of who you are.*

8. *To do my share to provide you a healthy human environment*—in which you can live, grow and realize yourself as a person. We talk much today about our need to clean up our polluted external, earthly environment. There's worse pollution—psychological—that adversely affects your life and being (Ram Dass). We humans are far more delicate (not fragile) beings than we yet know. I profoundly affect your being

and growth by the character of my presence. I'm responsible to clean up your human environment as provided by my presence. My capacity for doing that depends upon my cleaning up my own internal pollution, the unnecessary structures within my own being.

9. *To not underestimate you, your natural capacity;* to have appropriate ambition for you: that you be/come wholly yourself: self-aware, whole, free, innocent, trusting, self-esteeming, beautiful; to call your attention to yourself; to challenge you to realize all your potential; to be your loving critic, calling to your attention wherein you're not yet realizing your potential, being your fully natural, innocent, loving self.

10. *To challenge your taken-for-granted views of yourself and life and everything.*

11. *To enable you to recognize yourself,* your right to become yourself, your capacity to do so, to liberate yourself.

12. *To be present with you in a way that occasions your feeling fully trusted and safe*—so you can trust, relax and let go into being exactly, fully, spontaneously who you are; to accept you so totally that being with me is, for you, like coming home.

13. *To trust you.* Insofar as I trust myself, I'll not be worried about being invaded, overwhelmed by you. I'll trust you more readily.

14. *To accept you fully,* just as you are, no matter how different we may be. Accepting differences in other persons is a function of accepting myself: if I know and accept who I am, I won't *need* you to be like me, to make me feel okay.

15. *To love and nurture you.*

16. *To offer my love to you without conditions.* I'll do that to the extent I've overcome my own conditioning, my own fear of being loved, and of loving.

17. *To demonstrate my love for you.* It's not enough to say "I

love you." I ought express it visibly, by my presence, especially by touching you.

18. *To let you know you're important to me.* Friend Steve Wood, then 16, told me he tells a person s/he appeared in his dreams—letting them know they're so important to him, they're alive within him.

19. *To be present with you with a warmth that will nurture you*—not with a whip to beat you into shape, nor with a chisel to shape you subtly—thus enabling you to feel safe, relax your character armor, open up, melt down your rough edges, grow yourself your own nature's way.

20. *To be clear about what I want from you*—in our personal relationship.

21. *To be always authentic and honest with you.*

22. *To (learn how to) communicate directly with you;* to say to you directly what I want from you, in our personal relationship—trusting you to be able to take care of yourself, to respond as suits you.

23. *To play no role with you;* to be present as a person to you, being very personal. I play a role when I won't play as a person with you.

24. *To be non-chauvinistic toward you;* to not assume I know better than you what's best for you.

25. *To recognize your individuality, to not stereotype you.* Labels ("nigger," "politician," "faggot," "liberal," "Republican") are a head trip. It's my intellect that analyzes, separates, compartmentalizes. Labels are usually an excuse for avoiding, not encountering you as a person. If I'm careful to lift your masks, look beneath your surfaces, I'll find that we're the same inside.

26. *To respect your right to be yourself.*

27. *To respect your right to think for yourself, believe as you want, say what you believe, disagree with what I'm believing and saying.*

28. *To respect your right to feel as you choose, to express your emotions forthrightly*—so long as you don't harm any other person, including me.

29. *To respect your right to use your body and sexuality as you want*—so long as you don't harm any other person, including me.

30. *To not expect you to be always the same,* even the same as last time we were together; to respect your growing, even occasion it, even expecting you each time to be more grown, different—on account of our last being together.

31. *To respect your space, to not smother you.*

32. *To not perpetuate your dependency upon me;* to be clear, direct, strong and gentle in resisting your deficient, needy, power-play, manipulative efforts toward getting me to act, to keep on taking care of you—supplanting, forestalling your taking responsibility for taking care of yourself.

33. *To never try to plant flags on you, colonize you, own you, possess you, manipulate you, use you.*

34. *To not mystify, awe, intimidate you.*

35. *To not use my power over you—but to utilize my power to empower you.* I best do that by occasioning your changing and expanding your sense of yourself, your self esteem; you'll then expand your sense of your natural right to power for yourself. I best facilitate your self esteem by loving you.

36. *To be enough self-assured that I don't find my identity in my ideology—so I don't need you to believe like and agree with me;* so I don't need to judge your belief, so I can be fully present with you—listening to you, hearing you, sharing your experience, your belief system—without having to judge or interrupt you,

even by my nonverbal expressions (especially facial).

37. *To enable you to recognize and unlock your own locks.* The most wonderful gift I can give you is to contribute toward your expanded acceptance and knowledge of yourself.

38. *To become a psychedelic person, turn you on to yourself, reach for and evoke the spark within you.*

39. *To not be silent in the face of injustice to you.* To so be silent is to be accomplice in that injustice.

40. *To not compete with you.* Most religions instruct me to love you, my neighbor, even if you're my enemy. That leaves no room for competition in our relationship.

41. *To cause you to confront your true state of satisfaction with your life*—even though it may involve your feeling your pain. I don't intend to *create* suffering for you—though I may unveil its presence in your life. I'll ask you to look honestly at your own behavior, assess its personal costs to you. I'll not let you be beguiled by society's typical justifications: "That's the way life is," "You can't have it any better," "Someone else knows better than you what's good for you, how you ought to be." It's up to you.

42. *To not be defensive and guarded with you*—but instead to convey the message that I trust you.

43. *To be gentle—rather than violent—toward you.*

44. *To not play the "retaliation game"*; to not strike back at you for how you treated me, nor for how someone else did. Instead of blaming or dumping my anger and resentment, to take responsibility for outgrowing it myself.

45. *To include you in, never exclude you from my pondering of any decision I'm going to make that will affect you.*

46. *To teach you everything I know of import,* at the lowest dollar price possible, especially that which empowers you,

especially enabling you to carry on by yourself, no longer needing me.

47. *To (be willing to) risk our relationship, by being always open, authentic and self-disclosing.*

48. *Upon meeting you, to ask you more than "What do you do?"* Instead, to ask you at least *"How are you?"* And to mean it, and to care about and listen to your answer. A certain capitol elevator operator routinely said "Good morning. How are you?" To the reply she routinely responded, "That's nice." One morning, when she asked, I was in an especially depressed mood. I answered "Not very well." She responded, "That's nice." I felt worse. The next time she asked and I was feeling down, I responded very, very slowly: "I'm . . . not . . . feeling . . very . . . well . . . today." She responded, "That's — Oh, I'm sorry." From then on she listened for my response.

Even further, on meeting you, to ask *"Who are you?"* Provided I truly want to know, and that I'm willing to be asked, and answer, that same question.

49. *To challenge you to engage in politics,* to involve yourself to see to it that your world becomes a more nurturing environment for your continuing human growth and development; to lead you to that opening of your self-awareness in which any real politics involving yourself must be grounded. I best accomplish this by adding to your self esteem, by the quality of my presence. With enhanced self esteem, you'll be more aware of your rights, less intimidated by those who are constraining you, more insistent on acting to improve your situation.

50. *To measure carefully my words to you*—not to edit what's going on within me, but to be as sure as I can that my words present you what's happening within me, as precisely as I know how; to be sure I say what I mean, and I mean what I say.

51. *Altogether, to provide you a faithful, attractive, intriguing, invigorating, empowering model of healthy humanness.*

In my life I accept these responsibilities to you personally.

And I live them as best as my current state of my own development permits. I'm not yet grown enough personally to fulfill them perfectly. And I'm aware of several situations that cause me special difficulty or dilemma. I want to share them with you—as part of my own growth process.

First, for example: if I experience you being irresponsible, what do I do? I remember that your irresponsibility comes from our old culture, just as mine does—and that beneath that, you (as I) are naturally responsible. I am not responsible *for* you, but I am responsible *to* you—to recognize your state of readiness for taking full charge of your self and your life. I am responsible to be with you in a way that occasions your growing more responsible. I do that best by demonstrating to you a responsible way of being. In the meantime, I should neither abandon nor smother you, but be present with you in a way just beyond your current reach of responsibility, so that you will gradually stretch and grow your own responsibility. Especially if I'm in a position of authority (e.g. parent, teacher, clergyperson, governing person, law enforcement person) I'm responsible for facilitating the transfer of authority and responsibility from me to you. I should be careful in accepting power over you, especially when you offer it to me. That often denies you the discovery of your own capacity and the further development of your own responsibility.

Second, what if you're afraid of me? I respect your fear. It's not my fault that you're afraid of me. But I should provide you a safe place in which to experience your fear. I'll suggest that what you're afraid of in me is in you instead.

Third, what if you defer to me, placing me above you, yourself below me? I have especial trouble here. I get nasty, like a dog which barks and bites if s/he senses fear. I need to search out my own fear, underneath my nastiness—so I can recognize your deference is fear, also.

Fourth, what if you're angry and attribute it to me? Anger should not be lightly dismissed. It's not irrational. It has its roots and reasons. I should be open, not be defensive, and try to hear the message within your anger. Anger is often the second feeling, put up to cover the first feeling, hurt or fear (Will Schutz). To return your anger will only cause you to put up your defenses. In that posture, armed, there's no way you can be persuaded my intentions are peaceful, that you ought trust me, let me in. If what I hear in your anger rings true, relates to my behavior, I should take responsibility. I should acknowledge it and attend to outgrowing my angering behavior.

If I believe your anger doesn't truly relate to my behavior, and that you're inappropriately dumping your anger on me, I ought tell you that. I should do that in a clear and gentle way that conveys to you that I'm rejecting your anger, not rejecting you. At times I get into my own anger in return, and call it you. I need to work on this, for myself.

Fifth, what if I have something unpleasant to tell you? My responsibility is to be utterly honest with you. I ought not hold back. That puts a barrier up between us, blocks our relationship.

I ought immediately tell you anything unpleasant I'm feeling between us. Otherwise it'll just build up, and finally explode, cascading out. I should always be gentle in telling you whatever's unpleasant. Sometime ago I realized I'd developed a habit. Whenever I'm about to tell you something you won't like hearing ("no" to a request, something uncomplimentary), without thinking I first reach out, placing my hand on your arm, for reassurance, for us both.

I ought especially be sure to tell you that unpleasant matter first, before I say it to anyone else. If I've somehow first said it to someone else, I should immediately come tell you, so that you hear about my having done that, first from me.

If something unpleasant stands between us, let's deal with it directly.

Sixth, what if your culture is negative about human nature, and has conditioned you to think and feel badly about yourself? I'm responsible to accept your entirety, including your chosen culture and belief. With our expanded vision, I respect you more than your culture does. I care about you, and I don't want to see you demeaning, denying and repressing yourself. I put you before your acculturation.

I'll confront you with this issue. I'll tell you "I'm saddened. I don't experience you that negative way. Are you sure you feel that way about yourself?"

I experience this dilemma with my Chicana friend Lorenza Schmidt. Her Mexican-American/Catholic culture conditioned her to believe she was not good internally. Her Anglo schooling changed her name to Lorraine, conditioned her to believe her Mexican-American culture was not good. She's still not sure of her own goodness. But I am. It's fun to tease her about this dilemma—for both of us. I recognize it's a condition true for all of us, including myself. We're all still constrained somewhat by our old culture.

Seventh, how do I relate to you if you speak a negative outlook on life, if you're holding and living the vision contrary to mine? We see everything contrarily, even ourselves and each other. Our differences are foundational and functional—and irreconcilable. All that's reconcilable is ourselves. How do we get ourselves together? How do we engage in a loving relationship?

In the presence of such a person (commonly called a "cynic"), I have trouble. I find myself feeling threatened, even poisoned. My system tightens, tending toward protection and withdrawal. I need to recognize that's *my* problem, *my* responsibility. I need to struggle with my own negativity, my own insecurity—free myself to be with you in a loving, reconciling way.

Then I can recognize your cynicism as your protection device, on account of your fear of yourself. Then I can be with you in a positive and accepting way, reassuring you, enabling you to feel safer, fear less, become more positive and, open. That's the simplest, fairest way I can enable you to expand your experience of yourself, then your vision of yourself. That's the basis of our reconciliation.

Eighth, and related—what do I do when we experience and perceive differently, even contrarily? Perhaps you and I are in exactly the same geographic place, in the same moment in time, observing the same event—and we see and interpret it differently. Sometimes when I conclude a speech, the audience has some combination of the following reactions:

a. Some persons nodding, grinning, applauding, even standing to do so;
b. Others sitting glum and hostile;
c. Others inert, believing I've said nothing more than glittering generalities;
d. Others believing I've spoken to the core of our problems;
e. Others saying "Wonderful," then by their next action contradicting my message.

For example: In a recent speech in Southern California, I recited all the difficulties occurring in the Capitol regarding school finance legislation. I proposed we needed to acknowledge them in order to overcome them and succeed. One man heard my presentation as utterly bleak, two women heard it as optimistic.

Again, I owe it to you and myself, to be honest. I ought not hold anything from you. I believe the best hope for overcoming our difference is to disclose it to you. I'll tell you "I'm not happy about this, but I want to tell you we have an enormous difference. I hope that by getting it in the open between us, we can resolve it, it won't stand in the way of our relationship." Sometimes that works.

Sometimes though, you respond: "What do you mean? We don't have any difference at all" or "It's not a significant difference, why worry about it?" I find myself saying "Oh." You shrug off our "difference" as unimportant, while I believe it crucial. I find this especially exasperating, for I know no way to continue our verbal discourse, since you don't think there's anything to talk about. Again, I ought be patient. I should take responsibility for myself—and my need to resolve every difference, with every other human being—right now.

I should recognize that our differences in perception have roots and reasons. I should avoid rejecting you, instead engage you lovingly. I should recognize that how each of us perceives is a matter of projection, of our respective internal states of being. The most we can do is engage ourselves, at that foundational level.

Ninth, what do I do if I experience you as being turned off to life. I sense that you're so remote, so detached from yourself, that a direct appeal strikes almost no accord? I'm appealing to some long lost, believed-to-be-present, all-but-still presence within you. I'm speaking to your unconscious, where you've gone to sleep.

It's like wondering whether there's life in our universe, in outer space. On the hope there's life out there, we bounce radar signals off distant objects, hoping for the slightest response, more than an echo bouncing back, to signal life. Here it's the same. I believe there's (common) life in our universes of inner space. I'm hoping to discover there's a subject in there. How can I make contact with you, if you are out of contact with yourself? Unwilling to forego my hope, determined to try, I put out positive signals. My most availing message is a simple "Hello, are you in there? Yoo hoo—can you hear me? I'm out here, a common kindred person. It's safe to come out. Let me know you're in there.''

I ought do my best, be my best—enable you to feel safe, comfortable, relax, open up, lower your defenses, let me in. I'm a friend, come to reassure you, to excite and inspire you. I'm hoping to facilitate your coming out. I offer an alternative world view. If adhered to, it leads to greater love, joy, health, satisfaction and fulfillment—for us both.

Tenth, is it fair to preserve your innocence, in a world which presumes you guilty? Will you be able to cope with our cold, cruel world? (Recall the story of my friend Mary Sweeney and her non-fighting son.)

I'm responsible to not be naive about the current state of our world. But if I love you, I can't simply prepare you to succumb to it. Rather I should trust that you and your innocence can overcome our world, rather than the contrary. I should support you as you make your way through it. I'm responsible to grow myself more, so I can love you better, further empower you and your innocence. Then you'll convert our world, rather than succumb to it.

Eleventh, what if you're needing me to be with you, ratify you, to make you feel okay? This poses a theoretical problem. If I simply fill your need, I'll postpone your developing your own responsibility for ratifying yourself. I also find this a practical problem. For whatever reason deriving from my earlier experience, I am extremely sensitive in this situation. Sometimes even before I consciously recognize what's going on, I find my system tightening in the presence of a person who is so needy. I automatically retreat. All I so far know to do in this situation is to immediately tell you what I'm experiencing, how I'm resisting, and keep on trying to grow myself more, to outgrow my condition.

Twelfth, what if you're wanting to be with me, and I'm not finding myself feeling I want to be with you? This occurs increasingly as I meet more persons and get busier. I know no easy, comfortable, satisfactory solution. I try to make *some* time for being with you, trust you'll understand my not having more time to spend, and hope you'll not take my choice personally, as a rejection of you.

These are difficult and touchy matters. I hope that if you're ever experiencing yourself in these difficult ways in my presence, you'll do your best to be with me in these supportive and liberating ways.

That's how I see my responsibility to you personally.

Having reviewed my rights and yours,
my responsibilities and yours,
how does our Liberating Vision
apply to our personal relationship?
How should we be *with* each other, together?

chapter 20

reciprocal reflections: responsibilities to and for each other

> *"The moment we cease to hold each other, the moment we break faith with one another, the sea engulfs us and the light goes out."*
> —James Baldwin

> *"Love...consists in this, that two solitudes protect and border and salute each other."*
> —Maria Rilke

> *"When centers meet, it is called love."*
> —Bhagwan Shree Rajneesh

Who are we to each other?
How are we with each other?

As humankind is our social frontier, so are you and I our human frontier. We are co-responsible for our co-evolution—affecting, whether we like it or not, for better or worse, each other's continuing evolution as a person. Intrapersonal, interpersonal, societal and human evolution are mutually and reciprocally interconnected and reinforcing. Let's fully commit ourselves to our progress and realization.

As we are appropriately concerned
about our brothers and sisters
in the materially underdeveloped nations of our world—
let's recognize
we human beings are underdeveloped.
Let's take responsibility
for developing the people of our world,
beginning with ourselves.

Let's recognize each other as fellow members,
brothers and sisters of the same one human family.
Let's recognize our bond,
a basic empathy, an ecstatic joy
as each of us discovers in the other
a sameness meaning "I'm not alone here."

Let's have a truthful relationship.
Let's always be true to ourselves and each other.
Each time I'm not true,
I raise a barrier within me.
It's a barrier between us.
There's never reason
to lie to each other.
Our reason for being together
is to enable each other
to become more true.

Let's let ourselves come together in openness and love.
Let's not carry our protective roles and titles into our
relationship.
Let's shed them and relate instead as persons,
friends, fellow searchers, pilgrims, together.
Let's help each other find our way, and ourselves.

Let's care about each other
as members of one family.

We're not responsible *for* each other, but we ought naturally
feel responsive *to* each other. Let's immediately identify with
each other. Let's recognize our humanness and ourselves in
each other. Let's be open to each other's suffering, loving,
laughing, hurting, needing. If you're without food, I'll feel your

hunger; without shelter, I'll feel your homelessness; without health, I'll feel your illness; without friends, I'll feel your loneliness; if you're not fully liberated, I'll feel your repression. If I don't naturally feel so, I owe it to myself and you to wonder "Why?" I should attend to outgrowing that "Why?" within me, so I become more humanly responsive to you. If we're enough open and close to each other, we'll be unable to tell whose experience it is. Nor will it matter.

Let's attend to our continuing liberation and growth: our self-actualization, community feeling and love. These ought be matters of morality, desire, goal, commitment and passion for each of us.

It's not enough to pray on weekends about loving our neighbor and pledge our flag on weekdays about "liberty and justice for all." It's not enough to exert ourselves for justice for peoples oppressed in Viet Nam, in our ghettos, or on our farms. That's right and good and holy, but we owe more to ourselves and each other: No more warring against our *nature*; no more warring against our *neighbors*—here at home, every day. Let's operationalize our ideals in our everyday lives. Let's discover how we can grow ourselves to be/come able to live our ideals. Let's become more intelligent, caring, loving and gentle with ourselves and each other.

We've given up much of our lives to persons and institutions which refused us permission to be ourselves. Let's give each other permission to be ourselves with each other. Let's give each other encouragement to become ourselves. Let's give ourselves permission to change, grow, move and stretch. Let's take the risk—to become risk-takers. Let's search together for the roots of our fears—of ourselves, of each other, of life, freedom, truth and love.

Our dialogue should not and need not be shallow. We can go beyond our surface differences, to open and show each other our common depths, our humanness. The more we do that, the less we'll notice our differences. Beneath the ideology of our politics, the faith of our differing religions, the internalized conditioning of our diverse cultures, the external color of our skins, the difference in our sexual organs—we'll find we have a common human nature.

We deepen our dialogue best
by opening and deepening ourselves
in each other's presence.
Let's open ourselves
to our common ground of being,
our common human nature.

Let's believe in our inherent trustworthiness.
Let's trust each other.
Let's trust enough to drop our roles, masks and defenses.
Let's experience each other naturally.
As we trust each other, trust will turn to love.
It'll prove contagious. Let's start an epidemic.

My sense of boundaries between us
derives from my experiencing apprehension in your presence.
When I'm feeling safe in your presence,
I'm not conscious of there being any boundary between us.

As we've split ourselves, we split from each other. Let's struggle to overcome our separateness. Let's liberate ourselves from the structures—internal and external—that imprison us alike. Let's un-spoil each other—by "spoiling" each other with a healthy human environment.

Let's provide each other the best possible environment for our human growth and development. Let's be with each other in invigorating rather than violating ways. Our lives are gifts of nature. Let's make the most of our gifts. Let's make the most of our lives. Let's make the most of our nature. Humanness evolves when naturalness is nurtured—through relationships providing loving, caring, trusting, touching. Rather than relating our "interlocking neuroses," let's be interdependent with each other, cherishing each other's independence. Let's recognize that each of us may not get everything we want from any one other person. Let's be bound together enough for loving support, yet loosely enough for us each to pursue ourselves, our own ways.

If we're open and growing more whole,
we'll be present with and for each other in the most healthy way.

Sharing makes our joy more joyful, our pain more bearable.
Let's recognize, believe in, open up and reveal ourselves to each other.
Let's not be afraid of ourselves, or of each other.
Let's not fear whatever may happen between us in our relationship.
Let's not be afraid to explore everything, discuss everything—even our differences. True friendship is based on affiliation and affection, agreement or not.

Let's give ourselves more credit. Let's not think so little of ourselves, that we can't get along. Let's open ourselves and relate intimately. Let's challenge the old saying "We shouldn't discuss religion or politics with friends." I opened a 1962 letter urging friends to support the re-election of Governor Pat Brown, with that saying. Former classmate IBM engineer Jack Kuehler wrote back: "You're right, you shouldn't discuss politics with friends. You lose friends that way. P.S. There's another old saying: 'You're only a Democrat until your income rises above $10,000 a year!' Apparently you aren't doing well as a lawyer. P.P.S. Give me a call, let's have a beer." A mutual friend, expecting fireworks, invited Jack and me to dinner one evening, without telling each the other was invited. Instead of fireworks, Jack and I became fond friends, and worked together politically to elect a city councilman. We *can* discuss politics with friends.
Let's discuss everything with each other—politics and religion, vision and values—and especially ourselves, our own growth and development, our own experiencing, our hopes and fears, our feelings and our bodies, our loving and our sexuality, our satisfactions and frustrations.
We talk much today about discovering how to communicate with great apes and dolphins. Let's focus our attention on discovering how we humans can communicate with each other!
Let's learn (it's okay) to be silent together. Too often, to cover our discomfort, we talk and talk and talk—to assure ourselves everything's okay. Let's instead assume our being together is positive, unless otherwise stated. And if we're uncomfortable, let's confront and disclose our discomfort, and outgrow it.
Let's open and explore the depths of our feelings, fully respecting each other's current limits and fright. Let's provide each other reassurance.

Let's work together with our bodies. We have little awareness of their realm. Let's discover their potential. Let's hold each other reassuringly, enabling each other to let go more. When you hold me and I let go more—I inspire more, inhale more, get exhilarated, dizzy, even giddy. I'll get nervous, even laugh to cover it—as I think of what more there is to experience. How readily I transfer my energy to my head, translate it into "safe thoughts."

Let's acknowledge we are not disembodied spirits. We have and are our bodies. So long as we are in our bodies, we'll each have our sexuality with us at all times, in every place and relationship. If we let our selves open, love and flow freely, our bodies may open as well. We need not do anything about that, except not pretend or be naive. We ought acknowledge our full selves.

Let's demystify and affirm our sexuality. "Sex" is simply what happens between two personalities who choose to let bodies touch, be touched in that way. Sexuality is a deep and wonderful display of trust!

Let's not perpetrate our hostility and anger, taking it out on each other. Let's each take responsibility for it in ourselves, work it out within us, in each other's presence. Let's recognize it as cover for our fears. Let's confront our fears, outgrow our anger—become our real gentle and tender selves. Let's turn ourselves from war to making love. Instead of the "battle between the sexes," we should love.

Let's commit ourselves to moral conscience. Let's quit competing in our traditional either/or, win/lose model. Let's quit believing that either you *or* I get the goodies, the other be damned. We, the human race, should outgrow our rat race. Let's begin loving in our new vision's both/and, win/win model, you *and* I together. There's more than enough "goodies" for all of us.

Another personal anecdote: I have another young friend, John—Christopher's older brother. About five years ago, when John was eight years old, I was visiting one Sunday with his mother Joni and her friend. John came into the room and interrupted our conversation. He told us he wanted to ask our opinion "on a serious question." He told us he had an idea about the answer, but wanted our assistance anyway. He asked: "Where did we humans come from?"

I made a wisecrack and was promptly, properly chastized by John: "This matter is too serious for joking." We settled seriously into addressing his question. Each of us three adults told all we knew about his question—which didn't take long. Then John said: "Well, let me tell you my theory. Once there was a female fish. A male fish got her pregnant. The other male fish got angry with her, chased her all the way up onto the beach. Not knowing how to breathe or live there, she gasped and died. The baby fish were ready to be born. Since they *had* to breathe in order to live there, they simply learned how to. That's how we got onto the land."

That's a marvelous metaphor for our times. We're coming up out of our own depths and darkness, opening ourselves up, having to learn how to breathe, how to be, in our new world, our new dimension. No less, just like those baby fish, we humans need to learn how to breathe, to grow ourselves—if we are to survive. Our current transformation is as momentous as that earlier one. We're changing ourselves into a totally new dimension of our humanness.

There's more to my story. For the next four days all John could talk about was "Where'd we come from? How'd we get here?" The fifth day John turned to his mother, with his large serious eyes and said: "That isn't really what I want to know. What I really want to ask you is: ' 'What's it all about? What's the purpose of life?' ''

Joni replied, in the year's understatement: "John, you ask very tough questions." After some thought, she continued, "Well, what I think it's all about is opening up, learning how to be a person and learning how to love." On hearing that, John turned to his mother, tears rising in his eyes, and said, "Do you know how tough it is to do that? Sometimes I try so hard, it hurts so much, I just want to lie down and die."

There's little hope for a society where it's painful for anyone, especially a child, to be an open, loving person. That's why we're changing our society. We have so evolved ourselves, we're unwilling to continue in this way. It's a hopeful sign that such questions are being raised by children, respected and responded to by their parents. We should encourage such engagement—amongst all of us, beginning with you and me. There's great hope for our survival, even for our thriving!

Friend Marc Christensen wrote of our relationship, in a way

that well describes our responsibilities, to and for each other:

"There runs a friendship true and deep
like hidden caverns beneath the earth.
There need be only a candle's flicker
to reveal more beauty than all the sun.

The path through these caverns is seldom straight,
more often does darkness prevail; but if
you'll walk beside me, together will
we go on a rarely traveled road." (April 20, 1968)

"Maybe it's his Portuguese blood that
Makes him sail his ship of life
In exploration much as Magellan
Did sail around the world.
Searching, looking, trying to discover
Something no other has discovered
For the beauty alone—and
The beauty to be shared with others.

No matter, I sail with him—
Also searching. The wind that
Fills his sails also catches mine
And we journey together." (January 14, 1968)

joint projections: responsibilities for our human institutions

> *"That's what's needed, don't you see, that; nothing else matters half so much...to reassure one another, to answer each other. Perhaps only you can listen to me and not laugh. Everyone has inside himself...what shall I call it...a piece of good news. Everyone is a very great and important character. Yes, that's what we have to tell them. Everyman must be persuaded, even if he's in rags, that he is immensely, immensely important. Everyone must respect him and make him respect himself, too. They must listen to him attentively...don't stand on top of him, don't stand in his light, but look at him with gentleness, deference, give him great, great hopes, he needs them, especially if he's young...spoil him. Yes, make him grow proud."*
>
> —Ugo Betti

Our human revolution logically has significant consequences for our society. Our liberating vision provides us new institutional responsibilities.

We may begin by asking ourselves: Why do we create and maintain institutions? What is their mission? What is their function? What do we expect from them?

The purpose of society is to enable every human being to fully realize his/her own potential. There's a spark of divinity in every person. Let's nurture it to its fullest realization.

The function of institutions has been to manage the relationships between and among persons in our society, where we believed we could not adequately manage that ourselves. The purpose of any *human* institution ought be more: *human liberation*—to provide environments for the healthy growth and development of human beings. Our institutions ought facilitate our growth toward self-realization, toward our becoming whole, healthy, fully-functioning humans. That's the mission of every human institution—home and family, church and religion, school and education, government and politics, and all others. These responsibilities are especially binding upon institutions in which other humans are involuntarily confined—schools, prisons, mental hospitals. We have a special responsibility to make that commitment and confinement experience an occasion for growth and healing.

Our institutions ought relate to us as the innocent and independent beings that we are. We should operate them so that they enable us to outgrow our dependency on and need for that institution and all institutions. An institution should support and stretch us—lovingly—to become fully grown, willing and able to accept our own freedom and responsibility in determining our own future. Then we'll all become able to responsibly exercise our human rights.

The world we inhabit is mostly a social construction: a set of institutions and rules not inherent in nature, but person-made. These systems have direct consequences upon our well-being. Our institutions aren't abstract. Their ways of operating become a concrete reality that profoundly affects us, our nature and our being. The choice of process—to fulfill the purpose of an institution—depends upon the vision and assumptions we carry about being human. Institutions operate precisely out of the images we intend for them. What do we truly believe about ourselves, about our human nature and potential? What do we have to work with? Are we human beings sinners by nature—or are we innocent? Is our human condition to be trusted—or is our human nature needing to be conditioned?

We need to explore the underlying mechanisms of social control and programming. Our traditional society maintains its hierarchy by altering persons early in life, internalizing morality so that ideology replaces biology as our motivating base. From birth we are conditioned to deny and distrust our own experiencing. Our traditional patriarchal family is the workshop which implants such guilt and alienation into us that we humans remain forever after outer-directed, docile, submissive to authority, incapable of sensing what's good for ourselves, even what we want. And if we do, we're often too frightened to act to get it.

In addition, a new vision institution ought help prepare, enable persons to lead moral lives. Let's admit it: our institutions now provide a subtle kind of personal and psychological, moral and political instruction—which profoundly affects our character development. Let's make it positive. We entrust ourselves to institutions for our growth. Let's make them positive.

We could all agree on what we desire: family, safety, peace, love, law and order. We could all agree on what kind of humans we want to grow and develop: healthy and whole, loving and peaceful, free *and* responsible, competent and productive, fully-functioning human beings able to lead fulfilling lives.

But how about our means? It's the *process* that makes the difference, that makes "the product." And it's the process that usually accounts for our differences and controversies. The fundamental question of our times is: "How do we grow healthy human beings?" That's the major controversy confronting and dividing us today. We are in agreement on goals, but we do not agree on how we should realize our goals.

Selecting the process for answering our fundamental question depends upon our basic assumption about our human nature. As our visions differ, our theory, practice and processes will differ. Individual and cultural beliefs about our human nature and potential have a profound effect upon our growth and development. They result in designs for institutions which are either life-enhancing and liberating—or life-denying and repressing. From those designs we create, manage and operate our institutions. If we believe human nature is negative, we'll believe that human "growth and development" is best realized through control. We'll operate our institutions for repression. If we believe human nature is positive, we'll believe human growth and development is best realized through nurturance. We'll operate our institutions for liberation.

The issue was clearly framed by friend Alex Sherriffs, former University of California psychology professor, then educational adviser to Governor Ronald Reagan. We met when I was appointed chairman of the Legislature's Joint Committee studying California's Master Plan for Higher Education. I dropped him a note, saying that most of what I'd heard about him I didn't like, but that since we'd now have to work together, we ought meet each other. His note back mirrored mine. We got together for lunch, liked each other enormously, thereafter lunched together regularly, and worked together enjoyably and effectively. One evening he told me he'd figured out where he and I differed: "You believe humans are born innocent and get ruined by institutions; I believe people are born guilty (he later claimed he said "neutral") and get saved by institutions." I agreed that was our difference. Then I asked him whether how he believed—reflected how he experienced himself. He called that "an unfair question." I call that "the only question."

Our Human Revolution shifts our human growth and development model from negative to positive. Our liberating vision chooses life-affirming processes. There's no more arguing "nature versus nurture." Let's simply nurture our human nature. Let's rebuild our human institutions on new foundations—our positive model of human nature and potential.

The issue is eminently practical. It operates in our everyday lives. A major ongoing controversy throughout our society is about how to grow responsible humans. We agree on that goal. Because of our contrary assumptions about our human nature, we choose opposite processes to achieve it. Our traditional vision—distrusting our natural responsibility—believes it ought protect us against ourselves. It invokes self-denial, repression, intimidation, fear, shame, guilt and conditioning to *make* us humans responsible. I believe it makes people irresponsible. We should stop doing that to ourselves.

Our new vision—trusting our natural responsibility—calls for institutions to foster openness, nurturing, liberation and self-actualization. The word "educate" derives from a Latin root meaning "to lead out of." Let's form our institutions so as to reach for and lead out each other's innocence.

What some persons see as license, anarchy and permissiveness—others see as freedom and self-determination. And all are equally sincere. But only one group can be accurate.

This controversy is current in our public lives. Recently the Creationists asked California's State Board of Education to include their doctrine in the science curriculum in our public schools. The Scientific Evolutionists strenuously objected. I didn't, I welcomed the request: First, because I believe in "free speech," "the truth will make you free," and "the market place of free ideas." I enough trust our natural capacity to ferret out and recognize and choose truth—when we're exposed to all versions of it.

I welcomed the dialogue for a second reason: it brought our basic issue out in the open, made it clear and simple: "What is the origin of us humans? Are we responsible for who we are—or is someone else? Does legitimate authority come from within or without us humans?"

I'd like every human—child and adult—to be exposed to all theories and versions of the truth—about our human nature. I trust we'll each and all eventually—perhaps after trials and errors like my own—come to the truth—that truth which most matches our inner truth, the (f)actual character of our human nature.

This issue is also current in a resurgence of concern about character, moral and values education. Again we share a common concern and goal: the development of moral human beings. Again, on account of our differing foundational vision, we believe in contrary processes to enable persons to be/come moral. Our old vision proposes that we are naturally immoral, that our becoming moral can only occur as the result of fear, guilt, shame—repressing our natural immorality. Our liberating vision proposes instead that our moral growth and development are consistent with, identical to our healthy human growth and development—including our intellectual, physical, emotional and sexual development. What a contrast!

Our liberating vision proposes that we have our own innate natural law. It proposes that consciousness is the seat of conscience. The more consciousness, the more conscience. And conscience is our natural responsibility.

Our choice of our vision is imperative because it is operating, whether we are consciously aware of it or not. We owe it to ourselves—and each other as affected by our institutions—to acknowledge, examine and take responsibility for our choice.

Our choice is crucial because if we guess wrong (none of us truly *knows*), we'll select the wrong institutional processes. All our efforts will be counterproductive. We'll harm whatever we intend to heal. If the infant arrives innocent and we assume it guilty—in need of containment—our efforts will necessarily harm the infant, contain its innocence.

Our choice is profound because it's so much a self-fulfilling, self-perpetuating prophecy. Persons who believe and expect the worst about us humans—act in ways that assure that's what they get from us humans. They'll reproduce the worst of humans. It's the Rosenthal effect, the Pygmalion effect. And we're having that effect, on each other, *whenever* we're together, in each other's presence.

We owe it to ourselves to reevaluate our institutions fully. Are they operating in ways that respect us humans, honor our rights, trust our capacity for exercising them responsibly, facilitate our full development? Or are our institutions disrespecting us, dishonoring our rights, distrusting our capacity for exercising them responsibly, stunting our growth and development?

Too often we operate our institutions (government, universities, social agencies, businesses, workplaces, churches, families) by departments, split up, dealing separately with the alleged parts of ourselves and our behavior, seldom recognizing our interrelationship, and theirs. We should operate our institutions—especially our families, churches, schools, universities and governments—for whole persons. Our universities especially should become the places where our society explores and encourages the *wholeness* of human beings.

We ought ask every institution: Are you relevant to the state of our awakening, growing, expanding human beings? Are you responding to our rising aspirations, our surfacing needs? Are you enabling us to resolve our problems—or are you perpetuating our problems? Are you our problem? Are you speaking ancient tongues to a narrow, dwindling congregation— or are you speaking to our present struggle toward a more human world?

We need to redesign our institutions so that they fit who we humans are becoming. We need to restructure our institutions so that they respond to us new humans, our needs and wants and aspirations. We must shift our institutions from the command/control model to a liberating, individualizing, personalizing model. They must foster our continuing growth as healthy human beings.

We should denounce social institutions which debase and degrade humankind, our humanness. Too often they substitute forms and appearances for our substance, anonymous relationships for human engagement. Let's indict unjust social hierarchies which continually threaten the non-hierarchical wholeness, the independence of the individual person. We each have the ultimate power, we owe it to ourselves—to delegitimize *any* institution that is enslaving us. After all, *it exists to serve us*. We created it for that purpose!

We owe it to ourselves and each other to undertake a radical transformation of our present social and political systems. We should not just tinker with adjustments here and there. That's like "rearranging deck chairs on the Titanic." We ought be bold. We ought act now.

Our modern culture and institutions comprise a single tissue of intertwined evils. They're based on our world macroproblem. No plan of partial, gradual reform from within or outside our system can produce a lasting human remedy. We simply must destroy the systems which destroy persons. We must challenge relationships based on mutual suspicion, distrust and fear. Our immediate and long-range task is to humanize our institutions, to recreate them based upon our liberating vision. We should faithfully carry our humanistic vision into all our institutional operations.

We've already begun to transform our heads and our public policy into our new vision. Our changing personal and public policies toward racism and sexism are examples: They're no longer thought to be acceptable; they're no longer our public policy. Now we face the more difficult, no less essential task. We must transform ourselves. We must transform our hearts and feelings, our values and attitudes, our everyday actions and relations. We've even already accomplished much of that. We need now to allow our human feelings of acceptance and love to slip up into our heads and destroy our old intellectual stereotypes.

Even though our transformation must be radical, we can expect our reform efforts to be gradual. We still need some vertical structure, some hierarchy, to support us in our still vertical, crippled condition. It's our bias that's important. We need to act according to our positive bias—believing in our natural capacity for responsible self-determination. We need to move, lean and risk in that direction. In doing so, let's trust the resilience and durability of our human organism. It's better to err on the side of freedom—than on the side of control.

How do we proceed? How far? How fast? We can't force-feed our capacity for freedom, that'll harm it. Nor can humans be abandoned as we now are—damaged, confused and irresponsible. How can we best evolve people into freedom *and* responsibility? It's been the classic problem faced by every parent from time's beginning. A mother doesn't give her baby matches to play with, nor does she continue holding her 18-year-old son's hand crossing the street. We best enable persons to grow when we are fully present with them—neither too far away (people will founder, we *do* have to hold baby's hand), nor too close for too long (people will smother.).

To "grow up" is to progress from dependency to autonomy. We grow from external, fear-motivated, locked-in control systems—to internalized control systems. We need to grow further—to let go of controls absolutely, allowing our innate self-guiding capacity to operate.

We must recognize that institutions are no more nor less than people, ourselves, the persons who operate them. It's seldom the institution, it's most often the people—who make the difference. Changing the persons who occupy the chart's positions makes more difference than changing the organizational chart.

This gradual shifting of responsibility requires wise persons operating our institutions. They must be able to trust, themselves and the persons they're ministering to. They must be/come able to discern readiness. They must not need to keep power to prove themselves worthwhile.

The persons operating institutions will do so precisely as they operate themselves. The institutions we do—are who we are. It's a self-fulfilling prophecy: we create institutions to perpetuate what we believe. We create the kinds of persons we intend to. Our institutions will be healthy for growing humans only insofar as the persons operating them are healthy, themselves. They must be into their own process of liberating themselves, believing in their own innocence and trustworthiness.

As we grow personally, we'll improve our vision about how far and fast we can let go of others, allowing them to take their own responsibility. We'll improve our sensitivity as to how ready people are for more letting go. We'll then make our institutions sensitive to the precise stage of human development of each person. That's true "individualization"—of our institutions, and of our programs.

Ultimately we all cherish freedom and we all need security. How can our institutions best balance these goals? Probably by gradually giving us a bit more freedom than we're used to. We'll stretch, develop our capacity for exercising that responsibility. In that process we'll also grow a bit more secure. At that point we're ready for more freedom, on and on—until we grow ourselves fully free—and secure.

Our traditional institutions are organized on the wrong premise. Hence persons who have made their way to the top of those institutions have often done so for the wrong reasons, at the expense of their natural selves. Typically they're the most edited, scared, rigid, self-surrendered, repressed persons. As a result, they're usually left with less than good vision. As a result they're usually the most needing to hold power to make themselves feel complete and important. We must discover how to enable our traditional institutional leaders to recognize that our liberating vision is good for them, as well as for us. It lifts from them the burden of responsibility for everybody else. They can look inside themselves for the source of their own importance. They won't any longer need to depend upon others needing them for their own self esteem. They must have the psychological strength to give away power. Then they'll become the best leaders, the healthiest institutional operators.

There's a tremendous responsibility on any person who presumes to hold a position of influence over the life of other human beings. That includes especially parents, clergypersons, educators, politicians, public servants, therapists, physicians, judges, policepersons, business and labor leaders. We're responsible for becoming ever more self-aware, innocent, insightful and trusting. We should not use or manipulate each other. We should not maintain each other's dependency upon ourselves.

Every person operating any institution is responsible for being a growing person him/her self, all the time. That's especially incumbent upon any person operating an institution entrusted with the development of human beings. We must become masters of ourselves, so as not to need to master others. We must lead them in ways that enable them to realize their innate capacities for becoming their own masters, of themselves. We must lead people to themselves. In turn, people will then select leaders who will further that reciprocating liberating process.

The best teacher so turns a student on to his/her own curiosity, s/he no longer needs a teacher for motivation, direction or learning. The best cleric so turns a person on to his/her own innocence, s/he no longer needs a cleric for instruction, absolution or salvation.

Again, we can recognize the convergence of responsibilities. Our responsibility to other humans in operating our institutions—is identical with our responsibilities to each other interpersonally. And those are identical to our responsibilities to ourselves: to grow ourselves fully, wholly human, to become fully-functioning humans, to attend to human growth and development, beginning with our own.

We must be changing and healing our selves and our society—simultaneously. Who I am determines how I'll operate our institutions. How our institutions operate determines who I am. It's a circular, inescapable process. The most direct way to break into that circle is to take responsibility for going inside, changing myself, thereby starting the circle changing.

Whenever and wherever we look for answers, the trail again comes clear. It all begins with ourselves—with myself, and with each of us, with our own human growth and development. I am responsible—from and for the very beginning, *and* for going all the way!

VI.
POLITICS:
FOR
GROWING HUMANS

mainstreaming
our vision

"Only those who have already experienced a revolution within themselves can reach out effectively to help others."

—Malcolm X

"The great, the beautiful and the good things are done only when one is good, beautiful and great."

—Antero de Quental

We've explored our liberating vision, in our individual lives and relationships. It's time we bring this new vision into the mainstream of our society. We need to humanize our government and our politics. We have an answer to propose for the dehumanization and inhumanity of our times. We've got to make our personal policy our public policy.

We're going bankrupt personally, emotionally, socially, politically, morally—precisely because we're destroying persons with our old vision processes. We're going bankrupt fiscally—precisely because we're spending dollars in counterproductive efforts to contain and/or cure our human casualties. We're bankrupting ourselves, dollarwise and humanwise.

Our times require a conscious and continuous reexamination and revision of our society, our institutions and our everyday

lives. We must examine, and reexamine, everything—in
keeping with our new vision, and our expanding humanness.
There's a bigger risk in clinging to our old ways than there is in
changing them. Clearly our old ways no longer work. Clearly
they no longer serve us.

Our unifying social fabric used to be our fear—of want, of
authority and of hell, of the unknown, of death and of life itself.
That's no longer enough. We're outgrowing those fears.
Instead, we find ourselves driven apart—by fear of ourselves
and of each other. We need to outgrow those fears as well.

We need a new positive basis for our unification. Initially it
can be our shared liberating vision. Then it will be our trust—in
ourselves and of each other. Ultimately it will be our love—of
ourselves and of each other. We have to put aside our
differences and recognize we're all the same human family.
We're wasting too much of our energy, time and resources
resisting—ourselves and each other.

It's not enough only to attend to our own growing on
weekends at Esalen or elsewhere. It's only enough to involve
ourselves in our public effort to humanize our society. Since the
turbulence of the 60's, many seem to have abandoned (hope in)
politics, some retreated from it, others sought to transcend it.
Many of us were bright enough to recognize that something's
wrong, but not yet deep and connected enough to recognize
what to do instead. It's now time we bring our expanding selves
back into politics, to infuse and transform it, according to our
new vision, our new selves.

It's no longer enough to keep our deadly machine going. It's
no longer enough to cure our crippled, rehabilitate our harmed,
one by one. It's no longer sufficient to adjust them, so they can
"make it" within our crazy, sickening and deadly system.
That's futile. That's immoral. We need instead to help persons
grow—so that they can recognize their situation, who is friend
and who is foe. We need to enable them to outgrow their fears,
so they can more freely act to change the quality of their lives.
It's only enough to actively involve ourselves in challenging
those crippling forces in our society. We must initiate efforts to
transform our institutions into agencies of nurturance and
liberation.

It's not enough to pray on weekends or pledge the flag on
weekdays. It's not enough to fight against injustice in social

causes, distant or near. We must stop warring against our neighbors. We must cease resisting our loving nature. We must enlist our loving selves in an effort to achieve justice for all humans, in our everyday lives and relationships.

We must come together at our own roots, our common humanness. We have a common goal—to make ourselves and our society more human. These changes are necessary for our society to survive and become decent; they are essential to our own personal meaning and fulfillment.

We owe it to ourselves to figure out why our society isn't working, to actively involve ourselves in making it work. We need to develop a public awareness of the causes of our dehumanizing relationships and conditions. We need to provide leadership that leads us out of our human misery.

Our motivation is more than warding off disaster. We have a *positive* reason for acting: to open up to and enjoy the experience of life. That's possible when we shift to a positive vision of ourselves. We serve ourselves positively by creating a society that nurtures our further human growth and development. We grow ourselves—in a society based on love, rather than on fear.

We should ask ourselves not *whether*—but *when* our vision of universal peace and love and brother/sisterhood is going to come into reality? We might prefer to have lived another time, but we might as well take the time that we have, now. What's keeping us from realizing our universal vision? What can we do about it?

There's no reason things have to stay the way they are. We can change them. What keeps the ideal from becoming real is only our belief that it can't be so. We can change that. It's time—and it's essential—that we generate and legitimize a belief that we humans can be/come more than we now are. We need to verify, through our personal experience, the possibility that we humans can live differently.

Today only the ideal will prove pragmatic—for making things right, in our lives and society, now and for our future. We owe it to ourselves to try.

Let's develop programs to learn how we can get along better with ourselves—less alienation and apathy. Let's create programs to learn how we can get along better with each other—less estrangement, hostility and war. We must become more gentle, caring and intelligent in our dealing with ourselves, each other and our earth—or we may perish.

What will make the difference is whether enough loving persons have the wisdom, compassion and courage to commit themselves to public action. We must speak to the deepest needs of our human brothers and sisters—love, understanding, respect and companionship—in our mutual adventure of growing and learning. We need to begin with ourselves, to grow ourselves into actively loving persons, to overflow our love into the mainstream of our society and our public-policy decision-making.

How do the everyday concerns of our lives connect to the larger issues of human evolution and social transformation? Healing our earth requires an evolutionary transformation in human consciousness, beginning on a personal level. A healthy culture based upon loving and sharing can be achieved only by persons willing and able to invest our values and ourselves in our world. However difficult this struggle may look or be, we humans are, by our nature, each uniquely suited to the task.

We're becoming fascinated by and committed to revitalizing ourselves. We need to become fascinated by and committed to revitalizing our society and institutions. We must acknowledge our personal social responsibility to become more active participants in creating a more human environment. We need a vehicle for such participation, to enable us to discover how we humans can live together better. We ourselves must become that vehicle.

To solve our problems—we need a moral revolution. We need to become life-affirming—supportive of life. We need a moral revolution, not just changing our beliefs and ideas and institutions, but developing our capacity for leading loving lives, and transforming our personal moral values into action.

How do we accomplish our transformation?

We shouldn't wait for some leader or government—anyone or anything else—to do it for us. They can't do it. It's up to us.

There's no better place we can begin than with ourselves. Each of us has the capacity to make a difference in our world. We need to take our responsibility. Self-help is the ideal. That's revolutionary!

Each of us is personally responsible for a public demonstration—a political embodiment—of our vision. I need to become a greater participant in our human family and community—a planetary citizen, a co-evolutionist, a moral agent, an agent of social change.

The best way we can facilitate our transformation of our old vision culture into our new vision culture is by making it safe for persons to do so individually, in their own way, at their own pace. Each of us must make our way ourselves, and each of us should support each other's effort.

In order to assure our humanizing our institutions, it's essential for every person to be/come political. Our inward journey isn't all there is. We must, and we will, manifest our personal transformation in all our relationships, in every aspect of our daily lives. It's only enough if we're living models of our vision—innocent, trusting, open, caring—in every moment of our living with/in our human family. That's our only hope!

If there's a "manifest destiny" for us as a nation, it's to help underdeveloped people, beginning with ourselves. We owe it to ourselves and to each other—to see to it that our public policy is in full support of our personal policy of healthy human growth and development.

We need to recognize that politics is more than what happens in the Capitol, more than what happens in the voting booth. Politics is how wo live our everyday lives and relationships. Political and personal are one and the same. The politics I do is who I am.

Each of us humans should involve ourselves politically. Let's turn off our television sets. Let's become creative *participants* in our human evolution. Let's become cheerleaders for life. We must be/come the prime time actors ourselves. Every night live! This is the big leagues—the leagues for growing persons. And we are all stars!

Let's bring our expanding selves and our liberating vision into our political mainstream, into our public-policy decision-making.

The primary sociopolitical issue of our times is "How do we grow healthy human beings?"
How do we provide an environment in which a human being can most readily, fully grow and develop him/her self—
to be/come self-aware and self-esteeming, self-realizing and self-determining, free *and* responsible,

wholo rather than fractured,
hopeful rather than cynical, open rather than closed,
revealing rather than concealing, gentle rather than violent,
motivated   rather   than   apathetic,
democratic rather than authoritarian,
cooperative rather than competitive, competent and excellent,
ecologically responsible, loving rather than hating,
moral rather than immoral, political rather than apolitical?

Human development must become the primary effort of our society.

Simply said, we need a politics for growing humans.
We need a politics that's about human growth and development.
We need a politics that's appealing to growing, developing humans.

Since our issue is a matter of "How?"—it's essential we come to understand human beings. We must understand
the character of human nature,
the extent of human potential,
the origins of human behavior,
the entire process of human growth and development.

We must go beyond our traditional science. It's proven stupendous in answering the mechanical questions, like "how can we send a rocket to the moon?" It's not answered the more essential question: "Can we humans learn to love each other, to truly believe that every human being is a part of ourselves?"

We need to turn to psychology. Many persons still don't recognize the inherent connection between psychology and politics. Old vision persons even argued there was no connection (See John Bunzel's *Anti-Politics In America*).

But politics is just human relations, nothing more nor less. It's our policy about growing humans. It's choosing the persons who will choose our policy. It's choosing ourselves, who will choose those persons. It's all about us humans.

And our politics will be just like us humans. If I am cynical, my politics will be cynical. If I am idealistic, my politics will be idealistic. If I see life as struggle, I'll expect politics to be that way as well. And I'll act to make it so, again our self-fulfilling prophecy.

The more whole persons we become, the more holistic politics we'll have. The more loving we become, the more we'll have a politics of love. We must legitimize a human politics—by the models and the mottos of our lives.

We've surely got to go beyond our traditional psychologies and their diminished vision of our human nature and potential. Their view is our problem. It's the problem we humans have to solve. Let's look instead toward a politics based on humanistic psychology. Let's wonder about humanizing politics. Let's not let skepticism serve as excuse for our not so acting. Too many persons grimace or grin on hearing the term "humanizing politics." They find it inconceivable.

But if politics isn't humanistic, it's anti-human. If I'm not into humanizing politics, I perpetuate dehumanizing politics. Our skepticism about our liberating vision is likely just our fear of love. We owe it to ourselves to outgrow that fear.

We owe it to ourselves to look at the social and political implications of humanistic psychology. It originated as a psychology of individual health, in an effort to better understand our human behavior, our human growth and development. It grew out of our need for understanding what constitutes and contributes to the development of a healthy human personality. Now we must ask ourselves whether it can grow further, expand beyond its disciplinary boundaries. Can humanistic psychology become an ethic for *social*, as well as *personal* change? Can it contribute to the creation of an art and science of healthy human evolution?

The natural development of humanistic psychology is both a scientific and social necessity and challenge. We need to further our knowledge and experience of our humanness. Humanistic psychology provides the best hope for answering the major issue of our times—"How do we grow healthy human beings?" We need to demonstrate a humanistic alternative to understanding our human behavior and attending to our social problems. Applying humanistic psychology helps us understand what's going and gone wrong in our society, and how we can make it right. It suggests how we humans can right our wrongs, and ourselves.

We owe it to ourselves to explore the implications of humanistic psychology for our society at large, for the future of life on our planet. We must bring it and ourselves to bear on the crises of our lives and times.

Neither major political party has updated its platform to fit who we humans are becoming. Neither is providing hope for solving our most disturbing problems. Neither is providing us what we expanding humans need and want. We have to do it for ourselves. We need to bring our liberating vision to our politics and our public-policy decision-making. We need to humanize our government. We need a humanistic, holistic politics.

Humanistic politics presents an entirely new "third force" in American politics. It represents what our country has *claimed* to be about and, at its best, has been about: personal responsibility, self-reliance and freedom of choice. It represents what our religions have *claimed* to be about, at their best have been about: love. "Inhumanity" and "dehumanization" are the central social problems of our time. Humanistic politics is the best antidote for those.

Humanistic psychology offers a radical political ideal: self-help. It believes that a human being is a naturally responsible, self-sustaining organism. It legitimizes self esteem and self-determination. The best alternative to big government and government control is a self-reliant and cooperative people. Grown self-esteeming humans least need government to be our saving authority figure, doing it for us, perpetuating our dependence. We need to bring this awareness into our mainstream. It's time we bring our human growth movement out of the closet, into the open, into the mainstream of our lives and politics and government.

Humanistic psychologists believe every child is born with innocence, and a million glorious possibilities already inside him/her. Our challenge is to elicit as many of these possibilities as possible, by the creation of a life-climate that will nourish these inner potentials. We need a society that will provide such a positive climate for life. We need institutions that will tell every person, in deeds as well as in words, "How beautiful you are. What a wonder of nature. What a joy it is for me to watch your own special, unique flowering. Let me share in the wonders of your unfolding. Let me support you in your fully realizing yourself."

Our public decisions must become fitting and appropriate for today's humans. They must be based upon our liberating vision. We need to integrate our human growth, liberation and consciousness movements with our political efforts.

To humanize our politics, we must activate ourselves. We best do that by humanizing ourselves, developing ourselves personally. That's how we first overcome our apathy. We exercise our capacity, right and responsibility for involving ourselves in our society and our future.

We must show that humanistic psychology applies to our real lives, that it provides answers for our seemingly intractable social problems. We need to create programs that fully respect both our ideals and our reality. Then we'll not be naive in our search for solutions. Yet we'll move wisely to close the gap between reality and our ideals.

We need to "spread the faith," our faith in us human beings. We must develop a public political consciousness about our liberating vision and its ramifications. We must present our human agenda to our people. We must find ways that are appealing to them, ways that enable them to recognize it as credible, realistic and valuable for them personally. Then they'll activate it for themselves.

We new vision persons must be committed to human(itarian) action. We're faced with a tremendous challenge: to live our stated beliefs. Then we'll be convincing in our efforts to touch and enlist other persons. We must act publicly, through our political processes, to assure our vision manifests throughout our world. Our goal is to develop responsible citizens, capable of creating a real human politics.

As we become active participants in our individual lives—our own growth and development—we'll become more active participants in our social lives—our government and politics. We'll recognize how much they affect our personal lives, and those of persons we most deeply care about. We recognize the political dimension of our personal vision. We recognize the human dimensions of the persons who are politicians. They'll recognize the human dimension of the policies they're deliberating. They'll reexamine and disclose their own vision, make themselves open, available and vulnerable to the people. We'll all do politics and government in a more human way.

Our personal searching is far more than a luxury. It's a necessity. The survival of our selves and our society depends upon our growing (our) selves more human. The best contribution we can give our society is our healed and grown selves. Healing self and society is all one operation. Persons and institutions and culture are interrelated. Changing ourselves changes them all. And I can begin that, by myself, and no one can prevent me. Growing myself further constitutes the most truly effective politics.

More and more persons in our human growth movements are becoming interested in politics. That's not surprising. It's a natural development, since politics is precisely about human growth and development. More and more such persons are involving themselves in politics. And it's contagious: many persons in politics are becoming increasingly interested and involved in our own personal development.

We need now to bring ourselves—fully idealistic, fully realistic, clear thinking, deep feeling, bold acting—into our political arena.

We all have to become personal and political. They affect each other, they are one, they are inseparable. The reason many persons so isolate themselves from politics is that government so often isolates itself from healthy human growth and development. As we make politics about healthy humans again, healthy humans will make themselves political again. Our internal and external worlds must change simultaneously, if a reconstituted, *human* society is to develop. We need to develop programs for implementing our liberating vision. We need programs that enable persons to become self-aware, self-esteeming, self-sufficient, and responsibly self-determining.

If we'll all take a more active role in politics, we'll see a rapid change in our government and institutions. We'll have institutions that nurture us more, enabling our further growth and development. The dynamic process will be on.

How do I get you to be/come more political? The best way is by my being present with you in such a way that you develop a deeper sense of yourself. Then you'll change the model of humanness you have, your model regarding the kind of world you want to live in, the kind of person you want to become. Then you'll trust yourself more, have more faith and hope, become more idealistic and loving. Then you'll feel you deserve more rights, and you'll be more insistent about exercising your rights.

I do all that best by accepting, loving and touching you so powerfully that you have to reexamine your own negative sense of yourself. I do this by modeling it, by openly loving *myself* more, and by giving you support for your loving *yourself* more. I do this best by accepting, loving and touching myself.

Finally, we must create the opportunity for all new vision persons to come together and create a human politics, a politics of love. Our humanistic alternative deserves a broader airing, our widest public audience deserves to hear about it, to hear about themselves.

From my personal political experiencing, I suggest three ingredients are essential, for realizing our liberating vision, through our politics and government, throughout our society:

First, *inventory our social problems and apply our liberating vision to discovering their root causes;*

Second, *propose a human(istic) agenda for resolving our social problems; and*

Third, *mobilize ourselves toward realizing our Human Agenda, our Liberating Vision and our Human Revolution.*

a new vision, stereoscopic look at our old problems

"Our economy is out of control, our currency is in danger, our institutions of government...(are)... unresponsive or inept. We are at war today—with inflation, with unemployment, with lack of education, with racial discrimination. We are, furthermore, not winning. If we lose, our system of government may not survive."

—Felix Rohatyn

"If I were to search for the central core of difficulty in people as I have come to know them, it is that in the great majority of cases they despise themselves, regarding themselves as worthless and unloveable."

—Carl Rogers

With our expanded vision, we can now look more deeply at our problems. We can recognize that what we *see* are mostly surface symptoms. If we're to have any hope of solving them, we can and must look more deeply, searching out their root causes.

In this chapter I will catalogue our most pressing problems, and propose a critique of each, based upon our Liberating Vision. My critique suggests what's going and gone wrong, in our lives and society, now and in our past. It will be brief and simple, describing what seem to me to be the most significant (not singular) and least understood causal factor(s). It needs to be expanded and acted upon.

Hopefully, you'll undertake that for yourself—now. I'm experiencing some difficulty with this allocation of responsibility between us. Something in me keeps saying that I ought to do more leading. But according to our new vision and its leadership model, it's enough for me to point the way, turning it over to you for your consideration and action.

I won some reassurance on this point at a recent parenting workshop. I began my address by telling the audience I was exhausted, that if I seemed to lack energy and enthusiasm, it was not indicative of my feeling toward the good cause for which we were gathered. During the question period, one person asked with some hostility, "Is it true you aren't going to stay with us all day?" I answered, "That's true. I'm going to spend the day recuperating myself." Many in the audience applauded. As I left, one woman thanked me, "not just for your message about parenting, but for your modeling what you said, feeling free enough to tell us you weren't going to stay here and take care of us."

My critique is based upon the following premises:

- There are reasons for our problems, they are not natural;
- The problems we experience are surface symptoms with deeper root causes;
- Solving our problems requires we go beyond attacking, containing our surface symptoms;
- We must search out and eradicate the root causes of our problems;
- Knowing the root causes doesn't provide any excuse for human inaction, continuing irresponsibility, continuing inhumanness;
- Learning the root causes provides reasons we can deal with, to prevent harming future persons and to enable already harmed persons to better understand and rehabilitate themselves;
- Our problems and our incapacity to solve them all derive from our basic macroproblem: our old inaccurate and inadequate vision of human nature, and the processes we've thereby imposed upon ourselves;
- The interplay of social and personal factors is direct and inescapable in the origin of our distress, as well as in its necessary remedy;
- If we were more open to, in touch with, and appreciative of (the wonders of) ourselves, we would not be, could not be, racist, sexist, ageist, violent, competitive, insensitive, or

indifferent, toward each other.
- Each troubled person came out of one of our individual human families;
- Each troubled person is still a member of our entire human family.

Take a new vision look with me at the personal/political/social problems we are experiencing. I've labeled them as "my" or "our" problems, because we all share them as members of our human family.

1. *Alienation:* consists of my alienation from myself, being out of touch with myself. It results from my separation from myself, on account of my repression of myself (especially my emotions, body and sexuality) at the hands of an alien culture and institutions.

2. *Loneliness:* consists of my longing for the missing parts of myself, missing as a result of my repression of myself. I'm the long-lost person, most missing in my own life. I'm the missing link; the missing links are within me.

3. *Anxiety:* consists of my feeling uncomfortable with/in myself. It results from my being unnatural within myself, on account of my repression of parts of myself.

4. *Apathy:* consists of my not actively involving myself in life. It results from my being out of touch with my energy and passion. I've been conditioned to deny, withhold and contain myself, my passion for life, my life energy. My earlier experiences leave interlocking impressions, acting yet within me:
—Fear of punishment: if I assert myself and err, I'll get punished;
—Need for reward: if you want me to do something good, you'll promise me a reward first, give me a reward after;
—The world's too big and set in its ways, there's nothing can be done about it;
—I'm too small and inconsequential, I can't make a difference anyway.

5. *Stress:* consists of my feeling pressure. It results from my

not being open to responding naturally and fully to each life situation. I especially don't respond appropriately to the unnatural pace and pressure of our competitive rat-race life style. My energy builds up unnaturally inside me.

6. *Cynicism:* consists of my negative belief and feeling about human nature. It results from my having been taught to distrust myself. I learn that while repressing myself, leaving me less than innocent and trustworthy.

7. *Low self esteem:* results from the negativity I'm taught about myself. I thus repress myself and my body and, being somewhat shut down, I don't feel my full worth.

8. *Depression:* results from my being put down, repressed, especially in my body.

9. *Emotional illness* (in epidemic proportions: California, for example, spends $450 million per year on state mental hospitals and local community mental health programs). My repression, especially my mind/body split, leaves me fractured. Naming it "mental" rather than "emotional" reveals our bias, and a reason for our cure efforts failing. It suggests my problems exist in my mind, and we treat it by endless talking. My problems were imposed and persist in my gut.

10. *Physical illness:* results in large measure from my not fully understanding, owning and inhabiting my body and emotions. That results from the mystification and repression of my body and emotions. I got little health education, plenty of unhealthy education.

11. *Arrogance/pomposity:* results from my being and feeling insecure within myself, on account of my not being self-possessed. I need them to pump myself up, appear bigger than (I feel) I am, elevate myself above you (in my own eyes), to make myself feel important again.

12. *Authoritarianism:* results from my being structured and organized vertically within myself, a part of me elevated above and ruling the rest of me. I don't trust my full being, so I don't

trust yours either, and I structure and organize our relationship vertically.

13. *Elitism:* consists of believing a certain group of persons is better than the rest of humankind. It results from believing a certain part of me is better than the rest of my humanness.

14. *Prejudice/discrimination/stereotyping:* consists of my judging, labeling and pigeon-holing you—instead of engaging you as an individual person. It results from my judging, labeling and pigeon-holing myself—instead of engaging my entire person.

15. *Chauvinism:* consists of my believing I know better than you what's good for you, that you need me to take care of you, to protect and save you from yourself. I get to define your value and your role. It results from my deficient self esteem, distrusting my own natural capacities, unwilling to trust yours. Chauvinism operates at many levels, will continue to do so as long as we structure ourselves on levels. Several forms are evident:
—Intrapersonal: intellectualism (my head's wiser than the rest of me);
—Interpersonal: paternalism, maternalism, racism, sexism, ageism;
—National: war;
—International: imperialism.

16. *Irresponsibility:* results from my having repressed, alienated myself from my own natural responsiveness. Our culture proposes "accountability systems" as a substitute. "Accountability" is a symptom and statement of distrust. In a world so changed, we're insecure and grasp at objective measurement to assure ourselves things are really going okay. Accountability is never sufficient. It doesn't reach or improve my natural responsibility. It's always mechanical. It's not healthy for dealing with humans. Instead we must get to know and trust each other, face to face. I don't impose accountability on persons I know and trust.

17. *Uncaring/lack of compassion:* results from my being

turned off to my natural responsive feelings toward other living beings. I've lost my sense of my own oneness within myself, destroying my grounds for feeling oneness with each and every other person in our human family.

18. *Sexual dysfunction:* (including unresponsiveness in women, impotence in men): results from
—our culture's enormous negativity about our sexuality;
—the mystification of sexuality in and by our culture;
—our having been poorly educated about our sexuality;
—our enormous guilt about our sexuality; and
—our having repressed our natural sexuality.

Our typical family transmits strong messages before puberty that sex is "off limits", even for discussion. Our average family is all but mute on the subject. In a recent study (Liz Roberts, Harvard) of 1400 Cleveland parents, less than half had talked about menstruation, even with their older daughters; less than 15% had mentioned intercourse or masturbation; less than 6% contraception; 75% had talked about pregnancy and birth, but the vast majority did so in terms of "the birds and the bees." As a result of this family conditioning, I become unable to fully, freely, naturally let go, let myself experience and express my emotional and bodily energy and vitality.

19. *Family breakdown/disintegration/divorce:* results from persons changing and growing at different rates, and/or in different directions, outgrowing stereotypical roles and/or each other. We have little education for family living. Our individual sexual problems aggregate. A person competitive at his/her job is unlikely to turn that off and become loving on the way home. After all, the persons at work and at home are all members of the same human family, only more or less closely related.

20. *Troubled/disturbed/runaway/suicidal children:* results from parents not being fully grown, self-aware, self-esteeming and self-possessed persons. We want and need and use children for our own life, often to make us parents look good, seem worthy. We have little education regarding child or human growth and development. Most parents prefer to present ourselves to our children as doubt-free authorities, rather than

as candid loving friends. We don't trust our children to make wise choices for themselves—if we provide them ourselves, our loving support and the best information we have. We're afraid to reveal our uncertainties. We turn away their questions. Instead, we allow misinformation and confusion to percolate into their lives from friends, television and back streets.

21. *Incest/child molestation:* results from our sexual ignorance and repression, our resultant incapacity to satisfy ourselves sexually, in a normal mature manner.

22. *Pornography (including "child"):* results from our same inability to naturally get sexual satisfaction in touching; instead choosing to excite and/or relieve ourselves through pictures.

23. *Rape:* results from a combination of sexual repression, incapacity to fulfill ourselves naturally and voluntarily, hostility toward a woman, on account of earlier self-denying, enraging experience, and our societal conditioning to accept violence as legitimate behavior toward another person.

24. *Child abuse:* results from
—our needing our children to behave or be/come a certain way to make us feel whole and worthy;
—our not knowing enough about normal child growth and development;
—our using available, less powerful persons as outlets for our frustrations, anger, lack of self-love;
—our conditioning to violence as an acceptable means of expressing our misunderstood needs.

25. *Drug abuse (including alcoholism):* results from being incomplete on account of repression, physiologically and emotionally. I reach for a chemical to alter my state of feeling— either to dull the pain of repression, or to energize my repressed feeling. Experts believe that whatever experience drugs occasion is naturally available to open, fully-conscious, fully-functioning humans. A U.S. House of Representatives task force returned from Europe in December 1978 and reported that conservatively half the U.S. Army soldiers there use hashish, one of every four uses heroin, and the use of drugs is growing.

26. *Violence:* results from my bodily repression, my energies being distorted, my expressions becoming contorted, my efforts at touching becoming inhuman. If I disrespect and hate my body, I'll hate and disrespect yours as well, I'll have no compunction about hurting your body. Any person who could harm any other person—except in immediate and actual self-defense—is "sick." If I take a nice, gentle being and beat it around, s/he won't be gentle anymore.Sooner or later, s/he'll get back, get even—with me or by putting it onto another person, or by withdrawing (furthering the violence against her/himself). As a society we have so glamourized violent acts as to make them seem not only acceptable but admirable, in the eyes of some.

27. *Recidivism:* results from the dehumanizing environment of our prisons, which doesn't heal me but makes me sicker and more dangerous. Often prisons are operated by persons who don't believe we humans can truly change our character. They're neither educated nor grown to be self-aware and positive, able to provide a growthful presence, relationship and environment.

28. *Greed:* results from my being incomplete, on account of my repression, needing to accumulate/hoard things to make me feel more sufficient, important.

29. *Materialism (wealth, property, money):* results (Norman O. Brown) from my being repressed bodily/sexually, needing substitute gratification to restore my lost sense of self-importance. Money brings power, becomes highly desired if I believe myself inadequate otherwise. Having repressed my natural motivation toward life, self-realization, union and love, I believe in, need, promote substitute gratifications.

30. *Poverty:* results from (among other events) an interplay of the exploitation of the needy by the greedy, and my lacking enough sense of self to care for myself economically. If I were grown naturally, I'd share all I have with my human brothers and sisters. I'd trust life—as per the Biblical instruction regarding the lilies of the field. Grown naturally, I'd be able to care sufficiently for myself.

31. *Consumerism:* results from my being repressed, needing to possess things for substitute gratification, needing "to have" and "to do" on account of my not knowing how "to be". I am not self-sufficient, able to simply enjoy my own being.

32. *Crushing Competitiveness (our "rat race"):* results from my mind/body split, being down on myself on account of my own repression, needing to beat you, to (re)elevate myself to my lost natural position. I need to prove myself, to make myself feel better. Such competition is wasteful, especially of humans. When I beat others, I destroy their self esteem. When I beat myself, I destroy my own.

33. *Polluted Environment:* results from how I treat my own human nature—with scorn and disrespect, horribly. How I treat my outside world depends on how I treat my inside world. I've lost touch with (my) nature.

34. *Energy Crisis:* results from my having repressed my natural capacity to enjoy, be satisfied with simple natural pleasures. If I'm out of touch with my own energy, I'll not feel alive and satisfied within my own being, I'll use more energy having and doing.

35. *War, Militarism, Massive Armaments:* results from my assuming I'm naturally dangerous and untrustworthy. From my repression, I'm left feeling angry, defensive, frightened, untrusting, paranoid. I'm assuming everybody else is angry like I am, and I arm myself to scare you. The major roadblock to disarmament is the war within myself, living the assumption that I am the enemy.

36. *Big Government:* results from my having lost my natural (sense of) responsibility and being unwilling to take responsibility, to act for myself and with others. By my irresponsible actions or inactions, I create or perpetuate problems which no one but government will try to solve. I expect government to do too much *for* me, and too much *to* other persons.

37. *Apathetic Bureaucracy:* results from a combination of —insecure persons heading agencies, unable to tolerate talent,

creativity, dissent, boat-rocking;
— a civil service system based on a distrust of human subjectivity, replacing individual choice with "objectivity" —
assuring "standardized mediocrity;"
— employee persons who lack self esteem, are timid, hiding,
playing "don't rock the boat," "cover my ass."

38. *Inflation* (43% in Iceland; 50% in Israel; former President
Ford called it "World Public Enemy #1"): results from the
reciprocally escalating combination of:
— massive government defense/armaments spending ($123
billion by our United States, $500 billion worldwide,
annually). This results from my paranoia; my distrust of
myself, and my subsequent distrust of other humans;
— other excessive government spending. This results from my
personal irresponsibility, expecting government to do things
for me and for those "less fortunate." I don't do enough for
myself and with others. I hurt and harm others, leaving them
needing rescue. This results also from insecure, frightened
politicians, trying to please the voters, make themselves popular and maintain themselves in office and power.
— massive wasteful spending in our private sector. We spend
$80 million annually on advertising of processed cereals. A
television network paid $10 million for rights to show one
movie one time. Corporate executives get paid up to $800,000
per year. All this results from my being so much into having
and doing, into a materialistic, consumer lifestyle. Inflation
may be the great capitalist booby prize. Capitalism operates
largely off our morality, of denying our natural selves, conditioning us to want more and more goods and services. With
our ever-increasing demand, we outscale our ever-
diminishing supply. We drive up prices ourselves.
— the rising aspirations and standards of living of (persons in)
developing nations. We're exporting our lifestyle.
— their refusal to continue subsidizing our luxurious lifestyle by thier substandard, inhuman wages and working
conditions.
— depletion of our world's nonrenewable physical resources: as
the supply dwindles, the prices rise.

39. *Unemployment:* results from our allocating so much of our

money to producing things, including weapons—leaving insufficient money for growing people. Dollars spent in human services create more jobs than dollars spent in producing things.

40. *Underemployment:* consists of not enough jobs available to match the developed talent and aspirations of searching workers. It results from our allocating resources to unfulfilling production activities rather than fulfilling human services.

41. *Structural Unemployment:* consists of many open highly-skilled jobs and many unskilled, enemployed workers. It results from my not extending myself—individually and through my institutions of education, business and government—to support my less advantaged brothers/sisters in developing themselves to qualify for available jobs.

42. *Job Dissatisfaction:* results from the dehumanization of work, especially unfulfilling impersonal assembly-line production, allocating our resources to production to fulfill our consumerism, rather than to our unmet human needs, matching our expanding human aspirations.

43. *Poor Treatment of Our Disabled Persons:* rcoults from a combination of
—my valuing humans only to the extent they are materially productive;
—my bias against the human body, accepting it only if it looks perfect; and
—my having lost my natural compassion, my responsiveness toward my fellow humans.

44. *Poor Treatment of Our Older Persons:* also results from my lack of compassion, and my not valuing humanness, valuing human beings only if they can produce. We assume that with age comes debilitation, and we disallow older persons from continuing to work, forcing them to retire. We're likely to be remembered as the generation committed to saving our whales and redwoods, uncommitted to helping our own kind.

45. *Educational Failures:* results from a combination of conditions and circumstances:

a. Our over-expectations about education. We've made it the new American religion, the key to good jobs, secure family, abundant culture, and prosperity—the good life. We expect schools to do it all for us.

b. Schools are in the middle of our Human Revolution, caught between two contrary visions with contrary learning theories: stuff information in from outside, or draw wisdom forth from inside.

c. Insufficient understanding of human learning and motivation. Children learn by themselves and naturally to walk and talk, two very complex processes, before they enter school, from persons without formal training in teaching. Schools don't facilitate curiosity, creativity, autonomy, responsibility, self esteem or full personhood.

d. Our old vision's schools and educators don't respect the individual whole child. They're designed still to socialize children of unsophisticated immigrants of diverse cultures— to make them uniform. They still focus on the cerebral and intellectual, "educating the mind." They scorn and disregard the child's emotions and body. They drill him/her to learn only our traditional 3 R's—reading, writing, arithmetic. They distrust natural curiosity and motivation, they threaten and scare kids into "learning."

e. Our new wave of educators, our "free school" people, offered an alternative. But too often they focused only on the child's emotional and bodily development, to the disregard of his/her cognitive capacities and need to learn the old 3 R's, often in resentment toward their own narrow education. They over-reacted. They failed as well to respect and deal with the whole child.

f. Either way, the child is split, within him/her self. S/he's left with no sense of belonging, trust, safety, self, or natural motivation—or is left without the skills necessary to be/come self-sustaining in our world.

g. School is an autocratic rather than a democratic experience. Schools are vertically organized and governed: trustees over administrators over teachers over parents over students. Children learn what's practiced more than what's preached to them. Democracy is not learned in the theoretical and abstract, it's learned (or unlearned) by experience.

h. Schools pay little attention to moral and character

development. If they do, it's done by indoctrination, superimposing a set of values over the child's natural valuing system. There's no recognition that moral development derives from healthy human growth and development. Moral issues get lost instead in the endless, stand off debate regarding who gets to implant their value system within the child.

i. We keep passing kids through school, ready or not academically—because we don't want to "damage the child's psyche" (as well we shouldn't). We believe their self esteem is vital (as well it is). Unfortunately the theory and practice of our schools equate self esteem with "passing." We don't understand self esteem. We think it resides in how we compare with others, rather than in knowing our own inherent value. We fail to nurture internal self esteem, which enables a person to not be traumatized by being "held back" in school. We owe a child both self esteem and honest academic advancement.

j. Many school administrators are bland and neutral, sitting on the school scene to keep the boat from rocking.

k. Many school business managers treat education more mechanically than humanly, putting dollars before humans. They're more into balancing the books than developing balanced humans.

l. Many academic theorists are too abstracted from the realities of children.

m. Many teachers lack self esteem, are afraid of children and of parents.

n. Many parents are too preoccupied with their own lives, too obsessed with having and doing. They aren't present and participating in facilitating their children's learning and development.

o. It's common practice to isolate cognitive and affective learning and development. We're creating many half-persons, brilliantly developed on the intellectual side, severely retarded on the feeling, affective, valuing side.

p. We overload children with so-called "objective tests" (there's no such thing—the test-maker creates them out of his/her own subjectivity). What tests primarily indicate is the economic status of the parents. Those are their only clearcut correlations. The more measureable something is, the less human it likely is. (Russ Kent).

q. School vandalism, truancy, misconduct result primarily

from kids not feeling they belong, being resentful for how they're treated at school.

r. Traditional liberals propose that if we educate people enough, they'll grow up to be/come good citizens. "If schools do that well, all our problems will be solved." But they conceptualize education at the intellectual level, and fail to recognize whole healthy human growth and development, covering cognitive *and* affective domains and capacities. Only with an integration of cognitive and affective development will we be enabled to solve our problems.

s. Traditional conservatives propose that schools are only for training the child's intellect, learning the traditional 3 R's. All else is to be learned elsewhere, if at all. "If schools do that well, all our problems will be solved." But the rest of us doesn't get developed. They err as do the liberals.

t. Blaming our education failures on lack of money—rather than recognizing they derive more from our lack of sufficiently human vision and practices. "If God had known what schools were going to be like, S/He would have made kids differently."

46. *Postsecondary Education Difficulties:* Again, result from a complex combination of conditions and circumstances:

a. The university is our institution most epitomizing our old "heady" vision, wherein the intellect is all that's valued and attended to. It operates on our negative, narrow model of humanness. It disrespects and disregards the rest of ourselves, our emotions and bodies, our whole human growth and development. It's bound to experience challenge and conflict by expanding humans.

b. "Higher" education has created a "myth of objectivity." It honors and attempts to operate from a supposedly value-free objective perspective. It operates off a faulty, fractured epistemology (philosophy of learning), rather than a holistic epistemology: cognitive and affective, intellectual and intuitive. It has a particular mind set: the mind is set; the set is the mind. The university almost never encourages, seldom tolerates diversity of thinking about *thinking*, about feeling, about other ways of knowing. Academic freedom is rarely accorded persons researching or teaching this other epistemology. Academia scorns such persons, it doesn't tenure them, it pushes them out. Programs not fitting the traditional model of epistemology don't get respect or position in the university.

c. The university is vertically organized and governed, non-participatory. It is elitist in approach and concerns. Too often intellectuals have looked down on, scorned the masses of people. This scorn is coming back, to haunt them.

d. The university remains the isolated and isolating ivory tower. That results from its insufficient epistemology, its abstraction, its myth of objectivity, its lack of feeling.

e. Its leaders are often old vision persons, even more "in their heads." They're often arrogant and condescending. As then San Jose State University President John Bunzel and I concluded a discussion of philosophy and epistemology, he turned to his vice president and said: "I didn't know we could discuss such important matters with legislators." I told John "That's condescending." He replied, "Oh, no, it's complimentary." I found that even more condescending. University leaders commonly distrust the rest of themselves, distrust subjectivity and feelings, are limited in vision.

f. The university claims to be "a community of scholars." It is more often a non-community of vertically structured individuals. Instead of seeking the much-talked about "meeting of the minds," they should attend to the remeeting of all of themselves, and each other as whole persons. Then they'd develop a full, real sense of community.

g. The university remains preoccupied with judging, measuring, grading and comparing human beings—rather than supporting, nurturing and celebrating human beings.

h. Academics tend to be anti-status-quo in their view of everyone else's operations, advocating radical change there. They're status-quo oriented regarding their own operations, opposing change there. Curiously, business persons tend the other way: into radical research and development of their own operations, conservative regarding the operations of others, especially including government.

i. Academia divides itself into departments and disciplines. It's scornful toward interdisciplinary studies. It fails to recognize that *reality* is interdisciplinary, our universe is one, each of us persons is a whole. That results from academics often having repressed the rest of themselves, finding their identity in their department, their discipline. The university specializes in analyzing, further dividing itself and all knowledge. It makes little effort to synthesize, largely a function of our emotions. It fails to recognize or respond to our need for getting ourselves, individually and societally, back together. We desperately need a commitment by our brightest scholars to research and develop our knowledge about the healthy development of our emotions, vision, synthesis and human action. We need our brightest scholars to be fascinated with those matters in their own personal life and being.

j. The university is not enough concerned and involved with matters of public policy, especially in its research. Instead it's focused on researching distant times, places and cultures. It gives too little attention to the many persons, cultures, problems and pains among us humans here and now. Again, this likely results from their abstracting from life, from themselves.

k. The university claims to be the most open place of research, the institution which mosts discovers and develops valuable new knowledge. Yet it has more secrets than any institution except the Pentagon. It's often the least-well-informed institution about its own internal operations, the least curious about researching how to improve its own operations. It seems to be the least curious about researching the purpose for which it exists— human learning and how it best occurs. It seems to assume it knows all there is to know about that. And if its School of Education does learn anything about that, the rest of the campus is the last to listen and learn.

l. An uneasy relationship exists between the university and government, especially legislators, and especially the legislators who were its strongest allies, defenders and protectors during the campus tumult of the 60's. These have become its most vocal, insistent critics in the 70's. There's too little trust between the university and legislators, each suspects the other.

47. *Ineffective government:* results from a combination of forces, especially the groups of persons who constitute it:

a. Many of our legislators and other elected officials are not sufficiently self-aware, about our own human dimensions. We fail to recognize the human dimensions present in our every policy-making decision. Too many are still committed to our old vision. We're enacting repressive laws to protect us humans from ourselves. Too many are too insecure to conduct our deliberations and decisions in public.

b. Many of our media persons likewise reflect our old vision's cynical view of human nature. They're more interested in reporting alleged intrigue, scandal and in-fighting. They don't enough recognize and report the significance of the subtle shifting of foundations and relationships which are occurring as a result of our Human Revolution. Their cynicism sees our liberating vision as naive and irrelevant. They're more into sensational selling of papers and time—than into human development. They look for and report the worst of government, perpetuate the cynicism that is its downfall in a free society.

c. Many of our special interests and their legislative representatives (lobbyists) are too little aware of the human dimension in themselves. They're more enamored of property and profits, concerned with economic development. They're less concerned with human beings and human growth and development.

d. Many of our public employees are too little aware of their own human dimension. They're protected by a civil service system which elaborately protects against the risks of subjectivity, assures the mediocrity of blind objectivity. People can be trusted to make good judgments. They're locked into a system that rewards "fitting in" and "going along" and "not rocking the boat." It inhibits creativity and change. There's no person responsible for judgment, there's no personal responsibility.

e. Many of our citizenry—including you and I—aren't sufficiently aware. We're not enough aware of our own human dimension. We're not enough aware of the political dimension of our personal vision. We fail to see the appropriate purpose and role of government: to provide environments in which human beings can most healthily grow ourselves. And we're not sufficiently responsible. We need and want too much from government. We *need* government to do those things we aren't yet grown big enough to do for ourselves. We *want* government to do those things we don't yet trust ourselves to do. The day after I'd lost my bill to ban the manufacture and sale of aerosol spray containers, a woman thanked me for my effort. She added that she hoped I'd be successful next year, so she'd stop using aerosol. I suggested she could do that voluntarily, but she would have none of that. Additionally, most citizens won't exert themselves and go and see their elected officials at work. They let the cynical media "inform their judgment."

f. Overall, enormous distrust between and among all our above groups, especially between our citizenry and our elected persons. Neither recognizes the changes in the other, that persons in both groups are now more self-aware, aspiring, trustworthy and assertive. Members of all groups are still operating off our old vision—expecting government to take care of people, or not to care about people at all. Instead government ought care to find ways to enable persons, insofar as possible, to care for themselves, to become self-sustaining, not dependent.

48. *Bad Politics:* This also results from a combination of forces, especially the various groups of persons involved:

a. Many of our politicians are not enough self-aware to recognize the importance of our human dimension in politics. Our deficiency operates both in our campaigning and in our policy-making. We're disdainful of the people, secretive, needing to be traditional popular leaders, unwilling to let go of our power, willing to do or say anything to keep it, unwilling to utilize our power for empowering others. We're too willing to use any means—manipulating, lying, other deceits—to ingratiate ourselves with the voters—to the end of getting ourselves (re)elected.

b. Our political parties are often operated by persons whose identity is caught up in electing their candidates, at any price. Parties get caught in the game and competition, fail to recognize the deeper truths and values deserved and desired by growing persons in a free society.

c. Our media is often more fascinated by the struggle and intrigue of politics, titillating the public. It's less concerned with the development of substantive issues, and educating the public, especially about its own growth and development.

d. Our citizenry is too often cynical, distrusting and apathetic. They're unwilling to exert themselves to go and meet the candidates, then complain they don't know the people they have to choose between on the ballot. They deny themselves opportunities to make wiser judgments, choices for themselves.

e. Overall, our politics fails for the same reason our government fails: our cynicism, our unwillingness to recognize our own and each other's growing humanness.

That concludes my catalogue and critique. I hope it makes clear how our liberating vision helps locate the root causes of our problems. But it's not responsible to apply our expanded vision only to criticize what's going and gone wrong, in our lives and society, now and in our past. Instead, we owe it to ourselves to use our expanded vision to propose alternatives—how we can make things right, in our lives and society, now and for our future.

chapter 24

new horizons:
a human agenda

"Our task is to tame the savageness of man and to make gentle the life of the world."

—Robert F. Kennedy

"For every political purpose, but particularly for reforming and revolutionary ones, we need to understand our genetic constitution."

—Mary Midgley

With our expanded vision, we have a proper foundation for making things right, in our lives and society, now and for our future. We can envision our human alternatives, our ends and our means, our goals and our programs for attaining them.

Let's propose a specifically human(istic) agenda for dealing with our problems—an agenda for human action based upon our new liberating vision.

Our agenda is based on the following assumptions:
• "All persons are by nature free and independent," a vital belief voiced by the people of California in the first section of our state Constitution. When our constitutional revisionists were shortening our Constitution, they proposed deleting the phrase "by nature." Before we voted on the proposed revision, I persuaded them it was worthwhile to leave it. It remains our recognition that the declaration of our "freedom and independence" doesn't come from "the people"—for then

"they" could as readily take it away. Rather it has its source in our own nature. We are *by nature* free and independent!

• We humans must, and can discover how to end our alienation from ourselves, each other and nature itself. Either we break through and discover how we humans can live together more caringly, gently and intelligently—or we may perish from our earth.

• The emerging primary personal and sociopolitical issue in our lives and times and society is: How do we grow healthy human beings? How do we provide an environment in which a human being can most fully grow and develop him/her self to be/come self-aware and self esteeming, self-realizing and self-determining,
free *and* responsible, whole rather than fractured,
hopeful rather than cynical, open rather than closed,
revealing rather than concealing, gentle rather than violent,
motivated rather than apathetic,
democratic rather than authoritarian,
cooperative rather than competitive, competent and excellent,
ecologically responsible, loving rather than hating,
moral rather than immoral, political rather than apolitical?

• Even as we attend to the underdeveloped nations in our world, we need as well to attend to the underdevelopment of our selves. We are underdeveloped persons. *We* are an underdeveloped nation!

• We humans have too much focused on our intellectual development, to the neglect of the rest of ourselves. We've intellectually outgrown ourselves. Without sacrificing our intellectual development, we must attend to the development of our total organism. We need fully developed hearts and bodies and intellects. We need to become moral persons.

• The central emerging event in our lives and times and society—is the emergence of our Liberating Vision. We must install this vision in place of our old negative vision of ourselves. We must make this vision our way of life.

• We must incorporate our new vision into our problem-solving efforts. We must develop a specifically human(istic) agenda— for reforming our society, our institutions, our relationships and ourselves.

• We must focus our attention, energy and resources on researching healthy human growth and development. We know more about how we grow and develop corn, tomatoes and cows—than about ourselves! Our research will enable us to design environments for growing healthier human beings in our future and for healing the damage in ourselves and each other now. Our research must be fully credible, thorough, careful and solid. Its results must be recognized as significant, valuable and acceptable by every human being and by our institutions.

• All our research should be totally open, for all of us to observe, criticize and learn from. The information it discovers should never be used for the indoctrination, manipulation or subjugation of humans. It must be available for the enlightenment and empowerment of humans.

• We need a series of institutions based upon our liberating vision—to facilitate our natural healthy human growth and development.

• We need a series of programs that acknowledge our current scarred and scared human condition. If a person is bleeding, immediate intervention is necessary to stop the bleeding. But it is only a temporary solution. We must perform it in a way consonant with our vision, so as not to hamper eradicating the real cause of the bleeding. Then we must proceed toward that permanent solution.

• Our major political need today is to bring our Liberating Vision into the public-policy decision-making of our entire society.

• Such efforts are not to be done primarily by government, certainly not by its mandate. Each and all of us human beings are responsible for acting, individually and informally—as well as jointly and formally through our government.

My proposal for our Human Agenda will be extensive, but simple. It needs to be expanded and acted upon. Hopefully, you'll undertake that for yourself, now. I'll include some readings and operating examples of humanistic programs. They provide assurance that humanistic alternatives are viable. They provide you a lead (names, addresses and phone numbers are as of March, 1979, subject to change) to facilitate your further exploration.

My entire agenda is listed on the next page. I'll discuss each item in some detail. I invite you to consider each item of this agenda, how it relates to your own life and growth. I invite you to add items and take action on your own, to help implement our vision and agenda, to humanize our society.

A HUMAN AGENDA

1. Our birthing
2. Our parenting
3. Our infant care
4. Our child care
5. Our diet and nutrition
6. Our touching
7. Improving my intrapersonal relations
8. Developing my healthy human emotionality
9. Developing my healthy human body
10. Developing my healthy human sexuality
11. Developing my personal freedom and responsibility
12. Developing my capacity for loving
13. Improving our interpersonal relations
14. Improving our family relationships
15. Making our health holistic and our medicine humanistic
16. Promoting our emotional health
17. Making our education holistic/humanistic
18. Humanizing our postsecondary education
19. Revitalizing our human services
20. Ending our prejudice and discrimination
21. Undertaking our affirmative action
22. Saving our environment
23. Overcoming our energy crisis
24. Humanizing our work and work places
25. Utilizing our underemployed persons
26. Overcoming our competitiveness
27. Humanizing our economics
28. Overcoming our inflation
29. Overcoming our poverty
30. Preventing our pornography
31. Preventing our incest and rehabilitating victims
32. Preventing our drug abuse
33. Preventing our crime and violence
34. Preventing our criminal recidivism
35. Humanizing our law enforcement
36. Preventing our wars and armaments
37. Improving the lives of our disabled persons
38. Improving the lives of our older persons
39. Humanizing our dying
40. Humanizing our government
41. Humanizing our politics
42. Humanizing everything

1. *Making our birthing processes gentle, human, natural.*
French obstetrician Frederick Leboyer highlighted the significance of the birthing process in the life and formation of the
newly arriving infant. Childbirth is a profound and intimate
experience, a healthful and natural process. How birthing takes
place powerfully affects the child, the mother, the father, the
entire family. In an environment safe, caring and supportive,
the full potential of the birth process can be realized, facilitating
the infant's full realization of her/him self.

Leboyer criticized the normal Western birthing practice,
wherein the infant is rudely received amidst bright lights and
loud voices, with a swat on the butt, cut of the cord and
placement on a cold metallic scale. He proposes that the family,
rather than the obstetrician, be the center, the stars of the
event. He proposes we welcome the infant with dimmed lights
(bright enough for seeing thoroughly) and whispers. He
recommends immediately placing the child face down onto the
mother's stomach, whereupon mother and doctor jointly
massage the child, whereupon the child begins to breathe
naturally. At that point the cord becomes limp, its subsequent
cutting is less traumatic. Finally, the infant is bathed, preferably
by the father, in a solution of water warmed to the same
temperature as the liquid environment from which s/he's just
emerged.

This is proposed as a basis for introducing humans more
gently to life. It provides them an initial experience which is
inviting and gentle, rather than traumatizing and violent.
Hopefully they'll expect more of life, expect life to be more
gentle. A report by Frenchwoman Danielle Rapoport surveyed
200 babies delivered by Leboyer. She found indications that
these babies more easily learned toilet-training and self-
feeding, are almost uniformly ambidextrous. The parents
especially cherished the experience, felt it brought them all
much closer together.

Additional related efforts are being explored, including
Bradley and Lamaze natural childbirth, breast feeding, home
birth, midwifery, fathers participating in the delivery, entire
family present, bonding (the process of tenderly touching the
infant immediately upon birth), and alternative birthing centers.

We should have a complete description of the facts, pros, cons
and availability of birthing alternatives distributed to every

expectant parent. Each could then better make the most informed, enlightened, wise choice for her/him self and for the new human s/he is about to welcome into our midst.

The California Legislature created a statewide alternative birthing committee, whose report is available from my office, State Capitol, Sacramento, CA 95814. Bob Plath's Gentle Birth Foundation (142 Calumet Street, San Anselmo, CA 94960) and Laura Huxley's Our Ultimate Investment Foundation (5615 West Pico Blvd., Los Angeles, CA 90019, Tel (213) 935-4603) are active in promoting gentle birth. William Staniger's Holistic Life University (1627 10th Ave., San Francisco, CA 94122) offers a major in holistic birthing. Three hospitals (O'Connor, Good Samaritan and Stanford) in my county have alternative birthing centers. Suzanne Arms (1175 Westridge Drive, Portola Valley, CA 94025) has produced a supportive film "Five Births." The Birth Place Resource Center (156 University Avenue, #201, Palo Alto, CA 94301, Tel (415) 321-BABY) exists to enable prospective parents to find the personal contacts, resources and information they need to have a fulfilling birth experience. Similar programs exist or are developing in other parts of our country.

Beginnings are so important. Nothing else comes before the priorities of birthing and parenting. I suspect we can trace every human social problem to how each human came into our world and was shaped from then on to adulthood. Becoming and being parents are among the very most fundamental acts we humans undertake. Birthing is a wonderful metaphor for our lives and times. It's a fitting place to begin our efforts to humanize our selves and our society.

2. *Making our parenting positive.* Our most creative effort is nurturing the growth of human beings. The quality of our future depends on the quality of the relationships experienced today by our children.

Every family ought be a growth center, for developing all the human potential of every member of the family. We only need a national or state department of "health, education and welfare" to the extent our families are failing to be the primary health, education and welfare providers for us humans.

We might be parents naturally, if we were natural persons in the first place. Instead of being parental—maternal and paternal—let us be natural and loving. Parenting ought be effortless. Sadly, we have little education in family living, in either becoming or being parents. We need to develop information, education and support services to enable persons to be/come healthier parents, to constitute healthier families, to raise healthier children. Parenting needs and deserves a more positive, supportive humanistic culture and society in which to flourish.

We need universally available healthy parenting education, to develop my understanding—as a parent—of: normal child growth and development; how my being and presence and behavior affect my child's growth and development; and how my self awareness, self esteem, and love of myself affect my presence with my child.

In raising children let's recognize we ought never punish feelings, punish only behavior. Let's recognize further that we might never have to punish at all, if we could love well enough to enable the child (or adult) to feel differently about her/him self, and thereby naturally alter, improve her/his behavior.

If we parent well, our children will be so well-grounded, they'll have a sturdy and sufficient foundation for undertaking all of life, even school. Parenting is the foundation of all relationships.

A major effort is underway by a 1200-member grass roots citizens group, the California Task Force on Positive Parenting: Recelebrating Families. It provides informal philosophical and moral leadership and technical information and support for individual and local action throughout California, to improve the quality of parenting. Its working paper is available from my office. Many public schools, community colleges and private programs are offering adult education classes in parenting.

3. *Improving our infant care.* We need to fully recognize and respect even the youngest infant as a unique human being, not as an object. Such a program has been developed by "educarers" Thomas Forrest and Magda Gerber (P.O. Box 32369, San Jose, CA 95152).

4. *Improving and expanding our child care.* Especially in a time of many single parents and two working-parent families, we need to have holistic childcare programs readily available.

They foster self-determination both in the child and in the parent. The parent is enabled to become self-sufficient economically (through work or schooling in preparation for work), without worrying about whether her/his child is being adequately cared for in the meantime. My Administrative Assistant, Susie Lange-Story, brought her newborn daughter, Sierra Liberty, to work with her almost every day their first year. No problems!

5. *Improving our diet and nutrition.* We need to explore the effects of what and how we eat on our human growth and development and human behavior. This has begun to show promise in our understanding of how to grow healthy human beings.

6. *Legitimizing our touching.* We must explore and legitimize the import of touching, as a significant factor in healthy human growth and development. Its absence is a possible causal factor in violence, alcoholism, other drug abuse and mental retardation.

7. *Improving my intrapersonal relations.* We need to make evident that the most important thing we do in life is grow and develop ourselves. We need programs to promote greater self-awareness and self esteem. We need to lessen personal alienation, loneliness, cynicism and despair. Let's honor our oldest educational dictate: "Know thyself." We must discover the roots of self esteem, wherein it is derived, how it is enhanced, damaged, regained. It's a crucial personal and public issue, since its absence results in so much inhuman, anti-social behavior.

8. *Developing my healthy human emotionality.* We must put a premium on openness, self-disclosure and authenticity. We should legitimize our natural feelings and their expression. We need to research emotional development and its relation to human development and moral development. Sid Jourard's *The Transparent Self* and Carl Rogers' *On Becoming A Person* are especially helpful.

9. *Developing my healthy human body.* Our bodies are an

important basis of our self esteem, as well as of our physical and emotional health.

10. *Promoting my healthy human sexuality.* From the moment of birth, a child is a highly erotic and sensual animal. S/he has a right to an appropriate education from birth—to become an honest, free, total personality. Such a child will have a healthy awareness of feelings of self and others, and no sense of fear, shame or guilt about expressing natural feelings. S/he will enjoy bodily and emotional experiences, reacting naturally to the stimuli of touch, light, air and total environment. Such a child's self-image will be good. The child won't be constantly preoccupied with self or sexuality, with only sexual interests and impulses. As his/her mind is free from worry and concern about cultural taboos, his/her body will be free as well. Children should be allowed full awareness of their five senses, including touch. If they aren't, they'll be crippled in their social relationships, moving against life rather than with and toward it.

We need to research and demystify our human sexuality. We need healthier sexuality education, affirming rather than denying it with fear and guilt and shame. We need to educate our health care professionals about sexuality (required by California legislation for prospective doctors and all psychologists, marriage and family counselors and psychiatric social workers).

Parents should be the first providers of healthy sexuality education for their children. To do so, they must develop themselves, their awareness, information and affirmation of their own sexuality. They must be aware of the significance of touching. They must be/come unafraid, unself-conscious about sharing information, anxiety, ambivalence and fears about sexuality with their children.

However you believe on the abortion/choice issue, we can all cooperate to minimize the issue. If we care enough to provide better sexuality education, more available contraception, more human support during pregnancy, more information, care and economic support, and less stigma to so called "illegitimacy," abortion won't be seen as a desirable choice.

The pioneering effort in human sexuality is friend Mary Calderone's Sex Information and Education Council of the United States (84 Fifth Avenue, Suite 407, New York, New York

10011). Programs on human sexuality are offered by the University of California Medical School (501 Parnassus Ave., San Francisco, CA 95122) and Ted McIlvenna's Institute for the Study of Human Sexuality (1523 Franklin St., San Francisco, CA 94109), and many colleges, universities, and clinics throughout our country.

11. *Developing my personal freedom and responsibility.* We need to research and provide experiences that enable persons to grow mature enough, developing our capacity for becoming both free and responsible.

12. *Promoting, developing my capacity for loving.* See Erich Fromm's *The Art of Loving.* We have a lot to learn about loving relationships.

13. *Improving our interpersonal relations.* We should further explore and legitimize ways of relating better with each other: non-chauvinistically (racist, sexist or otherwise), non-competitively, cooperatively, caringly, sharing.

14. *Improving our families,* including spousal/lover/family relationships. For any relationship to be successful, each person must have a healthy relationship with him/her self. Our nuclear family will expire if it doesn't expand its image of itself and humans, to match our expanding sense of ourselves and our humanness. The family will be preserved only as it becomes an agent for conserving and nurturing human beings.

15. *Making our health holistic and our medicine humanistic.* Our liberating vision assumes the whole human being is naturally healthy. We must shift our health consciousness from our illness model, wherein health comes from outside—the provider/expert, with her/his drugs and knives. We need a well-being support and maintenance-of-health model, based on a sound mind, body and emotions, all integrated. Owning my own body, shifting and taking responsibility within myself, are key elements of the holistic/humanistic model. Life itself then becomes the basis for better health and healing. Programmatic efforts shift correspondingly.

We're talking about grave matters of human public health.

The way we're living is killing us. We need good health education for all persons. We need especially to reeducate our "professionals" in holistic health. We need them to experience themselves in positive, holistic ways. Then they'll not need to maintain their power and mystique. They'll truly understand psychosomatic illness, and the import of a healthy human "bedside manner:" being present in a nurturing way that enables us to evoke our natural healing powers within. Holistic health is already becoming a broad-based social movement across our country. (See the *Holistic Health Review*, P.O. Box 166, Berkeley, CA 94701.)

16. *Promoting our emotional health.* We need to seek emotional wellness and growth—rather than just cure of our illness. Traditional therapies seek to change the patient and his/her attitudes so s/he may better accomodate to given external situations. It's time we instead change those external situations, so they're no longer sickening us humans. We should grow persons able to withstand and change unhealthy situations. Our "professional" people-helpers must do more than cure the crippled, rehabilitate our harmed, one by one. It isn't enough to adjust us to be able to "hang in there," and keep our deadly societal machinery operating. They must actively involve themselves in challenging and changing our systems into life-supporting, nurturing ones.

17. *Humanizing our education.* Einstein said "Every kid's a genius. It's just that some get through school without being harmed." We need to outgrow the either/or, intellect or feelings bias of our traditional and counter-culture educators. We need to found education on a recognition of the whole child. "Each child is a unique person, with unique needs, and the purpose of our educational system is to enable each child to develop all of his or her own potential."

A holistically educated person is a self-educating individual, for whom the context of education is life itself. The institution is at best a facilitator of—at worst an obstacle to—the learning, growing process. We must fuse affective *and* cognitive development and learning. We must attend to the *6 R's: Reading, 'Riting, 'Rithmetic,* self-*Respect*, personal *Responsibility*, and human *Relations*. There's no more basic, fundamental, survival skill than loving oneself and others—the necessary competencies for *living*.

Education should include attention to moral and character development, values education, and education in self-awareness, self-esteem, sexuality, spirituality, parenting and other human relationships. We need to increase our in-service staff development. We need to make our teacher training and in-service holistic, experiential. We need to include parents and parenting education in the educational process. If all parties involved in the child's development are on their own human growth and development track, they'll grow together with the child, rather than warring over who gets to "colonize" the child.

A major purpose of education is to prepare human beings to be/come critically conscious (Paolo Friere's *Pedagogy of the Oppressed*), fully aware and able to accurately assess and act upon her/his life situation, to make it healthy for her/himself. We need to grow good citizens, moral beings. We can't accomplish that abstractly, by teaching about it only cognitively. The medium is the more powerful message—the *process* is what really teaches. We must allow children to *experience* what it means to live in a democracy, to be/come self-governing, to have responsibility. School must be/come a participatory democratic experience—if we're to have and be/come good citizens.

There's an old quarrel between conservatives and liberals— about the purpose of public education—whether it's to socialize students into (maintaining) the status quo, or to transform students into change agents, who will challenge the status quo. Both demean the student. They see him/her as a *thing*, to be manipulated/molded to serve the desires and purposes of others.

We should instead respect and trust the student, enable him/her to be/come him/herself: free, responsible and whole. S/he can then properly decide for him/herself whether s/he wants to maintain the status quo or change it, all or in part.

There's another quarrel about priorities. Liberals seem more concerned about feeding needy people now. Conservatives counter "Teach a person to fish, and s/he'll be able to feed him/herself." Instead we should teach a person to fully be/come him/herself. Then s/he'll become fully self-sufficient, learn how to fish, feed him/herself and do all else as needed.

The major components which facilitate my learning are:
—The natural curiosity of human beings (student *and* teacher *and* parent);
—A safe, supportive environment. I'll feel trusted. I'll let go, reveal myself and discover my own truth;
—Totally trusting relationships. Then I'll trust the information you give me *and* trust you when you say it's vital for me to learn it. I'll let go from within, allow my inherent wisdom to surface;
—Individualized programs, tailored to meet the individual learner and his/her needs, strengths and weaknesses;
—Personalized programs, fitting the development of the whole person/learner;
—First-hand experience (experience is still the best teacher!), rather than the third-hand experience of the teacher and textbook describing someone else's experience;
—Recognition by the learner that the proposed learning is valuable for him/her.

We should be/come more patient, less demanding of immediate evaluation and results from non-traditional programs. Traditional programs are failing, they're already spending billions. It takes time to make education human, for its healthy results to show. We should be careful not to make learners into achievement-oriented test-takers. We should attend to developing the whole person, assessing only insofar as it helps us diagnose strengths and weaknesses and develop individualized programs.

Teacher friend Steve Ross teaches children who are far behind in their reading skills. He asks them to relate what's most exciting happening in their lives. He tapes and transcribes that. Then he asks the child if s/he wants to learn to read her/his own words. The response and progress are dramatically affirmative.

The best teacher education program I've found is George Brown's Confluent Education Program at the University of California, Graduate School of Education, Santa Barbara, CA 93106. Jack Canfield's Center for Humanistic Education (Box 375, Amherst, Massachusetts 01002) offers good programs.

18. *Improving our postsecondary education.* The primary purpose of a university is to empower persons to lead moral lives. That entails making our universities into human growth centers. We discover and develop our compassion, our sense of

right and wrong, within our emotions. Our universities ought
grow beyond the solely cerebral, intellectual, to a holistic model.
They should continue their efforts to develop minds—and offer
opportunities for developing all human capacities: academic,
vocational, emotional, moral, affective. Graduates should be
able to find fulfillment in both work *and* personal life. Holistic
programs include the Holistic Life University (1627 10th Ave.,
San Francisco, CA 94122), and Will Schutz' newly accredited
master's program in holistic studies at Antioch West (1161
Mission St., San Francisco, CA 94103).

Especially our universities should provide us the forum our
society needs for testing both models of human nature. They
should foster public dialogue about how our old and new visions
affect our lives and future. University of California President
David Saxon and California Governor Jerry Brown are
considering a proposal for joint sponsorship of a statewide series
of symposia on our old and new visions, and their respective,
competing application to various fields of crucial human
endeavor. These would explore their implications in various
fields of public policy.

It is not enough for our university researchers to merely
observe, measure and record our society and nature, as we
proceed toward extinction. We delegate to our scientists (as we
once did to our priests) our understanding of reality and our
discovery of how to protect ourselves from the forces that
threaten us. That's part of our social bargain with scientists. A
scientist should attend to facilitating our understanding how we
can take care of ourselves, humanity, all life and our planet.
Scientists haven't power to do that by themselves. But they're in
good position to help us discover our needs, directions and
methods.

David Saxon has moved the University of California in this
direction, especially by creating the California Policy Seminar.
He chairs its governing board which includes university
researchers, six legislators, the governor and two appointees.
Its purpose is to provide interface between our public-policy
makers and our university's researchers. It annually invites a
series of public policy research proposals from within the
University, and commissions the best of them for funded actual
research. For information, contact John Cummins, University
Hall, University and Oxford, Berkeley, CA 94720.

19. *Revitalizing our human services.* We have to apply our new definition of "human"—our liberating vision of human nature and potential—as the basis for reforming and revitalizing our human service operations. Our agencies should operate from the premise and with the intention that persons have the inherent capacity for becoming self-sufficient. We have created a "profession" of human development. We need to initiate programs for the further human development of the providers of our human services.

Let's demystify the human service process. Let's enable our human service recipients to become fully informed, more aware, and more responsible for making better choices for themselves.

20. *Ending our prejudice and discrimination.* The roots of prejudice reside far deeper in us, in our lacking self esteem, than we come close to imagining. Each of us needs to grow ourselves more human. Thus we can recognize our oneness with all members of our human family—regardless of sex, age, race, creed, nationality, size, shape, sexual preference, handicap, handedness, whatever. As I grow, my need to prejudge other persons will diminish. As I be/come less afraid of myself, I become less afraid of others. I won't need other persons to look like me or to look down on or climb atop.

We've already experienced movement away from social, politicial and religious elites. Now we're experiencing what's as vital—movement away from racial and sexual elitism. We need to end the elitism within ourselves.

21. *Undertaking our affirmative action.* As I grow, I'll increasingly recognize persons of differing color or culture or sex as members of my family. I'll exert myself more to assure that the lesser-advantaged persons in my family receive special opportunities, so they may fully realize their potential, as I fully realize mine. I'll even recognize their capacity for facilitating my broader experience, my further growth.

22. *Saving our environment.* I need to grow to know and respect my own nature, in order to better respect all of nature. As I grow, I'll be more into the simple pleasures of being. I'll be less into the polluting and littering that accompanies the pleasures of having and doing. As I clean my self up, I'll pollute our environment less.

We find ourselves living in a world of diminishing nonreplaceable mineral resources that are necessary to maintain our present way of life. Hopefully, we're finding ourselves—moving into a world of expanding human resources. We're more conscious, aware, informed, caring human beings.

We'll less need having and doing—to satisfy ourselves. We'll voluntarily lower our material expectations, as we raise our human aspirations.

23. *Overcoming our energy crisis.* At the time we're running out of our non-replaceable, non-human energy, many of us are discovering and developing our renewable human energy. Our bodies regenerate themselves naturally, both within ourselves and in producing offspring. Further developing my own being and energy diminishes my dependency on other energy, especially that expended for the substitute gratifications of having and doing. Simple examples: If I'm able to tap my own natural physical energy, I may walk or ride a bike at times I might otherwise have used a petroleum-consuming vehicle; if I value human relationships more, I may be with you instead of turning on artificial electronic entertainment.

24. *Humanizing our work and workplaces.* We spend large portions of our lives at work. We need to make our work and workplaces healthier for growing humans. Working persons need and deserve more than the boredom, anxiety and stress which is now often our daily work diet. We need to regain our sense of belonging and pride in our labor and product. We need to develop ways to make work, and being at work, more meaningful and fulfilling. We should explore rotating jobs, job-sharing, team-working, employee seats on corporate boards of directors, democratizing the work place, flex-time work, interpersonal relationship activities on the work site. California Assemblyman Bill Lockyer (State Capitol, Sacramento, CA 95814) is developing such a program.

We need more human, equitable pay and salary scales. We need to outgrow our silly waste of millions of dollars figuring out how much we're going to pay different persons and jobs, with no relation to their human needs. It's especially insane to set pay schedules just to keep an ''appropriate gap'' between persons in different jobs. That's merely a status symbol, for ego-deficient higher-ups. It's more economical and moral and human to pay everyone according to our human needs. Ironically, we now pay persons more, the further away from everyday people they work: we pay the person at the top of the organization (who's usually older, whose children have already left home) *many* times more money than his/her secretary (who's often a single-parent with young children still at home). Each does her/his job, each is essential to the success of the overall operation. And while we complain strenuously about paying taxes to subsidize the $50,000 salaries of executives of our public institutions—who are laboring to provide environments for people-growing—we cheerily, complacently subsidize, through the prices we pay and the profits they generate, the $800,000 salaries of executives of corporations who are making things, often hardly necessities of life.

25. *Utilizing our underemployed persons.* We humans have a right to work that utilizes our talent and potential, and fulfills us and our aspirations. We need to reallocate our resources to create jobs which fill that enormous, poignant gap between unmet human needs and rising human aspirations. Many persons need human services, many humans want to serve them—but we apply our dollars instead to producing things, to fuel our conspicuous consumption.

Too many of us work double-time, end up paying higher taxes to support others who can't find work. Too many of us who want to work can't find meaningful work.

26. *Overcoming our crushing competitiveness.* We need to grow ourselves more, to discover our own unique worth and beauty. Then we'll less need to compare ourselves, less need to compete to prove anything, to ourselves or to other persons. Let's become able to rejoice naturally in our own being, and in each other's. Let's love and share with other humans—rather than proving our capacity to beat each other. Erich Fromm's *The Art of Loving* proposes that competition and love are contrary. I find that true in my experience. I don't compete with persons I love. I'm told by religion and culture that I ought love *everyone*. I therefore ought not compete with *anyone*.

Such competition is wasteful of human energy and resources. It's time we humans abandon our rat race, and celebrate our human race. Let's trust our primo natural motivator, human caring! We don't need competition, "getting ahead," or making money to move ourselves to life.

27. *Humanizing our economics.* We need a new economics, derived from our growing into a differing sense of what it means to be human. We all operate from self-interest. As I redefine my self, what's in my self interest changes. My growing enables me to change my life style from competition to cooperation, from materialism to humanness. As I raise my human aspirations, my material aspirations lower. Let's grow into simplicity, appreciating and enjoying the finer things of life—our own and each other's being. We'll less feel the need to possess things. We may even grow to the point where we feel encumbered by possessions.

Much of the underlying root of capitalism is its morality of denying self. Denying ourselves, our natural beings, we compete to prove ourselves, to get the substitute gratification of things. Capitalism becomes less desirable and operational to fulfill our basic human needs, as we grow and expand ourselves. Enforced economics (like communism, state socialism) suit us no better. They are superimposed upon (and by) persons who themselves are not yet fully-developed or willingly sharing. In a sense, both free enterprise capitalism and socialism are more idealistic than we're yet ready for. The former assumes that if we're laissez faire, people will work everything out for ourselves wisely and fairly. The latter assumes we'll gladly share fairly with each other, from each of us according to our capacity, to each of us according to our needs. We're not grown enough for either system to work, for and with us humans as we now are.

We need to evolve a new form of economics, fitting for our current stage of our growth and development, to match us growing humans. Granted we need to have a healthy business climate; we as much need a healthy human climate. Our primary business is the health and development of humans. We need to outgrow our tendency to think in dichotomies, both are essential. (Cf. Willis Harman's "Humanistic Capitalism," and E.F. Shumacher's *Small Is Beautiful: Economics As If People Mattered*). New age businesses, founded on our liberating vision, are springing up across our country.

28. *Overcoming our inflation.* Our most hopeful way is to grow ourselves more human. As we become more human, our decisions about governing and about spending money, in both our public and private lives, will become more human, less wasteful. With our expanded consciousness, we need to reexamine our priorities, individually and societally. We must cut spending on non-essentials at every level: personal, local, state, federal and international.

To prevent inflation, each of us must act. We have to learn to live a more simple life. The best way to prevent inflation is to outgrow the psychological roots of our materialism, and of our paranoia that has us always preparing to defend ourselves, against each other—and of our irresponsibility for ourselves and with each other. If we overcome these, there'll be less waste, physical or human. There'll be less for government to do.

29. *Overcoming our poverty.* We need to discover the root causes of our poverty—our economic poverty and our poverty of caring. Persons who are "wealthy" must grow so they'll be less attached to things and money, more inclined toward being and sharing with other, needing persons. We must attend to the human development of persons economically impoverished, to enable them to become more self-sufficient. And we must all attend to our own growing of ourselves, opening ourselves and releasing our natural caring—so that we'll disengage ourselves from our preoccupation with being spectators of other persons' living, and instead engage ourselves with each other in improving the quality of all our lives.

30. *Preventing our pornography epidemic.* History amply demonstrates that so long as some humans desire and demand something, creating a market—other humans will produce it, creating a supply. Our efforts to curtail the supply are never enough. We must *as well* attend to curtailing the demand. We must search out its root causes.

Let's ask ourselves: "Why do we humans need and want to look at pictures, especially of children, of sexual activity?" Such desire must derive from a fear of being sexual and touching, naturally and satisfyingly. So long as we aren't comfortable with our own naked human bodies, we'll keep on wanting, demanding and buying pornography.

Only a new cultural attitude, affirming our human sexuality, will eradicate the root causes of pornography, adult and child. Healthy sexuality education will help.

31. *Preventing or rehabilitating our child sexual abuse* (incest, molestation). Again, the root causes reside in our underdeveloped or contorted sexuality. We are afraid to relate sexually with other adults. In our need, we turn to defenseless children. We should bear in mind that there's a fine line, requiring careful discernment, between the touching essential for the healthy nurturance of a child, and the touching which is instead for the sexual gratification of the adult.

Our only effective solution is persons becoming self-aware, emotionally developed and mature about our sexuality. Healthy sexuality education is a vital first step. We need to develop our capacities for sexual gratification and fulfillment through natural consenting adult relationships.

We should develop more and better diversion programs, to enable persons to maintain their home and work lives (at reduced taxpayers expense) while they are healing themselves. The finest I've found is Hank Giarretto's Parents United, Santa Clara County Probation Department, San Jose, CA 95110. (408) 299-2475.

32. *Preventing our drug abuse* (including alcoholism). Again, we must recognize that it is not enough to attend only to the *supply* of drugs. "Prohibition" proved that. We need as well to search out root causes of our *demand* for drugs. We need to grow persons so whole they won't be inclined to take a drug to make us feel whole, or to anesthetize our pain. We'll even be disinclined, because it's harmful to our bodies and ourselves. We need more reliable research, information and education about ourselves and drugs. Alcoholism is our most pervasive form of drug abuse. There are an estimated 10,000,000 alcoholics in the United States. I suspect that's the result of persons needing to take a chemical (alcohol) to ease the internal pain of our bodily repression and the stress of our rat-race lifestyle.

In our rehabilitation efforts, our traditional illness model is ineffective. We must apply our well being model of human growth and development. We must go beyond verbal, intellectual efforts. The drug abusers are not choosing from that level. Drug abuse derives from a deeper place in humans—that information doesn't penetrate. Experience—rather than words—created the problem. We must meet these people where their problem exists. Experience—especially the experience of love and touch—is the most likely remedy at that level.

As we grow our humanness, we grow our sense of responsibility for ourselves. We less need government to make our decisions for us. We should evaluate each drug according to our research and understanding of its dangers. We should decriminalize the possession and use of marijuana—not proven to be a significantly dangerous drug. I don't need our government to protect me from myself. I don't want our government to criminalize me, put me into a prison far more dangerous than the drug I used. Instead I need our government to sponsor better research and give me the honest information, so I can make the wisest choice for myself.

33. *Preventing our crime and violence.* First, we ought abolish all victimless crimes, where adults are consenting, or dealing only with themselves. That's not the business of government in a free society. We should focus our efforts on protecting us against each other's lack of responsibility.

Let's sentence criminals, where appropriate, to community service work and to efforts to aid their victims. That fits the punishment to the crime. That helps our society more than letting a person rot away in a prison cell.

We needn't extensively demonstrate our affliction with violence. We have random violence—shootings on freeways, bombings in airports, sniping into schools. Guyana left 900 persons dead. Former San Francisco Supervisor Dan White killed Mayor George Moscone and Supervisor Harvey Milk over a job. A San Jose father the same day allegedly killed his 6-year-old son over a dollar. Violence is touching all of our lives. Too many of us are too afraid—either to stay in our homes or to be out in our streets. These tragic events ought deepen our conviction and commitment to make violence prevention our number one priority.

We humans must discover how to live together more gently. We must discover how to stem the tide of violence that threatens to engulf us all, in fear if not in actual harm. It threatens as well the form of our government and free society.

We must go beyond our past and current efforts. They're not proving effective. Ask almost any police person.

To date our public efforts regarding violence have come after the (f)act: punishment imposed *after* the commission of violence, or punishment threatened, hoping to deter expression of the violent personality—*after* its formation. In either event, that's too little, too late. It comes after some person is made violent, and usually after that someone violates somebody else.

We need to transcend our liberal-conservative quarrel about who and what is responsible for crime and criminals. Conservatives usually argue that the individual human being should be blamed, society isn't to blame. Only punishment of the individual will correct the situation. Only punishment is proposed. Liberals usually argue that society should be blamed, the individual shouldn't be. Only social change will correct the situation. Only social change is proposed.

Neither is sufficient. Neither is accurate. Neither is effective. The problem exists in both the individual and society. Each and both are responsible. Only proposals for changing both offer *any* real hope of solution.

I find several problems with our conservative approach. First, it isn't working. The year after California reenacted the death penalty—homicides in Los Angeles County hit a new record high. The year after California enacted its "use a gun, go to prison" law (and before the State Supreme Court suspended it), it's reported the use of guns in crime increased rather than diminished. New York state has, in fact, reduced its harsh drug laws—because they have proven ineffective. Second, it's too little, too late. It comes after someone's been hurt. Third, it fails to recognize our social responsibility for violence, that the way we deal with each other personally contributes to our violence. Fourth, it's shirking our personal responsibility. Our government didn't create our violence, and it mostly can't prevent it. We do that ourselves. Only we can prevent it—by growing ourselves more gentle, so as to be that way with each other, in our every human relationship.

I find several problems with our liberal approach. First, it isn't working. Second, our people are terrified, and won't settle for that anymore. Third, it fails to recognize our individual responsibility for violence—that each of us is responsible for attending to growing ourselves nonviolent.

I propose instead that both society and individual human beings are responsible. We need to correct both. To the extent society is responsible for violating persons—making them violent—we must change our society. We individual human beings often provide the experiences that violate each other, result in each other's becoming violent. Each of us is responsible for being present with each other, in our daily lives, in ways that are healthful and nurturing, not violence-producing. See Chapters 19—21, discussing our responsibility *to* and *for* each other.

We should look at a person's early experience—not as an excuse for, but for an explanation of his/her violence. It helps us understand how we can cooperatively labor to undo those scars of earlier experiencing.

At the same time, the individual person *is* responsible for his/her actions. Society and other persons may have provided the experiences that planted the roots of violence in me. That's no excuse for my *expressing* my violence, nor for my *continuing* to be violent. I am responsible for who I am now, and for who I become. I must outgrow that crippling anger/rage/resentment/ bitterness contained and carried within me.

Toward such violent persons, what is our society's appropriate response?

Certainly we ought not allow persons convicted of violence to roam free. They're dangerous to others. We ought quarantine them, as we do other ill persons, dangerous to the rest of us. We should keep them separate from the rest of us.

How should we then deal with them during quarantine?

It's self-defeating to deal with them in ways that infuriate them, make them more bitter and resentful. When released they're then more dangerous, rather than healthier and safer. In fact by such action, we have cooperated in making them more violent. We have not served them, nor ourselves, well. Instead, we should provide them experiences that enable them to cure themselves, outgrow their violence, and emerge safer—for all of us.

You and I may disagree about the efficacy of punishment (capital or otherwise), more prisons, policepersons and longer, mandatory sentences. But let's agree that's not enough. It all comes after humans are hurt, initially making them violent or afterwards violating others. No amount of punishment or threat can bring back the lives already taken.

Of course we need to maintain our current containment approaches, considering the current state of our human beings. But alone—that's not enough.

Hopefully we can agree. We need an additional preventive approach. We must again ask ourselves the primary question in our society today: "How do we grow healthy human beings?"

We must focus our efforts on what underlies the formation of human personality and character, and on human growth and development. How is it that persons learn to become criminals? How can we enable such persons to relieve themselves of their violence—other than by dumping it on us? How can they heal themselves?

Here we encounter enormous complication, enormous controversy. Each of us chooses our prevention theory based upon the theory of human nature we hold. Do I believe that we humans are evil or innocent by nature, or perhaps neutral (the so-called "blank slate" theory)? The first and last beliefs are contrary to our new vision, *and* to my experience of my own humanness. I believe I'm naturally life-affirming, inclined toward gentleness—not naturally life-destroying, inclined toward violence.

From our basic assumption, we will conceptualize and operate our institutions, including our child-raising and child-educating processes. If our assumption is positive, we'll choose nurturing and liberating processes. If our assumption is negative, we'll choose controlling and repressing processes.

In either event, we'll be creating for ourselves a self-fulfilling, self-perpetuating prophecy. Suppose a child, in fact, arrives innocent. If we instead expect the worst, we'll edit, control and repress him/her. We'll have distorted an innocent infant into a pent-up, resentful, rageful human being, likely to become violent. We'll be acting in ways that will violate the nature of the young human, destroy her/his innate innocence and gentleness, and *make* him/her violent. We grow a child according to our expectations!

We must examine our assumptions—so *very* carefully! Each of us must begin our violence-prevention efforts by asking ourselves that most basic question: "What do I believe about my own human nature and potential?" With this beginning, you and I will be taking a significant first step along our long journey toward a gentle and safe society.

So what shall we then do? It's neither wise nor safe—to simply leave our human derelicts lying around, unaided. We have only three choices. The first is to simply exterminate them. That's immoral.

The second is to institutionalize them and perpetuate their disease. That's expensive and unsafe. It's dumb, only to try to contain the pentup violence, by penning up (or threatening to) the already violent person.

The third is to quarantine them in ways that enable them to recoup themselves and their innocence. That's our human challenge. We must discover what circumstances and events cause the formation of violence in human beings. We've got to discover how to enable already violent persons to release their violence in ways not dangerous to other persons.

Only then will we prevent the formation of more violent persons in our future. Only then will we cure the persons already violent in our midst. Only *then* will we have a gentle, safe society.

For some time now, I've been making violence prevention my primary legislative focus. I've been wondering whether and how we can grow healthy human beings—gentle rather than violent. My staff and I have been reading everything, consulting every expert we can find—on the subject of violence. My own personal therapy and growth experiences provide me a particular insight into this problem and effort. I've learned enough to propose a program: a non-violent approach for preventing violence, a gentle agenda—for gentle persons (persons committed to non-violence), to discover how we can grow more gentle persons. My "gentle agenda" parallels our "human agenda" discussed throughout this chapter, but focuses particularly on thirteen key suggestions for research on the root causes of violence. I propose we seriously study the possible contributions to violent behavior of the following:

Suggestion #1—THE BIRTHING PROCESS: How an infant first experiences life outside the womb may well determine that person's inclination toward violence. An infant immediately traumatized by lights, noises, a slap, a cut, and a sudden temperature shock may well be conditioned toward violence. References: Frederick Leboyer's *Birth Without Violence*; Danielle Rapoport study of Leboyer-delivered babies; the first report of California's Alternative Birthing Committee.

Suggestion #2—THE PARENTING PROCESS: How a child is treated, raised, touched, loved, rejected—by his/her parents may well determine that person's inclination towards violence. References: Virginia Satir's *People-Making*; David Cooper's *The Death of the Family*; the working paper of the California Task Force on Positive Parenting: Recelebrating Families.

Suggestion#3—NUTRITION: A person's diet and nutrition may predispose his/her body to violent behavior. Reference: "Working with Children with Learning and Behavior Disorders", by Michael Lerner (operator of Commonweal School in Bolinas, California, where proper diet is improving the behavior of disturbed adolescent boys).

Suggestion #4—TOUCHING: The human baby (being and body) has need for touching, its deprivation may lead to a personality that strikes out—to get touched. References: Ashley Montagu's "The Skin and Human Development;" Ashley Montagu's *Touching*; Sid Simon's *Caring, Feeling, Touching*; Helen Colton's "Touch: It's as Vital as Food."

Suggestion #5—FEELINGS/EMOTIONS: The more natural, open and expressive a person is with his/her feelings, the less likelihood there is of a building up of feelings, toward a potentially violent expression. References: Sid Jourard's *The Transparent Self*; Carl Rogers' *On Becoming a Person*.

Suggestion #6—THE HUMAN BODY: The more open, natural and expressive a person is with his/her body, the less likelihood there is of a distorted build up of energy, toward a potentially violent expression. The more a person accepts and loves his/her own body, the less likely s/he is to hurt another human body. References: Tom Hanna's

Bodies in Revolt; Don Johnson's *The Protean Body*; Michael Murphy's *Jacob Atabet*; Therese Bertherat and Carol Bernstein's *The Body Has Its Reasons*; Stanley Keleman's *The Human Ground.*

Suggestion #7—SELF ESTEEM: The more a person knows and loves him/herself, the less likely s/he is to harm another person. References: Jack Canfield's *100 Ways to Self Concept in the Classroom*; Pat Palmer's *Liking Myself.*

Suggestion #8—SEX ROLE STEREOTYPING: The more a person acts out an old vision sex role (e.g. "macho," never crying) rather than being natural, the more likely that person will be disposed to unnatural, violent actions.

Suggestion #9—SEXUAL REPRESSION: The more negativity, guilt and repression of the human body and sexuality, the more likelihood the person will become violent. Reference: Jim Prescott's "Body Pleasure and the Origins of Violence"

Suggestion #10—TELEVISION: The more a person watches and experiences the violence of television, the more likely that person will be inclined toward violence. Today's typical 14-year-old has watched 11,000 murders on television! Reference: Your local PTA—which has initiated a national campaign against television violence.

Suggestion #11—POWERLESSNESS: The more a person feels powerless, especially to make his/her own life more decent, the more likely that person is to engage in force to change his/her situation. Reference: Bob Alberti and Michael Emmons' *Your Perfect Right: A Guide to Assertive Behavior.*

Suggestion #12—POVERTY: The more a person experiences poverty, and inability to improve his/her situation, the more likely that person is to engage in a display of force to change it.

Suggestion #13—PREJUDICE: The more a person

experiences rejection, the more likely the person is to build
up resentment, rage, eventually to explode violently.

That's my proposal. Perhaps parts of it are new and
unfamiliar to you. They once were to me. But no longer. I've
immersed myself in the study of these matters. I've come to
recognize their significance in my own life, my own growth and
development, my own being who I am. I come to believe that we
can use this agenda to develop a truly effective effort to search
out and eradicate the root causes of violence in our society.

Of course government and the law and the police can help.
But they didn't create the causes of violence, and they can't
resolve them. Its causes derive largely, if not entirely, from
conditions in which human growth and development fail to occur
naturally. That in turn is caused largely, though not entirely, by
(our) human relations. We individual human beings caused
those roots of violence. Only we individual persons can resolve
them. Only we can truly prevent the formation of violent
personalities in our society. Each of us is responsible for our
human relations and how they and we affect human growth and
development, and human behavior, in our society.

Some persons might deem this proposal for the study of
violence to be wasted effort, because of their assumption we
humans are simply violent by nature. They believe the best we
can do and hope for is to discover more and better ways of
repressing and controlling ourselves and each other. I find that
belief cynical, and essentially hopeless. As essential, I find that
belief inaccurate—contrary to my own experience of myself.
Psychologist Albert Bandura of Stanford University is one of
many experts who believe that aggression is not innate in us
humans. I believe a healthy human being could not, much more
would not, naturally harm any other human being—except in
actual, immediate and necessary self-defense.

Some persons might deem this project wasted money. But
we spend *billions* on crime control and violence today. We spend
$765 million *daily* in California alone for the costs of crime and
violence and its control. It will cost less than one million dollars
to perform this study, about what it costs to imprison two
20-year-old convicts sentenced to life. It would cost less than a
penny a year for each Californian to finance the statewide study
I propose. I assume the cost would be proportionate for other

states or regions which might undertake a comparable effort.

I acknowledge our effort won't produce overnight results. But there's much research already going on. It's yielding some helpful results. It's time we brought all that knowledge together, and to our attention. We can discover and eradicate the roots of violence, within us and our society.

Many liberals propose we ban handguns in our society. They could better involve themselves in causes that prevent persons being violated, and enable violated persons to recover. Many conservatives oppose banning guns, "Guns don't kill people, people kill people." They're more accurate, to the point. But conservatives would help their cause (to keep their guns) if they would actively involve themselves in programs that enable people to grow so as not to be inclined to choose to misuse guns.

I made this gentle agenda for violence prevention my major platform during my 1978 reelection campaign. My opponent made his an increase in length and mandates of criminal sentences. During our television debate, we each repeated our proposals several times. Then he turned to me and said, "You really want to produce a race of gentle human beings, don't you?" I replied, "You finally got it, I do."

I am now making this my primary legislative effort. I've introduced legislation to create a statewide commission on Crime Control and Violence Prevention. Its purpose is to involve our public in a massive effort to search out and eradicate the root causes of violence in our society. The commission will have a three-year life. It will be composed of 28 persons from various walks of life—including street level law enforcement, religion, academia, psychology, labor, business and the public. Four members will be appointed by each of the following: the Governor, the Attorney General, the Director of Social Services, the Judicial Council, the Superintendent of Public Instruction, the Senate and the Assembly. It will hold public hearings throughout California. It is to search out and marshall all relevant research and evidence concerning the roots of violence. It will report its findings to the Legislature and Governor and the people of California. I hope also to make the results of its work available nationwide.

I am personally contacting, seeking to enlist persons influential in law enforcement, religion, academic research, health and the helping professions, business, labor, government, the media and the general public. I've already received the endorsement of the Peace Officers Research Association of California, various labor, education and senior citizen groups, two district attorneys, the State Bar, the California Council of Churches.

I am hopeful we are on our way toward making our society gentle!

34. *Preventing our recidivism.* We need penal reform, to make our places of quarantine humanizing. Our prisons must be operated by persons faithful in humanness and innocence. They must believe, from their own experience of themselves, that we humans are by nature decent and that we humans can change for the better, even for the best. Our prisons must become places which enable persons to feel safer, so that they can grow, especially by outgrowing, releasing their anger. It's the *only* way to enable them to *become* safer. Now prisons tend instead to enrage people, make them more dangerous.

35. *Humanizing our law enforcement.* We need to provide experiential courses in self-awareness and self-development for persons in law enforcement. That will enable them to more perceptively respond to every situation, especially the domestic incidents, wherein police are most often killed or injured. There is such a thing as "a good cop." The "best cop" is a policeperson who is self-aware, insightful, sensitive and perceptive. S/he is a true peace officer.

36. *Preventing our wars and armaments.* The survival of humankind depends on our making peace a priority in our thinking and in our actions. William James said: "We need a moral equivalent of war." That means more than "moral rearmament." We need more than war, more than armament. We need to become moral. We need to overcome our paranoia and distrust. We need to become our whole, natural, moral, loving, peaceable selves. Then we'd have no need for artificial "arms." We'd be sufficient, using our natural arms appropriately - reaching out to touch each other, shaking hands, opening to receive each other, closing only to embrace and hold each other. We'd then have no (need to) war. Innocence and trust and love are the most disarming of "weapons."

War is becoming an economic as well as human problem. The size of the cost of armaments has so much grown—that we're no longer facing our traditional "guns or butter" controversy: we're arguing "guns or bread." We have insufficient "bread" for many needy, hungry human beings in our society. We can afford the wages of war less than ever!

37. *Improving lives of our disabled persons:* We need to provide our disabled persons more dignity and opportunity. We'll do that naturally as we grow ourselves more human, caring, responsive. There's a chance we'll all be physically disabled some day. Seven million Americans are hurt on our highways alone each year. Many are disabled. We're all physically vulnerable. Our able-bodiedness is never guaranteed.

38. *Improving lives of our older persons.* We need to enable more meaningful and dignified lives for our older persons. That should include economic support, physical exercise, cherishing their bodies, emotional engagement—especially with other growing persons. Even if you and I manage to avoid disability, we're all advancing in years. Sooner or later we'll all be "old." Let's begin now to make those times decent for ourselves—by putting in place programs that support our older brothers and sisters.

Maggie Kuhn's Gray Panthers (3700 Chestnut Street, Philadelphia, PA 19104) have led the way, insisting on human rights for older persons. The SAGE project (41 Tunnel Road, Berkeley, CA 94705) is a fine pioneer in programs for older persons. Friend Ken Dychtwald has founded the Association for Humanistic Gerontology (1711 Solano Avenue, Berkeley, CA 94707, (415) 525-3128).

39. *Humanizing our dying.* We ought legitimize and expand our burgeoning hospice movement. We need to tenderly counsel persons dying, discover how to deal with loss, grief and mourning, legitimize home dying. The California Legislature has created a pilot project in hospices, authored by Assemblyman Gary Hart. Already operating are: the Shanti Project in Berkeley, the San Jose center for Living with Dying, and the Hospice of Santa Barbara. The hospice concept is rapidly spreading to other areas of our country as well.

40. *Humanizing our government.* We must humanize our government. To accomplish this, we must ask everyone involved—elected officials, agency heads, public employees, media persons, lobbyists *and* the citizenry—to attend to our own further human growth and development. The best guarantee of a small-sized, healthy government is a citizenry of healthy, self-esteeming people. All this will begin to restore the trust and confidence and credibility essential for a democratic/republican form of government. That will change our expectations of government, and of ourselves and of each other. That will move our government toward a truly human agenda—for the growth and development of healthy human beings.

The enactment of Proposition 13 by Californians, and similar proposals in other states and in our nation's capitol, puts us all to the test. Will liberals be demoralized and despair, giving up on efforts to improve the quality of our lives? Our human problems persist, still deserve our effort. Will conservatives rejoice, further their efforts at economic reform—without making the essential and moral correlative efforts at human reform? The enactment of Proposition 13 didn't cure one troubled person in our midst. Our problems are still with us. If we truly care—liberals or conservatives—we should go past our differences on Proposition 13, and cooperate in efforts to healthily meet the unmet human needs in our society.

Will Proposition 13 be an occasion for our returning to our old vision, expecting the worst of us humans, then acting and getting exactly what we expect? Or will it serve as a creative threshhold, in which more of us, of whatever persuasion, will take more responsibility for involving ourselves personally—to see to it that our society becomes more of a healthy human family?

The answer's up to each of us. We each owe it to ourselves and to each other to see to it that Proposition 13 becomes an occasion for further humanizing our society—rather than for further dehumanization.

There were many reasons, laudable and not, for 4,000,000 Californians voting for Proposition 13. What surprised me more than the numerical result was the emotion wrapped up in it. I wondered much about that, and finally got a hunch about its reason from my sister, Margaret. We'd had a painful falling out, over my non-relationship with her husband. She wanted him and me to love each other, and I didn't. When she attacked me for my attitude, I was deeply scarred, and avoided her for more than two years. When we got together for a reconciliation dinner, she explained the reason for her deep emotion. I was her "big brother," who'd always made everything okay for her. When I failed her in this most important situation, she was hurt and angry...and "got me."

I suspect the emotion behind Proposition 13 was much the same. Persons in our culture have been conditioned to expect that the authority figure will make everything okay for them. Today our society isn't working, people are hurt and angry. Government is our primary authority figure, and people "got government" with their "yes" vote on Proposition 13.

Yet, even after the passage of Proposition 13, our local Chamber of Commerce urged me to continue, even expand, fiscal support for the state office of tourism. When I suggested they handle that voluntarily, they assured me it couldn't be done voluntarily, that "the private interests involved won't cooperate without government intervention."

We can't resolve our dilemma unless and until we take responsibility *personally* for making things right in our lives, for resolving our own parental and authority relationships. Again, in order for us to improve our political situation, we have to attend to resolving our personal situation.

Each and all of us,
of whatever political ideology, party, role—
elected, appointed, public employees,
media persons, legislative representatives, citizens—
need to forge a new agreement
on what we want *from* government,
based on what we want and can expect
of ourselves,   and
for ourselves,   and
from ourselves.

Then we need to carry out our agreement!

We should open everything in government: meetings, records, whatever. Secrecy breeds only suspicion. If you don't trust me to know what you're doing, especially when it concerns and affects me— why should I trust you? How should I trust what you're doing? The public interest is seldom well served behind doors closed to the public. The restoration of trust, confidence and credibility in government is a first order of business for all of us. Growing ourselves—to recognize our own innate trustworthiness, best enables us to recognize the same in each other, including persons constituting our government.

We have constituted our government to be a "government of the people, by the people and for the people." Literally we have that. Our government is *of* people. It governs people, especially in our old vision belief that people are not self-governing. And it's *by* people (it's people who operate it, elected or appointed or employed). They're chosen *by* people (directly or indirectly). They (at least think they) operate it *for* people. Yet it's clearly not working—for anyone!

We need to update our understanding of our government. We should constitute a government *"by and for us persons."* It should be the personal "we" rather than the impersonal "the people"—who constitute our government. It should be individual growing *persons*—rather than an undifferentiated mass of *people*—who constitute our government. The difference makes a difference!

Our Liberating Vision provides us a blueprint for making our government human.

We need first to convert our government to be *for* persons. The prerequisite for that is our coming to understand what it means to be/come a person...then will our government's operations, programs and appropriations be committed to growing healthy human beings. That will truly be a "government for persons."

And we need a government *by* (us) persons. Insofar as we recognize that persons have the natural capacity for becoming responsibly self-determining, we'll less need to govern the people. We, the people, will be able to take care of ourselves.

For all that to happen, we must operate our government *by* (growing) persons. That includes all who affect our government's operations, in the three branches of government, elected or appointed or employed in our civil service ranks. That includes lobbyists and mediapersons. We all must become healthy human beings. We must all attend to our continuing growth and development. The government we do is who we are.

That will truly become a government *by* persons.

Yet "government by us persons" requires more than that. It requires real participation by all of us persons who constitute the citizenry.

We need to recognize that our government is *us*, acting jointly. It's our collective effort to accomplish the goals and tasks we either cannot or will not do, individually, for ourselves or each other. Insofar as we choose to live irresponsibly, with our fellow humans, we either cause or fail to cure their harm and crippling. Then we act jointly through our government to attend to the consequences of our own irresponsibility.

Our government is our "neighbor of last resort." It attends to those Good Samaritan tasks to which we're all encouraged, but few of us attend. Our government will have less to do—especially in prevention, containment or rehabilitation— insofar as we individuals do more. We need to become more human, caring, responsible, and involved in our human endeavor. The more grown and self-esteeming I become, the less I'll need or want from government.

41. *Humanizing our politics.* Humanizing our government requires we humanize our politics. We need a politics for growing human beings. Our government will be the best government by the people if the leaders of our government are elected by all the growing persons possible. If only a few of us participate in our elections—and especially if that few are old vision people—we'll have more of "government of, by and for the people," less of "government by and for us persons." The more healthy growing human beings there are in our electorate, the more will be our commitment to politics that implement our liberating vision of human nature and potential. That will enhance our human growth and development. In turn, we'll then more select candidates, and elect officeholders—who are themselves healthy growing human beings. We'll have turned the circle—to life.

To enable all this to happen, everyone of us must involve ourselves—both in politics *and* in our own personal growth and development. The final responsibility comes down to us. The government we get is what we deserve. The politics we do is who we are. We can no longer be apathetic. Our problems won't go away. They're so pervasive, we can't escape from them. They won't be solved without our participation. It's up to each and every one of us!

Neither of our major political parties is adapting itself to our expanded humanness, to our liberating vision. Neither has updated its critique to recognize who we have become as human beings. Neither traditional liberalism nor traditional conservatism can suffice. Both are bankrupt. They share a common fault: our old cynical vision. Neither trusts our human nature.

Conservatives exemplify this in wanting government to protect us from ourselves, our personal freedoms and choices in our personal lives. They would make us criminals, for what we choose to do in our personal lives. Liberals exemplify this in wanting government to keep on taking care of people, not trusting they can become self-sufficient. They would make us dependent on the welfare state.

Conservatives are mostly still committed to vertical authority and order. That doesn't · befit our expanding humanness. Liberals are mostly still committed to horizontalizing authority and order. But they do it without sufficiently attending to developing us into persons able to exercise our new rights responsibly. Neither is sufficient for us. We need a new politics—for growing healthy, autonomous, self-sufficient human beings.

Let traditional liberals recognize: The methods and programs you propose have gone as far as they can go, yet not deeply enough. You want human needs attended to, you now need to go deeper. Go deeper within yourself. Bring forth greater depth than you have heretofore allowed yourself to believe in, experience and trust. Discover there's more of your humanness, and bring it and yourselves into a politics for growing humans. That will best serve you.

Let traditional conservatives recognize that we humans have grown. We're into our transition stage. We can't be stuffed back inside our old vision. The methods and programs you propose have gone as far as they can go. You want human needs attended to. You too now need to go further. Go further within yourself. Bring forth greater innocence than you have heretofore allowed yourself to believe in, experience and trust. Discover there's more of your innocence, and bring it and yourselves into a politics for growing humans. That will best serve you.

I'm finding myself more attracted to the sense of individuality of our Libertarians and Anarchists. They appropriately call for a minimization of government—though in differing aspects. Yet I find their programs naive. Neither seems to recognize the practical reality of who and where we humans are today. Sad to say, but certainly true, we're not yet grown enough to live together peacefully, lovingly, fairly and safely, as members of one family. We still need some protections from each other. We've got to go about lessening government by stages, wisely, as fast as we realistically can. But certainly not in a single stroke.

We need first to have our personal rights and freedoms restored. In learning how to exercise those responsibly, we'll gradually grow. We'll become capable of responsibly exercising our social rights. At that time we can properly lessen—even remove—governmental, legal constraints on our social behavior.

Neither major party, Republican nor Democrat, provides us a truly credible, hopeful vision and promise for our future. Liberals have lost—for the time being—the three hottest political issues today: crime, government spending and inflation. Their critique doesn't offer credible essential short-range solutions. Their credibility won't be restored—until they adopt our liberating vision—which suggests credible both short-term (containment) and long-term (root cause eradication) agendas.

Conservatives have—for the time being—seized the three hottest political issues today. But their critique doesn't offer credible, essential long-range solutions. Their credibility won't last—unless they adopt our liberating vision—sufficient for both short- and long-term agendas, a holistic approach fitting our expanding people.

Let us liberals advance ourselves
into liberating our human nature.

Let us conservatives advance ourselves
into conserving our human nature.

That provides us—liberals and conservatives—
a common ground on which we can begin to come together
to help each other advance ourselves
into healthy growing humans.

That provides us basis for a politics for growing humans.

Such a politics has one more ingredient:
a citizenry fully self-aware, committed to our liberating vision—and willing to involve themselves—and clear on what's important. For the quality of politics—especially election campaigns—depends upon the growth and development, values and perceptions of the voters.

In my 1970 campaign, in our first debate, my opponent, Virginia Shaffer, attacked me by saying "John votes his conscience," and promising the crowd, "And if you elect me, I promise you I'll not vote my conscience, I'll vote the way you want me to." When it came my turn, I responded, "That's right, I vote my conscience. And I'm proud that I have a conscience to vote. If you want an Assemblyman with no conscience, I urge you to vote for my opponent." The crowd cheered, and my opponent never raised the issue again.

We need a new politics, based upon our liberating vision. We have a new politics to offer. We *are* the new politics.

We'll each achieve our social goals—only if and when we are all individually into our personal growth and development. We must live our liberating vision in our everyday lives and relationships. We will then overflow ourselves into our public arena. We will insist that our politics become a politics for us growing humans, and for growing all humans. We'll then have a government by and for growing humans.

42. *Humanizing everything*. Each of us must recognize that all our above efforts are linked by our common theme—our Liberating Vision. Even as we labor independently at the respective agenda items which most engage us, we should recognize and support each other's efforts, and their contribution to our own.

That concludes my specifically Human(istic) Agenda. I hope it makes clear how our Liberating Vision develops an alternative program for public policy and action.

But it's not responsible to only theorize. It's only enough to act. We've theorized thoroughly about our Liberating Vision and how it answers our world's macroproblem. Now it's time we *do* something about it all.

magnifying our vision:
a call to loving arms

> *"To leave the world a bit better, whether by a healthy child, a garden patch or a redeemed social condition; to know even one life has breathed easier because you lived. This is to have succeeded."*
>
> —Ralph Waldo Emerson

> *"This will be the first government founded on the principles of nature."*
>
> —John Adams

We humans are not satisfied with philosophy, nor with pious pronouncements. However good our thinking, however good our intentions—we must act to make our word come true. Having philosophized well, we need to actively apply ourselves to the realities and practicalities of our everyday lives.

Let's do that now. Let's mobilize ourselves for personal political action. Let's make our human agenda the public agenda of our society. Let's make our society healthy for human beings. Let's realize our human agenda throughout our world.

Several steps are essential—for us to make things right, in our lives and society, now and for our future:

• activate myself;
• link up with and enlist you;

- build our alliance of faithful lovers;
- equip ourselves with realism and hope;
- perfect our style; and
- approach, educate and enlist persons in positions of influence in our public-policy decision-making.

First, *I must activate myself.* I must assume personal responsibility. I must affirm my commitment to our Liberating Vision, our Human Revolution and our Human Agenda. I must recognize that the first item on our Human Agenda is myself.

My first responsibility is to attend to my own continuing personal growth. That's the most empowering activity, personal and political, I can engage in. The most revolutionary political act I can perform is to take full responsibility for my life. I will decide, define, design, determine and declare who I am. I will take responsibility for liberating and integrating myself. I will be/come my own vision and action. I will become wholly human myself. It's up to me to become a fully-functioning human being. I will be/come my own leader and my own model.

That's the foundation for human political action. There's an inherent connection between the personal and the political. My experience of myself provides me the vision I carry into all my relationships, interpersonal and institutional. The state of my human development determines how I'll affect our social development. How much I am personally intact will determine how much political impact I can have. My vision of myself determines my public-policy decision-making. The politics I do is who I am.

My hope and goal is to be/come a liberating presence in our world. I want to become a "psychedelic person," turning other persons on—to yourselves. The more I'm grown, the more I'll appreciate our Liberating Vision and our Human Agenda. The more I'll recognize how best to participate in our Human Revolution, to make it gentle, to give it human shape and speed.

Second, *I must link up with and enlist you.* The second item on our Human Agenda is you, your continuing growth and development as a whole, conscious, loving human being. I need to proceed from my assumption that deep inside you share my nature, my idealism and my caring. I see you as I see myself. My growth will enable me to be present with you in ways that empower you to become a fully-functioning human being. My growth will inspire your growth. The second most revolutionary political act I can perform is to facilitate your taking full responsibility for your life. You will recognize that *you are the first item on your Human Agenda*. You will decide, define, design, determine and declare who you are. And your experience of yourself will provide you the vision you'll carry into all your relationships, interpersonal and institutional.

I needn't wait until I've got myself wholly together before approaching you. In fact, I want you with me in my efforts to realize myself. I want your support in my personal growth. You and I should undertake these efforts together, facilitating each other's growth and development. Together, empowering each other, we can go forward toward humanizing our government and politics.

We can ally ourselves even if we don't agree about the *total* innocence of our human nature. It's enough that we agree there's more to each of us than we've known, and that we want to grow ourselves further. Precisely how much further, we'll discover as we grow.

We should link up with each other tightly enough so that we provide support for each other, yet loosely enough so that each of us retains our autonomy. We'll work together or independently, as it suits us, toward realizing our Liberating Vision.

I hope you read "first" above, in your first person, applying it to yourself personally. As we each recognize our being the first item on our own agendas, we can most clearly and effectively link up with each other toward manifesting our vision in our government and politics. It takes a lot of personal growth for two human beings to come together profitably. Connected by our shared vision, we can trust ourselves to do that. If we're willing so to act together, we'll be well on our way toward realizing our Liberating Vision, personally and politically.

Third, *we must build our alliance of faithful lovers*. The next item on our mobilization agenda is enlisting other human beings who share our Liberating Vision, who are willing to share themselves with us. We "explorers of humankind" owe it to ourselves to band together into a worldwide alliance for human action. We need to become a community of fellow searchers.

I believe the most effective way we can live this community into realization is through intimate relationships with persons of kindred heart and vision. Our society constructs devices to constrain us from relating at core level with ourselves and with each other. We must help each other free ourselves from those. We must open, reveal ourselves to each other and our entire world—with innocence, trust, truth and love. Love is the most powerful force. It provides the healthiest environment, enabling each other to feel accepted and safe. We'll open up and discover our common natural goodness. We'll enable ourselves and each other to grow in energy, vision, boldness and durability. Then we become the change we want to see happen. We will create our reality by the lives we choose to live. We become the foundation for a new and human society.

It's not an easy process for three or more of us humans to come together profitably. Yet we must, and we can. Michael Rossman best describes this sharing and growing process in "Notes on the Tao of the Body Politic." Michael speaks of "the politics of love."

Through our joined effort, we will infuse our Liberating Vision into our public awareness and decision-making. We'll carry our expanding selves into politics. We'll raise awareness that politics and government are most appropriately about human growth and development. We'll be on our way toward a truly human society. Every person will be the first person to know who s/he is. We'll all grow together, becoming ever more whole, present and loving with each other, with every other human—no matter sex, age, race, color, nationality, sexual preference, wealth, whatever.

We of our Liberating Vision may still be a minority. But we come from the ranks of society that are often influential in suggesting the directions for our coming society. And many of us occupy key positions of influence. We touch many other persons. In our changing, troubled times, people are yearning for direction, and for hope. They are ready for our Liberating Vision, which provides both.

As our vision is appealing, so will we be, as our expanding selves. Already our numbers are growing dramatically. If we mobilize, our numbers will mushroom. As our vision spreads contagiously, we'll reach a point of critical mass. There'll be enough of us that the majority will accept our vision, adopt it, adapt themselves according to it. Our society will become transformed. It will be a society healthy for growing human beings.

We need to change our culture's consciousness, person by person. Let's begin our enlistment by seeking those persons already visibly living our Liberating Vision, already growing themselves into fully-functioning human beings. It's already happening in the hearts and heads, by the choices and actions, of thousands of persons throughout our world. Consider all the persons who participated in the liberation, human potential, spiritual, drug, peace, student, consumer and environmental movements. Consider the persons and programs I mention in this book. Consider the persons and programs you know of yourself. Change is already happening. Humans are already changing. It's time we mobilize ourselves.

We need to create a mutually supportive and empowering public alliance—toward transforming ourselves and our society. We must develop a vehicle for our mobilization—through which we can get ourselves together, individually and societally, personally and politically.

Our form should model our Liberating Vision. The "networking" model provides a participatory democratic group in which information, support, and decision-making are fully shared. It brings us together in a lateral, largely leaderless way. As equals, we'll come together in a nationwide helping network for information, education, mutual support, personal growth and political/social action.

You can do this locally, on whatever basis you choose. You can join us in our effort—SELF-DETERMINATION: A Personal/Political Network (P.O. Box 126, Santa Clara, CA 95052, Tel. (408) 984-8134). It's a membership network, sponsored by many leading citizens. It's the foremost effort I know of precisely focused on our foremost public need: humanizing politics.

Fourth, *we need to equip ourselves with realism and hope.* We need to be realistic. We must recognize the enormity of actualizing our Liberating Vision, our Human Agenda and our Human Revolution.

This will be a vast populist movement, a true people's movement, by and for us persons. It's our effort to translate the hope and promise of our Declaration of Independence, our Constitution and Bill of Rights into our everyday lives and relationships. It's our effort to resolve our American political and religious paradoxes. It's a revolution.

We are recreating our sense of human community. We are healing our earth. This requires a large-scale evolutionary transformation of our human consciousness. We can only realize a healthy planetary culture based on loving and sharing if enough of us are willing to publicly manifest these values in our everyday lives. However difficult this struggle may be, there's no task more worthwhile. Whatever our seeming limitations, we humans are uniquely suited to this task.

We're in a time of birthing, experiencing birth trauma. We're in a critical time, with human life hanging in the balance. We can't even assure our survival, but we can improve our chances markedly. And only *we* can do that!

We need to be realistic about the time it may take. We need to be patient. We're the pioneers of a long-term process, a human revolution. It might take generations to accomplish. All the more reason we should act now. We can hasten the process. The character of our actions, our own character, will determine the pace. We shouldn't expect, or need, immediate results and gratification. Just this year I was invited by a woman to be her university graduation speaker. She invited me because hearing me speak four years ago had inspired her to go back to college at age fifty! Two work experience educators are developing a new set of regulations, curriculum and staff development for their program—on account of a speech and questions I'd presented them three years ago. We must grow ourselves enough to be willing to endure. We shouldn't be acting just for the desired result or reward, but acting for ourselves. Our own meaning and fulfillment are its own reward, the best reward. Our action must come from within. Our pace depends upon the depth of our faith, our hope and our loving. Our willingness to so live will enable it to happen sooner rather than later.

We ought not let ourselves be turned off to politics. That's precisely the way other persons maintain their power, by persuading us we have no chance of asserting our own power and changing it. We shouldn't surrender our power and our lives that way. We needn't worry we'll be "sullied" by involving ourselves in politics. Politics is only people. It's only as dirty as people make it. We ought trust our own strength and integrity to be in there, and not 'get dirtied. We need to grow ourselves to assure we aren't contaminated by our involvement, that we affect politics more than it affects us.

And we shouldn't worry that if we involve ourselves, we risk repression or cooptation. We simply have to take those risks. We can minimize them by our continuing growth as persons. We'll keep outgrowing our vulnerability to cooptation. We'll keep growing our desire for ever more humanizing institutions. We'll become ever more visionary, bold and insistent.

Recognizing the difficulty and the duration we may expect, we need to attend to our own hopefulness. We must equip ourselves with sustaining hope. We may as well be optimistic—since there's no going back, no matter how much we or anyone else would like. We can take hope from the many persons and efforts already underway. Many sharing our vision are mobilizing persons toward involving themselves in social change to humanize our society. The Association for Humanistic Psychology, Lifespring, Esalen and est are asking their members to activate themselves. The Institute of Noetic Sciences (Cogswell College Building, 600 Stockton St., San Francisco, CA 94108) has instituted a social change column in its periodic bulletin.

We should take hope from other signs of our Human Revolution already in process. The November 1978 edition of *Reader's Digest*—certainly one of our more traditional and widely read publications—bannered across its cover an article by expert Wardell Pomeroy on breaking through myths about sexuality. During November of 1978 I guest-lectured in a sophomore religion class at San Jose's Catholic Archbishop Mitty High School. The theme of the class is "self-discovery and self-actualization," a far cry from my senior high religion class, whose instructor kept reminding us "It's a cold, cruel world, kiddies. You better get used to it now." The Mitty teacher told me he was having trouble—learning that to facilitate learning, it's sometimes best he just stay out of the way. But he was enjoying learning it.

During fall of 1978, The California State Board of Education did a weekend retreat at Asilomar on California's Monterey Peninsula. Also at the conference grounds that weekend were MENSA (persons in the top 2% of I.Q.'s around the world) and

COYOTE (the Margo St. James prostitutes group). A marvelous combination of mind and body and our Board of Education!

Declarations of intention to humanize large public agencies have been expressed by key leaders: General Frank Schobur of the California National Guard, Max Cleland of the U.S. Veterans Administration, Commander Glenn Craig of the California Highway Patrol. Banks now offer personalized checks and personal bankers. Pepsi advertises "It's the real thing." Our government advertises "Find yourself in the United States Air Force." Television urges us to enjoy sharing the watching experience with a friend. We've progressed from Richard Nixon's "royal" salutes to Jerry Ford's buttering his own toast to Jimmy Carter's carrying his own "suitcase." Thousand of Americans watch "Saturday Night Live"—satire on our society, institutions, authority. Political leaders, to lure persons to their fund-raisers, stage "roasts," at which they're made fun of. Howard Craven, Senior Vice President of Union Bank in downtown Los Angeles, came in to ask me how to contact and help community groups in their area. Lobbyist Bruce Roberts (whose major account is the general contractors) has a policy of representing, at no charge, one nonprofit social action effort. Fifteen-year-old Addie Shepherd lobbied for funds for respite (weekend) care for her Down's Syndrome brother, "He's my brother, I live and play and fight with him. I understand him. Once in a while we need a break. Please help." Friend Dan Bryant and his Down's Syndrome 12-year-old daughter Colleen are featured in a front-page story of our daily newspaper, and he says of her: "She doesn't know the things she can't do. She's more boxed in by me and her teachers, than by her own limitations."

Bumper strips ask, "Have you hugged your child today?" Others declare, "I found it." Others respond, "I never lost it." and "I am it." We more readily greet each other with an embrace, even amongst persons of the same sex; we more readily part with "take care" and "have a nice day." Increasingly we sing and dance to rock music, awakening our senses, and—more recently—to disco, awakening our bodies. Persons flock to the theater to experience the self-disclosing "A Chorus Line." The season's top new television hit is "Mork and Mindy." The one episode I've watched closed with Mork reporting about the curious violence bent of us humans, beginning with our physical onslaught on the newly arriving infant.

We can especially take hope from larger, remarkably successful accomplishments by us humans. We've radically changed ourselves and our ways regarding population. Ten years ago Stanford's Paul Ehrlich and others were reporting our population explosion, predicting it was amounting to a "population bomb." They feared it was already too late to save ourselves from extinction on account of world overpopulation. They initiated Zero Population Growth, in an effort to make a difference.

Now, ten years later we humans have changed our child-bearing practices: our nation's growth rate is leveling off; our average family is having 1.8 children; a 1977 Gallup Poll reported 87% said they didn't want our country's population to grow any more. We've not yet solved this problem, but some reputable experts believe our population crisis is now resolvable. They suggest we may have already "turned the corner" on it.

We're moving away from legal systems (divorce and insurance) based on fault or blame, to human-need-based systems. Many religions are transforming from God the Enforcer—"the big cop in the sky"—to God is love.

Perhaps the most analogous and profound precedent is what we humans have been doing in our world with respect to religion. I was raised a strict Roman Catholic, taught to believe that if I dared to so much as set my foot inside a Protestant Church, I could go to hell forever. That belief is absolutely foreign to me now. Thanks to Pope John XXIII and other contemporary religious leaders, those days are now gone and, I'm sure, forever behind us. In these past twenty years, through our ecumenical movement, we've learned to live peaceably with our profound differences of belief about God—what's "out there, up there." We can hope that we can learn to live peaceably with our profound differences of belief about ourselves—what's "down here, in here"—our own human nature. It shouldn't be as difficult for us to get together about what's within us, since it's so close at hand, and becoming much more readily verifiable.

In 1963 friends and I initiated an annual weekend "retreat." It began as a silent, priest-led, meditative experience, open only to Catholic professional men. Over the years, as we've changed personally, we've expanded it to non-professional men, then to non-Catholic men, then to women—and from priest-led to our own leading, from structured agenda to developing our own agenda, taking responsibility for developing our own agenda, and from dwelling on our sinfulness, to dwelling on our pain, and in 1979 to spending one session in which each of us told of what especially fine thing we'd accomplished in the prior year. Without being naive or pollyannish, it was the most light-hearted of our 15 annual experiences.

Our churches were our first major institution to reform, renew and reconcile themselves. Perhaps that's because they're our largest totally voluntary (at least no external constraint) institution. Persons can't quit our economic system (they have to eat), can't escape our government, our young have to stay in school. No one is forced to go to church. There's no reason we can't as readily reform our other less voluntary institutions. In fact, there's all the more reason we should—we *have* to live with/in them!

I take hope from my personal experience of thirteen years in the Legislature. We've made much progress, in many ways. It's no longer "popular" to be a racist or sexist or environmentally destructive. Those are no longer our public policy, those are no longer our public's policy.

In my county alone, for example, many women ably occupy positions of influence and power: Mayor Janet Gray Hayes, Supervisors Gerry Steinberg and Susie Wilson, San Jose State University President Gail Fullerton, Agnews State Hospital Director Keri Procunier, Santa Clara Chamber of Commerce Executive Betty Hangs, and many others, especially on school boards, where they sometimes constitute a majority. They're doing so well that questions are no more being raised about the competence of women to occupy positions of leadership. The recent selections of Margaret Thatcher to lead the British Government and Carol Hallett as Republican Minority leader in the California Assembly—both by conservative, traditional constituencies—is subtle proof that women's liberation is succeeding, there's no going back.

It's much like when Willie Brown became Chairman of the Assembly Ways and Means Committee in 1971. He displayed so much intelligence, wit and grasp of everything, that our racist imagery regarding blacks could never again be credible in the Capitol. He demonstrated (to those not yet aware) that blacks are as able, active and energetic as anyone could be.

The late San Francisco supervisor Harvey Milk promoted the same shattering of stereotypes of gay persons.

We've already made some remarkable, wonderful transitions in our heads. We've changed our minds about racism, sexism and our environment. Now we have to change our hearts. We need to grow our natural capacity for loving, and make that real in our everyday relationships with human beings different from ourselves, and with our earth itself.

Some personal anecdotes add to my hope. Upon reading a newspaper account of an outrageous statement by Los Angeles Police Chief Ed Davis, I wrote him my disappointment. He responded, "You of all people should know not to trust the press to accurately report what is said. I'm enclosing a copy of my entire remarks, in hopes you'll find them less offensive." Thereafter we corresponded occasionally. He invited me to visit him in Los Angeles. When I had a committee hearing coming up there, I called to see whether he was free for lunch that day. He told me he had to officiate at the graduation luncheon at the Police Academy, and invited me to attend as his guest. I agreed, then asked whether my hair (then long) would pose any problem. He replied, "No, we'll just tell them you're a 'narc'." I sat next to Ed at the head table, and afterwards accompanied him on his field review of the graduates. We both enjoyed the occasion.

Los Angeles County State Senator (Republican) Newt Russell shares Billy Graham's religion, based largely on the assumption that "I am a sinner, by nature." He usually votes conservatively, traditionally, repressively. He's as utterly honest and earnest a person as any in our Legislature—or outside it. Before our Assembly Ways and Means Committee in 1978, he presented a staff-prepared justification for his bill promoting volunteerism, concluding "...and this ought help us to humanize our institutions." I immediately moved we approve the bill. Later he told me he knew that I'd respond affirmatively, as soon as I heard him use that word.

A former colleague, conservative Bob Burke of California's Orange County, served ten years with me on the Assembly Education Committee. He began by promoting only our traditional 3 R's, later began talking as well about educating "the whole child."

John Stull, a retired Navy Commander from San Diego, came to the Legislature with me as Assemblyman in 1967. He retired in 1978, as a Senator, having served as Republican caucus chairman for some time. In his work John usually puts up his gruff front, hiding as best he can his large heart within. In 1975, he included in his presentation to the Assembly Education Committee, "Of course it's important for a child to learn how to laugh and love, but s/he's also got to learn the basic 3 R's."

In 1977 John lunched with a member of our Capitol Press Corps, who shared with John his utter delight and excitement about having just participated in the birthing of his child. Since I'd been working on legislation about alternative birthing, John shared the experience with me. In 1978, I was short one vote for my bill to extend our statewide Alternative Birthing Committee. I reminded John of his experience. He switched and provided me the swing vote for my bill.

Upon his retirement John and his wife Babbie went traveling. He sent me a "new age consciousness" card from Mesilla, New Mexico. Its front pictured two seagulls flying toward the sun, and the Kahlil Gibran legend "I care about your happiness just as you care about mine. I could not be at peace if you were not." Inside John wrote: "Dear John—Noting the message on this card, naturally I thought of you! See your influence on me. Babbie and I are touring, happy in the thought there is more to life than the California Legislature. Peace. John."

There's a further ground of hope in our revolutionary efforts, one which we should recognize, but tenderly. Our Liberating Vision and our way—accepting, loving, liberating—is more appealing than our old vision's way of rejecting, fearing, repressing. And our way is subtle. Others won't recognize its capacity for "seduction," nor how to combat it. That recognition comes only with the recognition of our Vision. By that time, they'll find it captivating, they'll embrace it. They'll join in with us in building our alliance of faithful lovers.

There are plenty of signs of hope. Don't just take my word for it. Open your eyes, look around yourself, see for yourself!

Fifth, having gotten ourselves together, equipped with realism and hope, we have another preparatory task: *perfect our style*. Each of us must develop our own style, and make it and ourselves effective in our effort.

Our style should demonstrate our vision, by being innocent, faithful, natural, loving and liberating. We're most effective in spreading our message if we well model our vision in the sight and sense of other persons. We should be present in a reassuring, liberating way with each and every person we seek to enlist. The best way to "convert" others is not by the shrillness of our voices—but by the power of our personal presence and example.

We ought not be defensive. Let's trust the truth of our Liberating Vision. Let's trust the power of its message: it offers trust, love and liberation. It'll carry through and be recognized for what it is—the truth. Nor should we be offensive. Let's not confuse being an "advocate" for being an "adversary." Advocacy consists of *winning* people to our side, not backing them into a corner. Let's be present in positive ways, that occasion the other person's further opening, receptivity and growth. Let's not be scornful of persons holding a contrary belief. Let's respect and listen to them—so that they feel safe and listen to us. Let's not arouse feelings of entrapment, defensiveness. Let's not allow *our* anger to get in *our* way. Let's not resort to our old vision's methods of threat, reward or punishment. Let's offer a nurturing climate and engagement, in which the other person will feel safe, find hope, trust, open and risk.

A bad example: a woman came to testify in our Health committee in support of my bill to ban smoking in California's supermarkets. I'd talked with the committee members in advance, knew I had more than enough votes. Her approach was to angrily tell the committee she suspected most of them were "on the take" from the tobacco companies. That wasn't true, and so angered the committee members, she almost cost me our bill.

A good example: Brain researcher Jean Huston, President of the Association for Humanistic Psychology, recently met with some Texas legislators and school leaders. She spoke about the significance of researching deeply into ourselves, about our human growth and development. A woman asked: "Aren't you afraid that if we open up and look inside ourselves that deeply, we'll find original sin?" Jean replied, "Perhaps, but if we open up deeply enough, discover the proper connections of our left and right brains, perhaps we'll find original grace." The woman queried: "Do you really think that's a possibility?" Jean responded, "I do." The woman closed: "Well, if that's the case, perhaps we should take a look."

Let's trust every other person to be the same as us, by nature: innocent, caring, and desirous of life and self-fulfillment. Our vision is inherently valuable for him/her personally. Our task is (to discover how) to present it and ourselves in such a way as to enable the other person to recognize that fact, the truth about her/him self, for him/her self.

Let's be utterly open in our effort. Let's have *no* hidden agendas. Let's not hide *anything* at all from other persons. That only engenders suspicion in the other person. Let's invite everyone into our effort. There'll be nothing to infiltrate, nothing to be spied upon. Everyone's welcome, no one's to be excluded. In my experience, persons become most cautious, conservative, even reactionary, when they are left out, ignored, feel rejected. When I invite you in, your negative feelings are defused, a much more positive and hopeful relationship ensues between us.

And as we change and grow, let's not leave any of our fellow humans behind, without help or hope. Even if we "outgrow" some relationships in our lives—we ought be growing ourselves to be more caring, and more understanding, especially toward persons involved with us.

Let's let our idealism, feeling, caring, passion show. We ought not be hesitant or embarrassed to show ourselves fully. We'll most powerfully persuade by our authenticity, compassion and loving.

We must as well use our heads, and use them well. In presenting our Liberating Vision and our Human Agenda, it's essential to be thoughtful and thorough, well-informed and well-prepared. We must have done our homework. We must think and speak and write logically and clearly. To do less is to discredit our cause. We shouldn't make it easy for anyone to scorn, dismiss or reject us or our vision.

In my early days in the Legislature, many of my colleagues and others involved in the legislative process, chose to dismiss me and my proposals. They characterized me as a touchy-feely dreamer who talked lofty ideas and ideals. They figured I wasn't tough enough to make it in the rough-and-tumble world of politics. They thought I couldn't get reelected or, if I did, that I wouldn't prove effective in the Legislature.

Election to my third term in 1970 demonstrated I was viable and durable, politically, and drew me some respect. I gained far more when in 1973 I was appointed to Chair the Education Subcommittee of our Ways and Means Committee. We review in detail the several billion dollar state education budget. (What no one else in the Capitol knew—and even I'd forgotten—was that my father was a math teacher. He taught me so well that my math test scores soared off the chart.) I began picking up calculating errors of our fiscal advisers, and adding, subtracting, multiplying and dividing more rapidly than they. Word moved through the Capitol that there was more to me than expected, that I could be taken seriously. In 1977 and 1978, my efforts on our Joint Conference Committee on the State Budget, solidified my reputation, and enhanced my influence.

Even as we contradict our old vision's substance, let's make our case credible and persuasive by every traditional standard. There's no room for sloppy thinking or careless action. We must be sharp and prepared, the best. We must demonstrate to legislators that something nontraditional, something new is happening. It takes something new to understand, respond to and resolve our problems. And our Human Agenda is economical. It'll save dollars—too often the prime attention getter, the prime criterion for action in our traditional vision. And it'll save lives. Let's show how our Liberating Vision is to everyone's advantage, including theirs. In the long run, our Liberating Vision will serve us best, in both human and economic terms.

It's especially valuable to get to know the other person, his/her assumptions, beliefs, biases and values. What does s/he hold dear? What are the tenets of her/his personal philosophy and political ideology? An example: When our Assembly Republicans were opposing our School Improvement Program, I asked them "How come? You're for the individual, and our School Improvement legislation requires an individualized program for every student. You're for neighborhood schools, and it requires school site governing councils. You're for the family, and it requires parental involvement in school decision-making. You're critical of teachers, and it requires staff development.'' We recognized we weren't so far apart and, instead, found ourselves coming closer together in our efforts.

Let's not let stereotypes get in our way. Let's not assume the worst about any other person, let's not write him/her off. We're all in this together. We share a common human nature. We ought risk and reach toward each other, beyond the surface masks and defenses we've *all* been conditioned to wear in our society.

A young, ramrod-straight, terribly serious San Jose State University student, Charles Martin, came asking me to write a recommendation to support his Air Force officer application. I told him I liked just about everything about him, except I found him a bit too zealous about flying, as though nothing else in life truly mattered. He responded that flying was only his immediate goal and focus in life, that his long-range life goal was self-actualization. He'd just finished the est training.

More recently, in two Assembly floor debates within a week, I personally and directly challenged statements by a new Republican colleague, Bill Filante. After our second public encounter, I began worrying—lest he misunderstand my motivations. So I made an appointment and went to see him. I assured him that my comments weren't personal, and that I wanted to be sure he understood that, so we wouldn't have a bad personal relationship. His first sentence in response was: ''What I want most in life is to be loved. I know I can't have that all the time. I was raised in a discordant world, and I'm used to life being that way. But I don't carry scars from it.'' When we concluded our brief talk, he rose and we embraced each other.

And let's not stereotype politicians or persons in public office either. Polls indicate 75% of people trust their own legislators. A like percentage distrusts ''the Legislature.'' The parts make up the whole. Note the Republicans I described above. And note some Democrats...

One evening Assemblywoman Terry Hughes hosted a dinner party of four Assembly Democrats. Terry is a black woman from south central Los Angeles, a former T-group leader and professor of education. She told of growing up in a Catholic school in New York City. In the eighth grade she was chosen to crown the Virgin Mary at her school May ceremony. But she was replaced at the public ceremony—by a white girl. Later she inquired about becoming a nun. She was told she couldn't join the regular order, but she could join a begging order they had for black girls.

Assemblywoman Leona Egeland of San Jose told of growing up in Arizona. Her friends' parents wouldn't let her friends' pets play with her pets—because she was Jewish.

Assemblyman Floyd Mori of Alameda County is a Mormon High Priest, and former economics professor. He told of growing up in a small Utah farm community not far from a World War II internment camp which housed West Coast Japanese Americans. Since Floyd's family lived inland, they weren't forced to relocate. His wife's family in Los Angeles had to put all their belongings in a truck and move to Utah. Many of his friends were in camps.

I told of being brought up Catholic. When I was 26, law school classmate Al Knorp invited me to be an usher in his wedding. A priest friend advised me I shouldn't accept, because Al and his fiancee Sally were non-Catholics, it was taking place in a non-Catholic church, and my involvement might give credibility to the ceremony. I turned Al down. A few years later another friend asked me to be best man for his wedding. He was a 19-year old I'd been representing in a bitter family custody battle. From our first interview when he was downcast and barely looked at or talked to me, we'd developed a deeply trusting relationship. Now my caring for him proved stronger than my earlier religious dictates. I said, "Of course!"

Here we were, four human beings of vastly differing experience, of vastly differing backgrounds—of sex, race, color and religion. Here we were, four friends and colleagues, sharing dinner, and caring much about each other. And we were all elected by Californians.

My best legislative friend is Assemblyman Art Torres of downtown Los Angeles. Art was on the PSA flight that left Sacramento for San Diego, and crashed there. Art had gotten off in Los Angeles. After attending a meeting, he called his office. He was surprised by the response, "We're SO glad to hear from you." Usually we call our office to pile on more work. They're not eager to hear from us. Art said: "Come on, you're never glad to hear from me." At that point he learned about the plane crash.

The next evening Art flew back from Los Angeles to

Sacramento. When he got home, he hugged his 2½-year-old son Joaquin with extra vigor. Tears streamed from Art's eyes. Joaquin reassured him, "Don't cry, Daddy, it's going to be all right."

Art knew eight persons on that plane who didn't get off in Los Angeles. As one of the last living persons to see them alive, the following week he visited several of their families, to offer some consolation. I wasn't surprised to learn of this. When Art detects I'm in a jam, emotionally or politically, he drops everything to be with me.

Let's be patient. Let's bear in mind the trauma and time it's taken us to bring ourselves to where and who we are, to embracing our Liberating Vision. Let's recall it takes several exposures for demystification to occur, for familiarization to reduce the fright of the unknown, for vision to expand. Let's trust that when the other person is ready, s/he'll recognize for him/her self, the truth and value of our Liberating Vision.

Finally, let's remember the responsibility each of us has—to every other person (as presented in Chapter 19).

Sixth, *we must approach, educate and enlist persons in positions of power and influence* in our society's public-policy decision-making. This is, finally, the action that will enable us to bring our vision and dreams into realization throughout our society. We must bring ourselves and our Liberating Vision right to the persons who most influence other persons and their lives in our society. They especially need to understand, appreciate, adopt and live our Liberating Vision. We must maximize our conversion efforts. We must contact persons in positions of power, in every institution of our society, at every level of our government. Then our public-policy decision-making will be based upon a commitment to the well being of humans.

Let me suggest how you can do that with your primary public-policy decision-making bodies, at whatever level: city council, county board, state legislature, Federal Congress. Let me use the legislature as an example. I suggest the following actions—for making an impact on our political system:

1. Take the primary responsibility for lobbying your own legislators about our Liberating Vision. Every legislator should be regularly lobbied by her/his own constituents—

about our Human Agenda, about how it applies to solving our social problems. Constituents are more influential with a legislator than are colleagues. Legislators depend upon you—not us—for their survival.

2. Recognize that political power is thinly held in our society. Not many persons involve themselves. If you and a few friends make the effort, you'll be astonished at how much impact you can have.

3. Bear in mind the points about style in the preceding section. Recognize that legislators are human, no more nor less than the rest of us. Trust them to be just like us deep within. They, too, have a vision, values, ego, pain, a personal life, problems, insecurities, and basic good will. As individuals, they have the same rights and responsibilities we do. My responsibilities to others interpersonally are fully applicable when I'm relating to a person in an influential position.

4. Don't let yourself be intimidated. Your legislator is only human, like you; s/he's only there by reason of election by humans, like yourself.

5. Don't underestimate legislators. There's a new breed in the halls of government, at every level. You can take credit for that: they were sent there by the people. And don't overestimate what legislators can accomplish. They aren't super-human. And you have to carry your own share of responsibility. And don't depend on the media to give you your impression of legislators. Get to know them yourself.

6. Seek to establish an ongoing personal relationship with your legislator. That will enable you to assess her/his vision, trustworthiness, competence and responsiveness. That'll enable him/her to know that you are trustworthy, knowledgeable, caring and reliable. You can undertake this in many ways. A simple one is working in his/her election campaign. You can drive him/her around—providing you spare moments between appearances to talk

and get to know each other.

7. Approach your legislators one at a time. In groups we legislators tend to be especially aware of each other's presence. We feel especially self-conscious, and hold ourselves back. We feel competitive, and sometimes try to outdo each other with the crowd. With limited time divided among us, it's easier for us to avoid or evade your tougher questions. It's easier to keep from having to engage on a deeper level, or to disclose ourselves personally or our basic assumptions.

By inviting us one at a time, you can go deeper—both into a dialogue and into the deeper personal relationship.

8. Meet your legislator in a quiet, unpressured time. In the heat of controversy, time is short, pressure is on, emotions are high and guards are up. It's difficult to establish a relationship in a time of crisis or conflict over a particular issue. When the pressure calls for an immediate decision, persons don't hear as well. Besides, what a person hears in the moment of crisis will likely apply only to similar issues in the future. During a quiet time, we can take the time to explore in depth the assumptions underlying public policy. We can engage more deeply, personally. A legislator will incorporate the insight gained in such a time. S/he'll operate from that deeper insight at all future times, on all issues in his/her future decision-making.

9. Assemble a half dozen friends of shared vision and invite your legislator into the quiet atmosphere of your home. Sharing a meal there is even better. Tell him/her you have several persons who have something vital to discuss and who want to get to know him/her better as a person. Invite the legislator's family too. Make the occasion friendly and informal.

10. Get right down to the issue of basic assumptions. In choosing solutions for our social problems, we'll each choose processes pursuant to our vision of human nature and potential. It's most valuable to discuss our visions.

Cause the legislator to reveal, make explicit and examine his/her vision—from which s/he is already influencing the lives of others.

Set a stage, provide a forum in which legislators find it impossible to escape having to deal publicly with their own most basic assumptions. If their responses are not direct, full and fair, ask your question again and again— persistently, but not as an attack—until you get a satisfactory answer.

A legislator who doesn't want to answer your question will be embarrassed to admit that. Recognize that, and be gentle.

As we move our policy deliberations to the universal basic questions, we'll move beyond our parochial answers. An entirely different dialogue and engagement will ensue.

11. Frame your question properly. That'll leave the legislator only two options: come to agree with our Liberating Vision or disagree and acknowledge s/he's against humanization, against persons being and becoming whole, gentle, honest, loving and responsible. His/her only recourse then is to admit to cynicism. That won't leave him/her much of a following. Faith is far more attractive. Faith is a very moving thing.

Characterize the issue properly. Focus the dialogue clearly, humanistically. Examples: In a discussion of laws on sexuality, don't ask, "Are you for homosexuality?" Ask "Do you believe that what adults do voluntarily in private is any business of our government?" We called the legislation decriminalizing certain sexual activities "the consenting adults bill." In a discussion of marijuana laws, don't ask "Should people smoke marijuana?" Ask "Should persons be made criminals for what they do in the privacy of their own homes, especially when the act is far less dangerous than what they're exposed to in jail?" We call that legislation "the decriminalization of marijuana."

12. Teach your legislator by experience. Sensitize your legislators by exposing them to real people in their natural habitat, predicament and pain. Partly because of

attitude—more because of the pace—legislators tend to live in a contained, materially comfortable world. Many persons in pain are only stereotypes to many legislators. Invite your legislator to come spend time visiting a situation or a program. Try a child care center, an incest rehabilitation program, a halfway house. Provide an opportunity for observing, first-hand, other people's lives and pain. Let him/her experience those other people. They'll be revealed as flesh and blood—human beings— just like the legislator him/her self. Never again will the legislator be able to dismiss them as "those people."

In 1977 I spent a week as a teacher's aide in a high school remedial reading class in my district. Earlier I'd witnessed an execution in San Quentin's gas chamber. During my first Assembly term, I spent a weekend in Watts with black Assemblyman Leon Ralph and his family. The only white face I saw in two days was mine in the mirror. I got to see for myself what problems black persons commonly experience in our society. I got to know, in my gut, that black persons are human just like me. Those experiences had a profound, permanent impact on me.

Suggesting this technique has its surprises. Two years ago I appeared, together with the late, acknowledged-gay San Francisco Supervisor Harvey Milk, on a panel advising community college personnel how to be politically effective. I suggested they invite legislators to visit and experience their program. I cited my Watts stay as an example. Harvey spoke after me. He seconded my suggestion for experiential learning. He then said he'd gladly add to my experience by inviting me to spend a weekend with him. He did it in marvelous taste. I never got around to taking him up on his invitation.

13. Spend a day with your legislator—in the capitol (or at whatever comparable level) or in the district. Just "hang out" with him/her, be a shadow. Do it for the purpose of experiencing, better understanding his/her working life (which is most of life for most of us). Do it for the opportunity of establishing a personal trusting relationship between you two. Expect to be dismayed by what you see and experience—especially the pace, confusion, seeming

inattention. Expect to be heartened by what you see and experience—ordinary human beings trying their best to deal with extraordinary problems. (Being a legislator today is like being one of a few (120) persons sitting atop the funnel of a tornado composed of the rising aspirations, frustrations and anger of many (23,000,000) persons.)

14. Mobilize friends of shared vision and saturate your state capitol, or local government center. Such an effort works. Just after Richard Nixon ordered the invasion of Cambodia, 700 law students came en masse to the California Capitol to lobby for my bill to make it a crime to fight in an "undeclared war." They all wore coats and ties. They visited every legislator's office, talked with many legislators, staff and secretaries. The Capitol was moved. Over the objection and to the astonishment of the Assembly Speaker, the policy committee approved the bill.

15. If you can't get to a legislator—reach the person(s) closest to him/her whom you can identify and contact personally: staff persons, secretaries, campaign contributors, personal friends, family. Be considerate though, don't invade their privacy.

16. On your visits, leave material for the legislator or his/her associate to read—short, provocative and valuable—about our Liberating Vision.

17. If you can't get there in person, try a phone call. State your case concisely and forthrightly. Give reasons. Most legislators today want to make wise judgments. We want to know *why* we're doing what we're doing.

18. If you can't make it in person or by phone, write a letter. Make it concise and substantive, with reasons for your position. Make it clear. A few legislators still respond simply to pressure and numbers of persons, calling or writing. More newer breed legislators want to know why you want him/her to do a certain thing.

19. Don't let yourself be discouraged. Try and try again.

Become ever more-ingenious.

20. Actively support legislators who share our Liberating Vision. Involve yourself. Give your energy, time and money to their campaign. Involve yourself in their legislative efforts.

21. Actively support good legislation. Don't expect the legislator carrying a bill you like—to do it all him/her self. Take your own responsibility—to enlist your own legislators to support the bill. Then the bill's author only has to "round up" the votes. Your representatives will recognize and appreciate the proposal being made. They'll understand it offers hope of solving our problems. They'll gladly agree and vote "yes."

22. Enlist media persons, use our media. They instantly inform everyone, everywhere, of what's happening. Identify and inform the key media persons in your area. Be sure they know of your efforts to further our Liberating Vision. Be sure they recognize its human, political significance.

That concludes my mobilization proposal. I hope it makes clear how our Liberating Vision serves to mobilize us toward humanizing our politics.

You can make it work for yourself in whatever institution you choose to involve yourself: your local school, police force, city council, union, workplace, day care center, car pool, whatever. You simply need to decide, choose to activate yourself politically. Then raise our human questions—with every person involved. Propose our Liberating Vision. Be how you believe.

If you care enough, you'll figure out what to do, and how to do it. Where there's a will, there's a way. It's time we unleash our will. It's time we make our way—into a more human future for all of us!

chapter 26

seeing stars —
ourselves

*"To be a...(person)...is to feel, when setting one's
stone, that one is contributing to the building of the
world. It is another of the miraculous things about
(hu)mankind that there is no pain nor passion that
does not radiate to the ends of the earth. Let
a...(person)...in a garret but shine with enough
intensity and (s)he will set fire to the world."*

—Antoine de Saint Exupery

That concludes
my presentation to you.

I have no proper ending for my book.
It's more like you and me—
unfinished and unended.

Rather it's a beginning:
we're beginning to be/come ourselves;
we're beginning to recognize
how knowing and being ourselves
affects our fate and future;
we're beginning to liberate ourselves
from our old vision,
grow ourselves full size.

I've told you all I know 'til now,
as best I can so far.
I simply ask you let it
pass through your head and heart.

I intend my writing
to provide a proper beginning,
focusing our vision
that we may proceed beyond.

You and I together
will write the ending
whether we act or not,
whether we like it or not,
whether we know it or not.

Let's be conscious of our writing it,
make it suit our vision—
that we may choose our lives
rather than choose to die.

I ask a lot of myself,
I ask as much of you;
Our times demand that much
of each of us.

My asking is an offering—
an opportunity to participate,
in our needed effort
toward humanizing politics
and realizing our vision,
throughout our world.

A Liberating Vision,
essential as it is,
is only that—a vision;
it reveals our possibilities,
points our way,
then looks to us
for its realization.

Our realizing it
depends upon what vision
we choose to live by,

how we choose to live,
whether we begin liberating ourselves
individually and reciprocally,
personally and politically—
so we can
live our vision
into reality.

I believe we can do that.
I believe we must do that.
The question is
whether we will do that.

I invite you
to join me
in doing more
for ourselves,
and with each other,
starting
now!

I invite and welcome
your critique of my Liberating Vision—
your sharing and discussing it
with your family and friends,
neighbors and colleagues,
your own legislators
at every level of government,
and especially persons
who don't yet share our vision.

In the 60's
JFK led us in an historic effort
which then seemed an impossibility
to most humans.
It proved not to be.

Now it's our turn
to lead ourselves
in a *more* significant effort
which seems beyond possibility
to many humans.

It's every bit as possible.
All that might prevent us
is our own contrary belief.
That's hardly reason not to try.

Let's not do it
out of fear or guilt.
Let's do it out of motivation
in keeping with our vision:
our faith, our hope,
our joyous natural urge
toward self-realization,
self-fulfillment,
unity and love!

Our path seems difficult,
victory seems distant.
We must grow
our vision and energy,
boldness and durability.
Our faith and love
will make it easier,
sooner than we think.

   During World War II American soliders found a shattered
Christ statue in a liberated French village. They pieced it back
together, except its hands were missing. They mounted a sign
on it: "I have no hands but yours."

That's how
life speaks to us today.
The facts are undeniable,
so are we humans,
so is life!

Our future is up to us.
It's in our hearts naturally
to love and care,
to be/come one.
Let's open our hearts,
let our love flow through our heads,
reach out our hands
to make our world more human.

That's why
we so much need each other,
need so much of each other.
Nothing less
than all—
of all—
of us
is required,
nothing less deserved.

Let's come together—
toward ourselves.

I invite you
to come and share my vision,
come share yourself,
come share my life.
Let's link up
to make politics and government
and ourselves
more human.

It's up to us
to be/come ever more personal
and ever more political.
Let's you and I do it together
to demonstrate it can be done.
If you and I can do it,
so can we all.

John Kennedy had a favorite story about a person about to plant a certain flowering tree in his yard. His gardener cautioned him against it, advising such a tree takes a hundred years to blossom. He responded: ''All the more reason we begin immediately.''

Folk singer teacher friend Kevin McCarthy told me years ago, as we were discussing our human predicament: ''I just don't know whether we're going to make it. I guess it's best I don't. If I knew we were, I'd not worry about it, just laze around. If I knew we weren't, I'd give up, do nothing either way. Instead, believing it's possible for me to make a difference, I'll involve myself personally in our effort to build our human society.''

Our lives and our future
hang delicately in balance.

Each of us
might well be—
and make—
the difference.

Let us,
you and I,
begin together—
now!

chapter 27

your turn

> *"If each one of us loved ten persons, saw their beauty as human beings just the way they are, without wanting to change them we could form a network of love big and strong enough to hold everyone in the world."*
>
> —Pamela Portugal

The next chapter
is yours to write.

It's your turn
to act.

Will you come
tell me
who you are?

Do you share my vision?

If so,
come look with me,
at who and where we are.

Come be with me,
we'll make our dream come true.

JOHN VASCONCELLOS